DISTANCE PSYCHOANALYSIS

DISTANCE PSYCHOANALYSIS
The Theory and Practice of using Communication Technology in the Clinic

Ricardo Carlino

Translated by James Nuss

KARNAC

Originally published as "Psicoanalisis a Distancia" © Editorial y Distribuidora Lumen SRL 2010. Viamonte 1674 Buenos Aires, Argentina

Revised English edition published in 2011 by
Karnac Books Ltd
118 Finchley Road
London NW3 5HT

British Library Cataloguing in Publication Data

A C.I.P. for this book is available from the British Library

ISBN-13: 978-1-78049-013-7

Typeset by Vikatan Publishing Solutions (P) Ltd., Chennai, India

www.karnacbooks.com

Caminante, no hay camino
"Todo pasa y todo queda,
pero lo nuestro es pasar,
pasar haciendo caminos,
caminos sobre la mar.
       [...]

Caminante, son tus huellas
el camino y nada más;
caminante no hay camino,
se hace camino al andar.

Golpe a golpe, verso a verso ..."

—Antonio Machado

Traveller, there is no pathway
"Everything passes and everything stays,
But ours is to travel,
To travel making pathways,
Pathways upon the sea
       [...]

Traveller, your footprints are
The pathway and nothing more;
Traveller, there is no pathway,
The pathway is made by travelling along it.

Stroke by stroke, verse by verse ..."

—Antonio Machado

Whenever I travel along a new conceptual path, I always take inspiration from the wisdom of these verses by Machado. When facing something new, I also feel that the only way to the experience it is to make the pathway is by travelling along it: subject by subject, point by point, guessing correctly and being mistaken, stopping and thinking, moving on and continuing to think that, in fact, this is the path that has been trod by psychoanalysis, which has existed for more than a century.

CONTENTS

ACKNOWLEDGEMENTS

First of all, I would like to thank Dr Julian Hermida, professor of law, for his valuable, supportive, and generous collaboration in helping to write Chapter Eight: "Public and Private Law Considerations of Distance Psychoanalysis". His contribution, which was based on his expertise in international law, was clear, concise, and accurate. This contribution made possible a liaison between his legal expertise and my clinical experience in the subject. I also take this opportunity to express my deepest affection and gratitude to Julian for having edited this English version of the book.

I would also like to thank the Buenos Aires Psychoanalytic Association (APdeBA) for the conceptual and warm acceptance received in all scientific presentations. Many of them had great expectations for my position of researcher on this subject. This subject was also presented in several international congresses, symposiums, clinical sessions, academic-scientific meetings, clinical workshops, and supervisions. The permanent dialogue with them, both spontaneous and institutional, assured me of the psychoanalytic firmness of the subject that I was exploring. The criticism I received also stirred controversy and created doubts which became one more step in my analysis of the subject. This experience of critical exchange is the purpose of belonging to a scientific institution. I have done so within APdeBA, in one of the clinical workshops in which I have participated for ten years, and also in a private group that has been meeting for the last eight years.

For more than a year I had regular meetings with Ms Marisa Ludmer in order to discuss treatment by telephone, based on clinical material and our own abstractions on something so new for psychoanalysis. These exchanges have been very stimulating and fruitful and some of the ideas presented here experienced their first signs of life during these meetings.

I would like to express my most sincere appreciation to James Nuss for his patient and enthusiastic work in the complex task of interpreting and translating the text into English.

One last recognition. When thinking about these subjects, I immediately recall the numerous and spontaneous conversations on the subject of psychoanalysis I had with Diana Cantis-Carlino. Through almost half a century we were life partners: first, as a colleague in the Buenos Aires University School of Medicine, and later professionally as a fellow psychoanalyst in APdeBA. She also accompanied me as a professor of psycho-semiology in the school of medicine and as a thinker, which she was until the end of her days. She was my wife, the mother of our daughters, and the grandmother of our grandchildren. As testimony of our fertile dialogue and partly connected to the subject "dialogue" I want to highlight what we wrote together in 1987: *Diálogo analítico, un diálogo multiple* (*Analytical Dialogue, a Multiple Dialogue*). From there, I took the concepts referring to the *Inter* and *Intra space* of dialogue. This book is for me, in fact, a tribute to her, as a scholar of both psychoanalysis and of universal culture. One of her posthumous short stories, *Soñar con el número 230 y deseo de vivir* (*Dreaming about Number 230 and Wanting to Live*) (Cantis-Carlino, 2007) leaves a legacy that I can take today and make real: "To write a book is to leave fragmentary and re-created testimony of one's own life, to settle the debt with oneself and to reach others."

I hope that the reading of these pages introduces the reader to the joy of thinking while opening him/herself to new ideas regarding other possible ways of implementing psychoanalysis.

Here is my contribution.

Ricardo Carlino
distance.psychoanalysis@gmail.com
April 2011

ABOUT THE AUTHOR

Ricardo Carlino is a physician and psychoanalyst. He is also a full member of the Asociación Psicoanalítica de Buenos Aires (APdeBA) and a full member of the International Psychoanalytical Association (IPA). In the early years of specialization he worked as a psychiatrist at a general hospital. In the field of psychoanalysis, he served as adjunct professor of psychoanalytic technique and as secretary of the Commission on Seminars in the Institute of Psychoanalysis, APdeBA. In the academic field, as a "free professor", he was in charge of the subject of "psycho-semiology" in the medical school at the University of Buenos Aires. He also served as a professor and head of practice in psychiatry in the Mental Health Department. Dr Carlino is the author of several works published in psychoanalytic publications and presented at academic clinics, symposia, as well as national and international congresses, in which he has shared his thinking regarding the clinical instrumentation of psychoanalysis. Since his very first experiences of clinical treatment carried out by telephone, Ricardo Carlino has researched this topic in depth. His written works on this specific and novel method have been published on twelve different occasions. In several of these accounts he has included his reflections on treatment carried out in synchronous written form via chat and asynchronous written form via email. He published his first book on distance psychoanalysis in Buenos Aires. This is a translation of that book which contains some slight modifications from the original Spanish version.

PROLOGUE FOR THE SPANISH EDITION

Writing the prologue of a book is a great responsibility, both to its author and to its readers, given the multiple communication involved. A prologue also involves a subjective perspective, no matter how objectively one tries to describe the content of the book. Distance psychoanalysis is a subject which puts colleagues prejudicially "in favour" or "against", whether they may be the author of the prologue or the reader of the book. I will try to limit the enthusiasm I share with the author for this subject in order to transmit the scientific criteria with which Ricardo Carlino addresses the topic. I would like to avoid the feelings of passion and adverse politicization that are typically provoked when this subject is addressed in an institution or psychoanalytic congress, whether it be national or international. Likewise, I will avoid going into details about the treatment that most new ideas and authors of those ideas tend to receive at the onset.

To my knowledge, this is the first time that a book dedicated to this subject and written in the Spanish language has seen the light of day. Those who need to compare their similar clinical experience will find a text which serves as a wonderful source for finding the answers to their questions. Those non-believers who simply express that "Distance psychoanalysis is not psychoanalysis" will find here a great deal of theoretical, clinical, and epistemological material upon which to discuss and express their opinions.

In many opportunities, Zygmunt Bauman[1] has highlighted insecurity, vulnerability, and instability as being paradigmatic of contemporary society. This is in contrast to the objectives that were believed possible in modern society: stability, predictability, and coherence. As a response, the present culture places great importance on the material satisfaction of experiences. Furthermore, sensorial pleasure tries to compensate for the distrust placed in emotions that arise from bonds and are expressed with words. For this reason the rejection of what is symbolic in contemporary culture is the great challenge of psychoanalysis. However, we analysts also feel insecure and deprived of tools if sensorial elements of our framework diminish or disappear, as happens in telephone analysis. In order to face our clinical difficulties, we feel that we will apprehend the concreteness of psychic reality with less difficulty if we have assured the concreteness of the sensorial totality of the office and the material presence of the patient.

Without exhausting the subject, Ricardo Carlino raises the clinical and theoretical characteristics, chapter after chapter, "so that"—he emphasizes from the introduction—"psychoanalysts will have a base from which to release themselves from the idea that established theories are fixed and absolute, and begin to approach the idea that psychoanalysis can also be open to new conceptions due to the traversing and permanent reconstruction that socio-cultural transformations produce in human beings." This reminds us of Freud's definition (1923a) of the character of psychoanalysis as an empirical science: "Psycho-analysis is not, like philosophies, a system [...]. On the contrary, it keeps close to the facts in its field of study, seeks to solve the immediate problems of observation, gropes its way forward by the help of experience, is always incomplete and always ready to correct or modify its theories."

In synthesis, from this epistemic position, Carlino generously exposes his clinical experience as well as his theoretical-clinical elaborations and hopes for, like any author who dedicates his time to a subject that he loves, an exchange that will expand the extension of psychoanalysis. In Chapters Three, Four, Five, and Six he describes in detail and with clarity subjects referring to psychoanalysis as a clinical practice and the means of distance communication that are available at the present time—real and virtual voice communication, its influence on subjectivity, its articulation, realism through telephone dialogue, framework requirements, types of dialogue, analytical contract, characteristics of application, scopes, and limits.

Another of the author's interests is that this extension of the therapeutic possibilities of psychoanalysis finds a propitious field on which to be researched and tested.

We still lack specific theoretical-clinical conceptualizations for distance treatment. The implementation of psychoanalysis by means of these techniques is still in the research and experimental stage, and, like any modification of classic psychoanalysis being undertaken, it must be open to discussion and exchange with other psychoanalysts. It needs the reflection of peers in order to avoid becoming a dangerous "wizard's venture".

Presently, there are many psychoanalysts who practise this modality and consider it to be "the least of all evils" in a community that has been forced to emigrate in search of work or other opportunities. As these emigrants wish to continue their analysis in their native language, distance psychoanalysis is often the only choice.

It is high time that we carried out a grand scale evaluation of our scientific policy both within our institutions and beyond the walls of our discipline. Psychoanalysis must be concerned with how and for what reason it should evolve. Who authorizes this evolution and transformation?

This is also the concern of the author, like many other psychoanalysts, although from multiple points of view.

I believe that *Distance Psychoanalysis* by Ricardo Carlino is the first of a series of similar publications that will begin appearing in Buenos Aires. These will be challenges for psychoanalysis, both in its way of operating and in its objectives in unison with the new paradigms of the 21st century. Naturally their fundamental concepts will remain.

I will contribute some ideas in reference to this challenge, which I think is shared by all.

Psychoanalysis has extended the understanding of subjectification and became a re-founding piece of knowledge that questions itself about the context of reality. Most sciences advance without asking themselves why, for what reason, or for whom. In contrast, psychoanalysis questions itself and denies the existence of absolute truths. Therefore, we must plot our scientific, philosophical, and economic policies for ourselves.

We can no longer postpone the redefinition of time-space paradigms to be applied to our conceptual framework tools, transference and countertransference. There must also be a wide-ranging self reflection that incorporates us into world history and geopolitics, thus remedying the academic disassociation that has kept us isolated from other sciences. We must no longer believe that this isolation is the best way to protect psychoanalysis. The evolution of psychoanalysis is bound to the defence of humans in society. Psychoanalytic thought is concerned with the humanized use of technology, given that its primary concern is for the subject, his/her sexuality, and his/her emotionality.

For the establishment, any novelty is a threat to its power. In this case, the threat is a technological element: the telephone. This question has become political because it has brought about the possibility of redistributing decision-making power. It obligates one to consider the redistribution effect that so many social movements and colonizations have produced in the history of humanity.

It is essential to make contextual and time-space reconsiderations of the practice of psychoanalysis. These must be made with a pioneer spirit in order to undertake the risk involved in assuming psychoanalytic practice in non-traditional situations.

Carlino indicates very clearly that not all patients will be analysable by telephone, nor will all analysts be able to make use of the telephone in order for patients to be analysed. It will be necessary to reconsider the concept of "analysability", to re-study the new syntactic, semantic, and pragmatic distortions and to rewrite classic works of Freud (1912e, 1913c) such as *Recommendations to Physicians Practicing Psycho-Analysis*, and *On Beginning the Treatment*. However, who will write it this time? Who will give authorization? Will everyone accept the need to learn some things all over again? It took a long time until it was accepted that group, couple, and family relations could be understood and later operate on them with psychoanalytic thought. Many analysts consider that adolescents are unreachable. This is simply because these analysts cannot tolerate "disobedient" patients. Something similar occurs with borderline patients. This being the case, a good part of our initial efforts will be dedicated to the new features in the transference and countertransference of the analyst with traditional psychoanalysis (Freud and the pioneers). Therefore I consider that the publishing of this book is very opportune.

And finally, in reference to "What is the challenge of the 21st century?", first of all it is necessary to indicate that above and beyond psychoanalytic institutions, we must foster the concept that psychoanalysis must take on a greater importance in the culture of the 21st century; much in the same way that Freud's contribution traversed the 20th century without intending to do so.

Freud mapped out a *different contact* with the patient when, along with Breuer, he accepted Anna O.'s suggestion of the talking cure. As the years passed, many people who needed to be listened to and to be supported were benefitted. I believe that this need to be listened to has greatly influenced the spreading of psychoanalytic thinking and its rise to popularity—especially in Argentina and Latin America, where the type of governments throughout the 20th century listened very little to their citizens. Additionally, the region has not formed part of the "centre of the civilization" and has been listened to very little by Europe. Similarly, the psychoanalytic conception of bonds has not only dealt with the academic and therapeutic aspects, but has also served to alleviate social pain.

We are concerned, as psychoanalysts and as citizens of the world, about the negative consequences of globalization, which have placed the market economy and the financial activity of multinational companies above all other disciplines and interests, including those of nations. The mentality is governed by the price that is assigned to the merchandise. Thus many of the values held by psychoanalysis, such as creativity, search for the truth, solidarity, experience, responsibility, privacy, honesty, respect for diversity—whether it be ethnic, linguistic, religious or of social class—not only are "not quoted on the stock market" but are even scorned if they do not render economically.

One way to face the commercialization of ethical and moral values has been through the practice of religious fanaticism, which is based on faith, not on thought or symbolization. It has tried to resist the effects of this globalization by injecting spiritual values compulsively, or even violently. Psychoanalysis, which is supposed to understand these subjects because it contemplates them and analyses the causality and unconscious motivations, has the ethical obligation to promote the media that can try to offer the socially isolated the opportunity to reflect upon their internal and external reality, all in their own language. It is an invaluable anchor of subjectivity to be able to count on regular telephone encounters in order to have the opportunity to reflect and to resolve one's own reality as well as to analyse one's dreams—all in one's native language. One can observe a chain of singular subjectivities in regions threatened by globalization or fanaticism. One can bet that psychoanalytic reflection, multiplied by thousands of subjects, will become an antidote to the danger of ideological fanaticism. *Distance Psychoanalysis* by Carlino has a great number of passages that contribute theoretical-clinical material on this subject. Carlino generously encourages wide regions of the world to become equipped with our tool, which will facilitate their contemplation of their history as well as their historical realities. In this way, we will be able to say that psychoanalysis could "create a shelter within adversity", according to Diogenes Laercio (3rd century BC). From the present time and 50 years hence, I would like to think that psychoanalytic thought will continue generating and promoting culture—or should we decree that the people who remain several years in interplanetary stations will not be able to undergo analysis? It is necessary to think of our work as that of pioneers in remote and poor regions, with all the limitations and imperfections that arise at the beginning of their opus. This will also allow us to get to know them in the context of their situation.

It is clear that all this raises the need for a revision of the institutional functions of central authority, which habitually tends to safeguard whatever is institutional, thus striving to mitigate the danger that can be brought about by pioneering activities that question some of their beliefs. The power of permanence is therefore put in a situation of confrontation with the proposal of change. By definition, the establishment should go through revisions and changes, something that is often considered unnatural instead of enriching and transforming.

Asbed Aryan
February 2010

Endnote

1   Interviews with Zygmunt Bauman about *Society Under Siege* by Silvia Hopenhayn, Osvaldo Gallone, and Daniel Gamper in www.lanacion. com.ar, July 10, 2004.

INTRODUCTION

The intention of writing this book is to contribute to the establishment of a theoretical and technical framework for distance psychoanalysis, which is a therapeutic practice that in our society still has the taste of "individual daring", given that it is not a classically instituted technique. This book has the objective of making an important and significant contribution to this subject. Psychoanalysts will find a solid theoretical-technical base that will contribute to the decentralization of established practice as something fixed and absolute. I have observed that a way of implementing something tends to be "confused" with the essence of that "something". Psychoanalysis can and must be open to new conceptions due to the traversing and permanent reconstruction that socio-cultural transformations produce in human beings. It is necessary to stop and think conceptually about this new psychotherapeutic possibility, which, in fact, is already becoming a reality. I propose this in the hope that it will become a processed conception in psychoanalytic institutions. It needs this seal of authentication in order to be held with the necessary stature at the moment of implementation.

The book contains certain epistemological considerations which are necessary to give a framework to the field which is being traversed. The question is whether these methodological changes imply entering a new field of psychotherapeutic theory or whether it is an extension of the same theory, connected to the natural growth of its doctrinal base. My opinion is that any new conceptualization, no matter how original and/or innovating it is, is based on the basic foundations of a certain theory and therefore must be taken as an evolutionary step of that same theory, thereby making it legitimate and pertinent.

I set out to consider the effect produced by the connecting of psychoanalytic practice with modern means of telecommunication. When two heterogeneous elements are harmoniously connected, inevitably a multiplying effect will take place. This result deserves a thorough observation. Regarding its clinical implementation, there arises a concern for researching the "what, how and why" of this new method, its specific indications and counter-indications, as well as some specific recommendations. All these questions will be addressed thoroughly by studying some of the effects which may occur at the time of putting it into practice.

The illustrative commentary that is inserted is offered with the intention of contributing some examples taken from history, literature, and present-day life. Chapter Six, which I titled "Clinical Anecdotes", contains testimonial comments taken from clinical material. They are intended to grant a status of legitimacy to the pretension of giving validity to analytical dialogue which takes place outside the psychoanalyst's office. I also attempt to refute the effect of confused homologation produced by the conceptual superposition, to my understanding erroneous, that labels as virtual all communication that originates from beyond the direct reach of the voice.

CHAPTER ONE

Socio-Cultural transformations: their influence on psychoanalysis

Psycho-analysis an Empirical Science:
Psycho-analysis is not, like philosophies, a system starting out from a
few sharply defined basic concepts, seeking to grasp the whole universe
with the help of these and, once it is completed, having no room for fresh
discoveries or better understanding.

—Freud, S. (1923a)

This epigraph contains the view on psychoanalysis that Freud (1923a) included in "Two Encyclopaedia Articles: Psychoanalysis and Libido Theory". It summarizes in concise form the epistemic spirit that encourages any researcher.

Socio-cultural changes and technological innovations that settle into and circulate within society affect both reality and people's subjectivity. At the present time we see so many changes in so many social customs that we easily perceive their influence. It is up to each individual to decide how to receive them, contemplate them, and what to do with them.

1   Base logic

This term refers to an elementary and axiomatic position from which each person feels, thinks, reads, listens, and elaborates his/her own feeling and thinking. This *base logic* operates as a determining factor at the moment of adopting a decision or conduct. It is the product of a combination of knowledge, beliefs, norms, and values, which produce a mental stance and attitude functioning as an axiom or point of reference. It functions in the mind as a lens through which one can observe, understand, and give meaning. It is a starting point from which to interact with the world and with oneself. It works subliminally like a permanent transparent lens which goes unnoticed by the person who uses it. Observing reality through this lens offers a perspective which leaves proof of its existence. It produces a sense of orientation that promotes a tendency and determines a certain stance when facing stimulants coming from within or from the surrounding world (Carlino, 2000).

Presently, a great degree of social interaction takes place vis-à-vis modern technological media. Due to the introduction of ever-improving technology in everyday life, new forms of meeting and interacting with other people have been added to the traditional ones, thereby changing the customs and cultural paradigms of behaviour. This technology allows for an encounter or a contact which differs greatly from traditional ones. Communicating by telephone, internet, or text message is now a common way of meeting.

Over the last century, the technological resources applied to communication have gradually changed our conception of everyday life. They have also had a great influence in our feeling of involvement and responsibility about what occurs in once faraway places—those which no longer seem remote or detached.

In the contemplation of reality, one must consider the values and paradigms in force in each place and during each era. Freud and his immediate followers developed psychoanalysis at the dawn of the last century. At the beginning of this century, psychoanalysis is offered to those who believe, articulate, and operate with the conception of technological advances. This phenomenon cannot be ignored. At different times in the history of its development, psychoanalysis has needed to enrich its theory and its technique to be able to offer assistance to children, adolescents, couples, families, and groups. Due to the psychoanalytic demand of more regressive patients, such as those that are borderline and psychotic, it was necessary to conceptualize classic concepts from different starting points. Psychoanalytic praxis, albeit differently, has found its implementation in institutions. Its conception and its clinical operativeness are linked to the knowledge offered by neurosciences and current psychopharmacology. These elements do not play the role of mere additives, but rather change the entire panorama and therefore, its implementation. Antecedents of this institutional practice can be found in hospitals in the Buenos Aires area, where, since the 1960s, it has been implemented in the formerly named Hospital of Lanús (today called Policlínico Evita) directed by Mauricio Goldenberg. In the Hospital Neuropsiquiátrico Borda, the two-time president of the Argentine Psychoanalytic Association (APA), Dr Jorge García Badaracco, adopted a therapeutic approach for the treatment of psychotic patients by implementing classic individual psychotherapy with psycho-pharmaceutical treatment while adding multi-family group meetings with understanding and psychoanalytic operativeness. This way of applying psychoanalytic knowledge takes advantage of the contributions of other disciplines, allowing its confluence to operate in the general psychological well-being of the patient and his/her family.

The new conditions and perspectives of individual, social, economic, and labour development usually generate instability or discontinuity in the place of residence. This has affected some patients undergoing analysis who, having had to emigrate, wish to continue or resume their analysis once they are settled in their new country.

The present state of modern telecommunications and its demographic consequences must be taken as a new opportunity to allow for the implementation of analysis beyond the walls of the psychoanalyst's office.

Society moves within the framework of the new logic which arises from these neo-necessities that have found their way into its heart. This has arrived at the psychoanalyst's office, thereby shaking up a part of the established position of classic psychoanalytic technique. The demand for psychoanalytic treatment of those people who live the typical lifestyle of the present era pounds on the doors of psychoanalysis, obligating it to enrich its theory and technique with the purpose of accepting forms of therapy that occur beyond the physical limitations of the psychoanalyst's office. This is not unlike what occurs with so many other customs that require changes in their structure and development in order to update and modernize their implementation.

In the epigraph, we can observe Sigmund Freud postulating about psychoanalysis as an open doctrine which must be rethought when light illuminates a new reality. Every clinical experience involves an analyst and a patient—two people related to the values and the logic of the era in which that analysis takes place. There are so many gradually-developing transformational changes that it is sometimes difficult to digest them and to leave aside certain attitudes in order to replace them with more suitable ones.

Technology makes possible and conceivable what beforehand was not even imaginable. It is for this reason that technological changes are implanted more easily in people who are born contemporaneously with the arrival of those changes, given that they do not have to make any effort to adapt. Neither do they feel remorse for the fact that these technological changes have occurred.

2 The horror towards what's different

The introjected image of a clinical psychoanalytical session has the conceptual and imaginary design of an encounter with corporal proximity between an analyst and patient in a doctor's office containing a professional diploma, a couch for the patient, and an armchair behind for the analyst. This introjected image operates as a preconception that tends to portray any attempt to psychoanalyse with a different design or structure as something improbable, incredible, or even outlandish. Anything new runs the risk of being labelled and catalogued as *strange*, *non-familiar*, or perhaps even *dangerous*. A mental matrix reproduces this feeling of rejection whenever something from outside a previously established order arises. This has been happening since the dawn of psychoanalysis. For Freud (1912e, 1913c) and his direct disciples, the concept of telephone sessions would have been unimaginable. In its beginnings, psychoanalysis was designed in a spirit of exploring the unconscious. The ways of achieving this and putting it into practice have always varied throughout time. It has always been necessary to contemplate psychoanalysis and discover its possibilities of application, taking into account the values, paradigms, and technical resources of every moment and place. This leads us to believe that there is no reason to suppose that psychoanalysis has reached its maximum point of development. Even more, the rapid advance of science and technique permanently broaden and sometimes even transform the orientation and possibly even the very sense of its goals. It is therefore important to keep in mind that a process which is implemented through habit is not tantamount to a conceptual essence.

There exists a certain and widespread tendency to denominate anything new as *strange, rare, abnormal, exotic*, etc., as if it were some type of foreigner who provokes xenophobia and the consequent attitude of alarm and even rejection. An example of this tendency can be observed in some people, especially children, who automatically refuse to eat a type of food solely because it is unknown to them.

These comments should in no way be construed as a lack of acknowledgement that these changes can often be at odds with classic analysis. Thus far, new clinical approaches are an attempt to test new methodologies within the clinical field. Only when their results are massively researched will it be seen how much their implementation has been able to conserve the psychoanalytic nature that was desired from the outset, accepting the premise that neither a single success nor a single failure confirm a doctrine.

There are two schools of thought regarding the rejection or acceptance of the clinical implementation of psychoanalysis carried out with communications technology. A third position is that of analysts who have decided not to define their views on the matter, but rather observe its development and follow the research as it is presented. Those who reject this innovative method consider that only classic treatment is practicable, given its abundantly proven success. This epistemological and clinical position works like a Procrustean bed that only considers as psychoanalytic those treatments within classically established limits. Another school of thought is open to the possibility of an instrumental modification to include it as another clinical option and to observe its results. For this reason, it is necessary not only to modify its implementation technique, but also to be aware of the need to process new theoretical conceptualizations when the existing ones will not suffice.

3   Why distance psychoanalysis?

The decision to theorize about distance psychoanalysis arises from the increase in supply of online therapies in recent years, the advance of the internet in everyday life and the need of some psychoanalysts to show the creative spirit of testing, finding out results, and presenting them.

The present tools of distance communication must be conceived not only as facilitators of new applications of psychoanalysis but also as promoters of entirely new forms of science.

In the here and now, whether it be of a session or life itself, certain facts and situations can be considered as unprecedented. That is to say, they are not preceded by any significant load and therefore can acquire it at the moment of their arrival. Some people, when facing a present situation which they have never seen before, react in an astonished and disconcerted way, which often generates an irrational rejection to this situation. These feelings are often covered up by rationalizations that tend to calm their underlying anguish.

A century after the "technical writings" of Freud, it is necessary to review them and to reformulate those points that require specific attention, so as to make room for the neo-necessities arising from the establishing of a different social contract in the population. Should it be believed that Freud did not have this in mind when he wrote them? It seems paradoxical, given the contribution of psychoanalysis in the metamorphosis of thought and social values, that these new principles would now ask their old and generous contributor to update psychoanalysis and create new perspectives that take these transformations into account.

When one has the intention of contributing to the construction of a specific and novel aspect of psychoanalytic technique, it is necessary and enriching to share with one's peers the thoughts and the subsequent reaction whereupon it can be received. New theoretical elements and new theories of technique become necessary when establishing the practice of distance psychoanalysis. These must then be contemplated and processed institutionally, as well as be exposed to a manifold and permanent discussion. For an undertaking of such magnitude, many reflective contributions are necessary. Its implementation introduces concerns and queries that promote the search for a new conceptual framework in psychoanalytic thought, one that has not been explored before.

The elements provided by classic theory and analytical technique are not sufficient to meet the demands of distance treatment. It becomes necessary, for example, to redefine some fundamental concepts in this new form of psychoanalysis, such as "real", "virtual", "presence", "contact", and "encounter". These concepts are beyond concrete definition and must be considered in abstract and symbolic form. Notions such as "distance", "far", "close" will not be measured in length but rather in time. In distance treatment, one must accept the ideas stemming from the *"mundos superpuestos"* (superimposed worlds) concept (Puget & Wender, 1982), and add the notion of *proper and different context*. One must also consider what quality and name to give to an interview (inter-view) in which the protagonists begin a relation without visual contact. The question arises as to whether there is an analytical "encounter" in the *Inter space* and in the *Intra space*. These spaces may be defined as follows.

The *Inter space* is an interpersonal connected space: "place" without physical dimension in which analytical dialogue occurs in the space of time of the analysis session; transference area of conscious and unconscious communication, originating in the *Intra space* of each participant. It can be conceived as a workshop of ideas in which abstractions and constructions of symbolic and concrete realities take place and contribute to an analytical process. It is created and contained by the framework and supported by the structure produced by the analytical work of the material in each session.

The *Intra space* is an intrapersonal connected space. It is an "area" of internal dialogue of every person. It includes the primary process of the internal world and the secondary process of a reflective internal dialogue. It is expected that the patient publicly exposes the "secondary" content of this internal dialogue. Concerning the analyst, he/she will produce in this area the internal analytical dialogue with the aim of analysing the material of the patient. This area includes personal aspects of his private world that will not be divulged to the patient. Here new concepts, whose content are expressed through verbal, paraverbal, and extra-verbal signs, are constructed and will be qualified for a new exchange that will take place in the *Inter space* (Cantis-Carlino & Carlino, 1987).

Other subjects will be added, stemming from the need for new conceptual objects which are unknown today but will be discovered as *"The pathway is made by travelling along it"*, as the verse by Machado tells us.

All these concepts must receive some contribution in line with the present social era, which is the creator of new paradigms that entail different expectations and accomplishments. These subjects will be discussed in Chapter Four.

a   Reasons linked to order and social values

Today's human being is not the same as the one that Freud studied more than one hundred years ago. The accumulation of some changes and the adding of new premises, at a certain moment produce a qualitative jump in today's human being. After World War II, new human rights were established with a certain firmness throughout the world. Legal, political, and economic phenomena have occurred in social life, which have created a deep impact on the mentality of the population. How much of all this affects psychoanalysis and the psychoanalyst at the moment of implementing a psychoanalytic treatment? The omniscient figure of the "doctor", for the good of medicine and psychoanalysis, has been dethroned. There is a new position in patients regarding their own image inasmuch as they hope—and demand—when undergoing a consultation or treatment. Nevertheless, as I understand, there has not been a growth or parallel development referring to the responsibility of "doing unto others as you would have them do unto you", as the Bible tells us.

Nowadays, for the middle class, the term "earn a living" greatly exceeds the expectation of merely acquiring adequate clothing, food, entertainment, and a bit of reading material. In order to have access to a decent lifestyle, and furthermore add the cost in time and money that psychoanalysis entails, it is necessary for many patients to carry out long working days which do not always leave much of a margin to be used in long trips to the psychoanalyst's office. In certain patients, one can observe rotation and instability of residence or even a geographic migration towards another region or country.

As shall be addressed thoroughly a bit farther ahead, within this group of people, there are those who request distance analysis. It should also be said that new motivations are constantly being added as products of the new paradigms of communicative encounter. As can be observed, complex socio-cultural reality is constantly changing, much like a kaleidoscope. When this reality changes, it simultaneously transforms its inhabitants. Focusing our work with the philosophical idea of evolution—to come into being—is inherent to psychoanalysis.

Psychoanalysis, as a theory and as a technique, must take inspiration from real human beings and also have them as its ultimate goal. These must be humans in their own situations, their histories, their present lives, their family, and their transferential bonds. It must focus on the social development with which it is to work and consider the values which prevail in the generation at hand. If it were not to do so, psychoanalysis would run the risk of becoming a very interesting literary and scientific piece, only one which would appear on the forgotten shelves of the library. In its evolution, except for some brief moments at the local or regional level, psychoanalysis in its own evolutionary geneal- ogy has been willing to continue, as Freud stated, *"having no room for fresh discoveries or better understanding"*.

b Professional reasons

The internet is today an adequate instrumental resource for the trans- mission and reception of information, whether it be public or private, written or spoken. The variety of services offered there can even be overwhelming. It helps to give solutions to many procedures that, before their implementation, required personal transaction. However, this technical resource, by offering new operative possibilities, ends up creating new necessities. A great part of the productive, creative, and interactive life of many people is based on the use of the telephone and the computer. In fact, the computer and its accompanying accessories are becoming part of the mental resources of its users.

The use of *counselling* services and focal therapies through the internet is steadily increasing. These services grow constantly in research, in practice, and in supply. The possibility of different types of distance therapy also progressively increases the number of users. In this context, the idea, supply, and demand for distance psychotherapy are born.

The intention of publishing this book stems from the premise that clinical psychoanalysis in distance treatment must find its rightful tech- nical and ethical place, based on a solid conceptualization. This book intends to contribute to that objective. It is also necessary to create fora and discussion groups of clinical material beyond borders, in order to exchange clinical experiences and to theorize about them.

Psychoanalysis, as a therapeutic resource established in a culture, would be seriously compromising its opportunity of survival through- out the ages if it did not generate adequate clinical survival methods. Although this does not pretend to be an absolute statement, currently there are favourable conditions established in our professional field which can allow us to take advantage of a suitable encounter between psychoanalysis and technology. Analysts in considerable numbers are showing greater tolerance for leaving classic moulds. They understand that a considerable number of people, due to new existential and/or work conditions, either temporarily or permanently, require analysis carried out through the technological resources of communication.

4 Influence of technology in the analytical framework

In this section I will deal with the vicissitudes of the psychoanalyst in a changing society. Psychoanalysis is a theory of psychism and also a therapeutic method *conceived from this theory and applied to people* who are part of the society and of the era in which they live, grow, are educated, exchange, and share. If psychoanalysis does not develop the theoretical conceptions and the technical instruments that every social era requires, it will gradually lose the possibilities of clinical implementation. However, this does not permit the idea of "anything goes as long as one can adapt to the changes".

When a patient is in a situation of geographic migration and requests to continue or resume his/her analysis with the same professional, some analysts consider this to be feasible and resort to the idea of implementing some type of distance treatment. Others, however, consider it is impossible to undertake analysis outside the psychoanalyst's office and therefore the best alternative is to accept that fact and allow for a mourning process for the loss of that bond to take place. On this matter, Argentieri and Amati Mehler (2003) state that it is difficult for them to accept the idea that psychoanalysis, or psychoanalysts themselves, should be a step behind society and its changing times. Our task—they add—is to understand and interpret that change. This statement, although it may contain some acceptable conceptual ideas, does not have the totalizing and exclusive scope that these analysts try to give it: the concept that "society" includes in its very heart that of "psychoanalysis". Psychoanalysis cannot be an extra-terrestrial observer that is indifferent to the values and paradigms of the society in which it operates. It is society itself that makes room for or rejects psychoanalysis as a valid resource for its population. Changes that take place in the former will inevitably take place in the latter.

Psychoanalytic treatment cannot be based only on the amount of conceptual reality that its texts contain, but must also be applied to people included in this context. Psychoanalysis has roots and destinations that anchor and address human beings anthropologically and socially. This statement, although it includes the subject in his/her circumstances, is by no means intended to foster a position of mindless submission.

The inclusion of suitable technological advances in communication is an act of enriching freedom and not of submission. Any type of psychoanalysis that does not intelligently accompany the evolution of society can only continue being implemented in the more stagnant sectors of the population, in which perhaps it will be able to persevere without conflict. I say "perhaps" because the new prevailing logic in the modern world does not leave any corner untouched. A critical position or even one that rejects change altogether must be free of all obstinacy. A reflective position is possible and, whenever necessary, discussions among colleagues must take place.

The avatars in cultural habits provoke individual changes which, once they become widespread, become new paradigms of thought and social behaviour. If the resources that have been prepared to attend "the way things used to be" are not rejuvenated, they begin to lose central prominence and move little by little to a corner where old, strange, and finally excluded things are tossed. We must distinguish between a fleeting fad and a change that is "here for good". Regarding this topic, we analysts must always maintain a position of reasonable balance between new phenomena that notify psychoanalysis of the need to renew itself, and proven and established concepts that continue being very valuable. However, given the moment, the correct procedure is to evaluate and to decide according to each individual clinical situation. Psychoanalytic theory and technique need to be updated by creating new theoretical and procedural resources that allow them to face unprecedented situations for present patients. The globalized world makes its population more heterogeneous and also more unstable regarding its geographic residence, whether it be for a short time or a long one. The social marginalization which is brought about by economic models that privilege the accumulation of wealth for the few while marginalizing the many, provoke certain tribal, sectarian, and dogmatic isolation, which gives rise to the creation of distinctive paradigmatic guidelines for each group. The analyst must become familiar with these guidelines and to be able to include them in his/her understanding. It is very important to consider that the arrival of new paradigms does not cause the previous ones to disappear. These older paradigms remain latent in the mind and can eventually superimpose or even push aside the new ones. Distance psychoanalysis entails broadening the field of anthropology, as well as that of sociology.

Distance psychoanalysis justified its entrance into the professional field by providing a solution to the real life situation of some patients in reference to the geographic distance from the analyst's office. This was its first reason for being. However, once established, proven, and accepted as an effective clinical method, it can be chosen by the patient as an alternative form of psychoanalysis. In this case we would be attending the specificities of the patient's personality and/or a simple (or complex) choice among different ways to undergo analysis. It is very probable that among the so-called *"Digital natives"*, there will be a growing demand for distance psychoanalysis, no matter how far away the analyst's office happens to be. The groundwork for choosing one form of psychoanalysis or another will be considered in the diagnostic interview and it will be a *sine qua non* function of the analyst to contemplate what form of analysis is the most suitable, while encouraging the patient to do the same. A surprise for this premise is that certain patients will not consider it necessary that the analyst indicate the method specifically to him/her, but rather suppose that it is his/her free choice. Ludmer (2007) proposes to think of the distance treatment as one more option inside the offer of treatments and to analyse with every patient who requests telephonic analysis what sense it has for him/her to be analysed that way. Assuming that dialogue carries out a fundamental role in psychoanalytic treatment, it is feasible to conceive of and execute psychoanalysis with the help of communication technologies. When the analyst interprets the patient, he/she does so based on his/her theoretical-technical knowledge. The interpretation reaches out to the patient through his/her words to which he/she simultaneously adds voice intonation (Guiard, 1977; Zac de Filc, 2005). Even so, the conditions of use of whatever technological means is utilized will differ from those of the doctor's office. These differences must be taken into account, although both modalities function with the spoken word.

When the analyst in his/her clinical practice associates his/her word with the use of a transmitting apparatus, it carries him/her to a different colloquial position. These instruments, until recently extra-analytical, now become part of the framework, which requires the analyst to acquire a specific preparation.

5 The use of communication technology and its psychological repercussion

At the time of its clinical implementation, the user generally has some pre-established connection with these technical devices, to which we can add the one that is produced every time the device is used, depending on with whom and for what purpose it is employed. As can be seen, the established relationship with the technical device being used is not neutral, but rather contains a load comprised of the amalgam of the previous emotions connected with its use and what is established each time the device is utilized. It is logical to suppose and also to consider as transference this emotion that overloads with meaning all that occurs during a session in which this communication device is used. A well-known experience will serve as an example: whenever a patient treated in an analyst's office calls by telephone to give information about something linked to the framework, it is well received if his/her intervention is merely informative and it does not require great commentary from the part of the analyst. When this limit is exceeded, in general the analyst says that the subject cannot be dealt with by telephone. This makes sense because the dialogue takes place outside the setting of the session.

The analyst must take into account, especially in the beginning of treatment, the transfer formed around the device being used (which comes from a non-psychoanalytic use) because it will surely be put into play in the bond. It is necessary, at the time of agreeing to the contract, to clearly stipulate the use and the purpose that the communicational device being used in the analytical dialogue will have. If, for example, the device were the telephone, this tool of communication must be treated as the "meeting place" of the session, equivalent to the classic psychoanalyst's office. Therefore, other means of communication must be used to transmit information outside the session schedule. As much as possible, the telephone should only be used for the time of the session, avoiding its use outside the session. Should the habitual means be Skype, it should never be used outside the session, even if one of the two sees that the other is connected. For the patient, trying to use the means of communication employed in the session after office hours is tantamount to dropping by the psychoanalyst's office when he/she looks up to a window and sees a light on.

6   Legal aspects

When the venues from which the analyst and patient communicate are different jurisdictions—i.e., different states or countries—it must be understood that the legislation in force may not only be that of the analyst's location, but also that of the patient's. It is therefore necessary and advisable to have a working knowledge of the respective legislations that govern the practice of the profession as well as the norms of private international law which may influence the choice of law between the involved jurisdictions. For example, in reference to legal and tax obligations, the following question may arise: where does distance psychoanalytic treatment really take place? Psychoanalysts have yet to decide on this topic but, when they do, there is no guarantee that domestic or international law will accept the definition of the psychoanalytic associations. Topics regarding work permits, civil and criminal liability, and tax obligations will be discussed in Chapter Eight.

The ethical aspect of these analyses entails a professional bridge that connects it with the pertinent legal aspects. This can be seen at the time of accepting or refusing a treatment of this nature. At this point in time, the only requisite is that the analyst has adequate expertise in distance psychoanalysis.

CHAPTER TWO

Technology and its influence on subjectivity

1 Reality: its presentations and its representations

We are now quite far from the early stage of a culture which, at times, was very interested in recognizing its surrounding reality in visible and concrete terms. In that archaic evolutionary stage of our species it was a great cognitive achievement to be able to distinguish that which had a concrete, tangible, and perceivable existence from that which could be an unworldly entity and/or product of hallucination.

We can see that in this conception, all that was real and concrete was set against all that, although possessing some type of existence, belonged to the category of the imaginable or the evocable. The evolution of this latter category gradually gave rise to the concept of "the virtual". When mankind learned to distinguish that a drawing or a word evoked the original object—that is to say, it represented it but it was not the same as the real object—a true advance in knowledge came about. In the psycho-semiological examination of a patient it is necessary to observe whether he/she understands this difference, given that it acts as a dividing line serving to differentiate a perception from an illusion (deformed perception of an object) or from a hallucination (perception without an object).

Presently, both artistic creativity and technology offer us a series of objects for delight or for practical use. These objects represent a reality, albeit often very different from what reality is habitually considered to be. When one interacts with objects created through the use of technology, such as the images on a screen, the voice on a telephone, the moving images of television or cinema, or simply the remote control, one manages to produce perceivable effects as if he/she had rendezvoused with or somehow been in contact with the real objects that they represent. Due to this, some of these applications have received the name of virtual reality, as if trying to make both parties happy.

As we shall see farther ahead, the analyst in his/her function becomes quite familiar (and sometimes very intensely so) with both reality and creative fiction, as well as with delirium. It involves both conscious and unconscious fantasy as well as objectivity and subjectivity. He/she must differentiate the symbol from what is symbolized, the signifier from what is signified. He/she must be attentive to transference and to what is transferred. He/she must approach his/her countertransference and know how to differentiate it as something of itself, of the other, or as an aspect of each one.

When reference is made to the "as if" of the session, in relation to what the analyst represents for the patient in the transference, implicitly one is referring to something that was real and concrete before, but that now is a psychic reality. However, when it comes into psychic reality, it is also present in the here and now of the session, thereby acquiring at that same moment the quality of being.

The analyst permanently manages both ranges of the idea of reality: the *psychic* and the *material*. Nevertheless, it is not possible to encapsulate all the possible realities in these two conceptual elements. Let us take as an example the dialogue of a telephone session. It would be a pity to limit it to one of these two types of reality. That dialogue *per se* is a fact brought about by an encounter between two people. Its content only acquires analytical meaning within the space of time in which a session takes place. The ideo-affective aspect that arises within it is constructed on the basis of the contributions of its protagonists. This content can be long-lasting or ephemeral, in either its appearance or its disappearance. The phenomenology which takes place in the session is regulated by the analytical contract, the framework, and the psychoanalytic understanding of the material. All these elements constitute manifold realities of analytical dialogue that lack tangible materiality.

The reality of the session can be considered according to the point of view employed. If we consider what takes place there we are in the presence of phenomenological reality. However, if we consider the way of processing, we are in the presence of psychoanalytic reality, based on material reality or psychic reality.

In the first tests of the instrumental use of technological devices, one generally has a clear awareness of the difference between the reality that exists as a result of the device's use and that which would have existed if that device had never been used. A clear example of this can be observed in the use of cellular telephones when they first came into being. One was aware of the technological artificiality that this use implied. However, presently, the mobile phone is so built in to one's routine that it has entered the daily logic of communication. Although one understands the difference between speaking on a cellular telephone and doing so from a distance of one metre, from the communicational point of view it is considered to be equivalent. Something similar occurs with a document received by fax, which can acquire legal value if the sender has a receipt proving that it was received. The same situation occurs with emails that have digitally scanned signatures.

Upon reading a well-written novel, the reader buries himself in the plot, in the ambience, and in the characters, thereby feeling a sensation of reality that, at the time of the reading, does not cause him to consider whether it is fiction or reality. In fact, the more the writer has been able to obtain that effect, the better his/her literary qualification is. Regarding this, the writer and novelist Mario Vargas Llosa, recent winner of the Nobel Prize for Literature (2010), in one of his works, *La Verdad de las Mentiras"* (The Truth of Lies) shows how, with the tools that literature has, it is possible to reach faraway places where the nucleus of truth that human lies have are located.

What is fiction? It is a construction of images or facts that represent something created by the imagination. However, at the moment of making contact with a fictional story, they are experienced as real and even applauded when they achieve this end. The "lies" of the literary authors must have a certain power of conviction. In fact, therein lies their genius because they manage to make us experience reality or other vital experiences as if they were our own. It is as if they allowed us to live parallel lives in their well-achieved novelistic conviction.

Although the widespread conceptual use of the term "virtual" already has a specific nomination, I will introduce some ideas on this subject. Several authors outside the field of psychoanalysis have treated this subject. Each one contributed in a certain direction and arrived at the place where his/her conceptual route has carried him/her.

a Virtuality

For the aims and purposes of this book, I have chosen to contemplate the conceptualization made by Pierre Lévy (1995) in its titled work *Qu'est-ce que le Virtuel?* (What is the Virtual?). It takes as a starting point some conceptual terms that need to be known in order to enter into the development of his ideas. They are: "the real"; "the possible"; "the virtual", and "the present", to which he assigns a specific meaning. Let us examine each one of them.

"The real" (*le réel*): Habitually it is connected to the existence of something that occupies space and is perceivable by some or all the senses: sight, touch, hearing, smell, taste. This description of something real is that of a material object which confirms that it is not the product of imagination. Following this line, one denominates as authentic or genuine that which can be differentiated from something artificial or an imitation.

"The possible" (*le possible*): Lévy, supported by the concepts of Gilles Deleuze, accurately defines some terms that identify certain processes of transformation. He defines as "the possible" that which exists in latent form within a real object, or that which has the potential of becoming "real" without undergoing any changes in its nature. Due to this, its coming into existence will provoke no surprises. A univocal relation exists between the identity of "the real" and of "the possible". Although it still has not come into being, one can anticipate the identity of the latter because it is contained in the real object. If "the possible" comes into being, it will maintain its original characteristics without any change in the nature in which it was preconceived. Conceptually, "the possible" is considered as a potential goal of "the real" without any changes in its ontological quality. In synthesis, what is found at the other pole of "the real" is "the possible".

"The virtual" (*le virtuel*): This concept is defined by Pierre Lévy as an entity that at a given moment acquires the quality of "problem", which needs a process of solution. When "the virtual" begins to move and arrives at its desired goal, it is considered to have been transformed into another object, which Lévy denominates as "the present" (*l'actuel*).

It differs from "the possible" in that its very nature holds a potential force of transformation that allows it to arrive at its goal: "the present". In its development, it does not repeat a predetermined programme without undergoing changes—as occurs in the path and the goal of "the possible"—but rather is programmed to solve a "problematic" situation in any way that is feasible and advisable, adapting to the circumstances that it encounters along the way. It contains a transforming force of a complex nature, destined to solve a "problem". Its resolution implies a development that tends to transform that initial "problematic" matter into a different object: "the present", which has another nature and another way of being.

"The present" (*l'actuel*): This is the result at which one arrives after a process of virtualization, born as a necessary element for the solution of "the problem" of "the virtual". When this virtual aspect that contains a real object is in a "problematic" situation or circumstance, and one adds to its nature an extrinsic stimulative force or will, a virtualization process is triggered and eventually transforms itself into "the present" of the primitive virtual object in a "problematic" situation. "The present", as a final result, is another structure and another way of being of "the virtual" because the virtualization process produces an ontological mutation.

From these premises, which we could consider to be axiomatic definitions, a real object can contain a virtual aspect in a situation, which we could call embryonic, with the potential of developing until reaching its goal: "the present". Let us look at a couple of examples. In the object, the egg—product of a fertilized ovum—we can appreciate its real existence on the one hand, while on the other hand recognize the virtual aspect that contains its potential of developing into an adult member of its species. Something similar occurs when a biologist perceives a caterpillar. Although he/she identifies the caterpillar as real, he/she knows of its potential to become a butterfly. Between the caterpillar and the butterfly there will be a transforming process that Lévy denominates as virtualization. "The virtual" contained in the real object (the caterpillar) of the near pole of this process will eventually reach the opposite pole in "the present"—the butterfly.

Therefore, we see that both the fertilized egg and the caterpillar—as objects per se—contain the quality of real beings. "The virtual" contained in them, when it gets the chance to carry out its process of development, will become in "the present". The egg will become an adult member of its species and the caterpillar will become a butterfly, that is to say—"the present"—as an object in itself, will be also a real object.

An example that vividly demonstrates the virtual aspect of something real can be seen in the seeds found inside the pyramids of Egypt, which gave rise to the adult species corresponding to each one of them—"the present"—five thousand years after its own origin or birth. The seed contains a "problematic" aspect whose virtualizing solution will allow it to became a tree.

Some ideas suggested by the subject can find expression in the possible variables of the game of chess. This game contains in its structure and operation a richness that can serve as a potent modeller of the ideas that we are dealing with. When one looks at a chessboard as the setting of a game, the following can be observed: "the real", as the tangible object of this game, is found in a square board divided into 64 squares in which 32 pieces, each carved in such a way that their shape and size emulate a specific meaning established by the rules of chess—king, queen, rook, bishop, knight, and pawn, in "black" and "white"—have their place. After the game begins, the pieces become distributed on the board in a certain way forming the reality of any given move as a consequence of the previous one. If by accident the position of the pieces were to be altered, each one of them must return to its previous position, so as to recover the original situation of the game, which was involuntarily altered.

"The virtual" which contains the present distribution of the pieces is formed by the logistic and strategic value of their positions and by the functional relation established with those of the opposite colour, based on the plays that can emerge from them. This is the "problem", which arises and must be solved in the move that is about to be made. When the player thinks about the different plays that can be made, he/she is imaginarily trying to solve "the problem" that arises as a result of his/her opponent's last move. In each move that he/she imagines, he/she calculates the invading effect of that move and the situation to which he/she subjects the opponent after the move is carried out. At some moment, he/she will decide to make the play. This act is a phenomenological fact that acts according to the reality presented in the board and tries to give a solution to "the problem" that was raised by the previous play—thereby starting up a process of virtualization that will structure the new distribution of the pieces on the board offered for the following play. Let us remember (as seen before) that the real object contains "the possible" in a latent form and that the transforming process changed nothing in its original nature. This description of the present of the board offers four possible central themes of observation:

1. It is "the present" because it comes from a process of virtualization carried out in the previous play as a result of the positions of the pieces.
2. It is "the real" offered to the new play.
3. It is also "the virtual" of this play that contains the "problem" that requires a solution—that will take place in the current play.
4. "The possible" is in the type of movement that allows or prevents the rules of the game. It is fixed and does not change in its form or in its essence. It responds to a predetermination.

b   Language and virtualization of thought

The capacity for expression and communication in the archaic eras of history was manifested in signs and gestures, at times executed in rudimentary oral ways and at times by means of spontaneous body expressions which "spoke" for themselves. From these primitive corporal manifestations, the communicative resources of human beings undertook a process of constant development and improvement. No longer did these means of communication come solely from the body, but rather from instrumental resources that were constantly being added. As it became necessary to communicate from longer distances, either physically or through time, a more complex language with greater symbolic content was developed. Each generation, with the advances in its expressive development, served as a nutrient model of identification for its children, as a starting point for new and richer expressive developments, and as another example of the virtualization of the language. Every "present" moment is a new starting point moving towards another virtualizing development.

Writing has also undergone a process of development in complexity, given the need to leave recorded testimony of a message or conceptual speech so that it can reach a faraway place or a point in the distant future. These first graphic markings, given their primitive nature, gave rise to an interpretative reading, which in the process of human development has been transformed into writing systems with shared orthographic and grammatical rules. The development of language, both spoken and written, not only allows for human expression, but also introduces itself into the mind and aids in the construction of thoughts. A well-known aphorism illustrates this: "He who speaks badly, thinks badly."

Since archaic times, there has existed a human necessity for distance communication—even beyond the reach of the body and the present time. The present conceptual language, oral and/or written, allows for and also promotes a spectrum of communicational possibilities, especially when it is delivered massively through modern communication technology. The quality of distance communication is undergoing constant improvement, even surpassing the present and the very life of the transmitter of that communication. In recent years, it has breached the boundaries of our own planet and even had the pretension of reaching out beyond our galaxy.

The richer the language used, the greater the capacity to think and to express oneself. Language operates as a tool that allows one both to "design" and to perceive conceptual "designs". It can be conceived as a kind of germinating seed whose development (virtualization) allows one to reach suitable conceptual levels in order to communicate and learn as well as to transmit or receive ideas, desires, wills, agreements, and disagreements without having to resort to bodily force or an exaggerated degree of gesticulation. In this process of human development, the simple fact of belonging to the same generation and culture does not guarantee that all contemporaries will reach the same degree of development.

Technology, along with all of its resulting devices, carries great importance. Pierre Lévy defines it as a "virtualization of the body, action, and physical surroundings". Technology empowers man to pierce the *natural* limits of corporal action. It strengthens size, force, and sensory-perceptive capacity. It multiplies manual ability, speed, and distance reach while diminishing the limits that time imposes. The hammer has increased the power of the fist, the lever has increased the power of the arm, smoke signals have increased the reach of body signals; and printed symbols have increased the possibility of recording our messages throughout time. The wheel has enormously multiplied the action of pulling, pushing, and transporting. The development of human technical ability and its instrumental progresses imply an exponential multiplication of the natural, the innate, and the primitive within humans. In historical evolution, this exponential opportunity has gradually been transferred and applied to agriculture, writing, printing, electrical development, motor-driven machines, and even complex and rapid means of locomotion and present-day electronic instruments, including of course communication technology. Vis-à-vis the internet, it is possible to "go" to a library without leaving home or establish contact with a distant person just by pressing keys or touching a screen.

These comments, which refer to the evolution of the communicational necessity and capacity of the species, have the intention of showing the necessity—or perhaps the vocation—of human beings to communicate "beyond their own noses".

In its evolution, the human species has never limited itself to its biological possibilities. Although its development is based on the material reality that its genetics and biology entail, it also displays "the possible" and "the virtual" content from within. When from the biological matrix different processes of latent biological virtualizations are detached, one will arrive at the possible updates that can exist. For this process to occur, it is necessary to be immersed in a culture that offers language, values, education, habits, technological resources, training, etc. Technological advances are multiplying these possibilities. An example of this is the diverse and advanced operational capacities that modern electronic instruments have acquired. "Digital natives" have a more widespread use of these instruments because they have been brought up in the presence of electronic-digital devices. This gives them a great advantage over "digital immigrants".

When we reconstruct or proceed to replay a session in order to supervise or to exchange opinions among colleagues, we bring to the present the resonance of a dialogue of the past. Any session in the act of being discussed or supervised, although absolutely authentic, has undergone a transformation and exists as "the present" after having gone through a virtualization process.

In current linguistic usage, one tends to label as virtual anything that is exchanged from a distance and which is transmitted by hi-tech means of communication. It is for this reason that we find virtual courses, virtual classrooms, and by extension, voices, writing, or figures that, in order to be communicated to an addressee, require a technological means of communication. One calls them conversations or virtual images or, in the case of psychoanalysis sessions, virtual sessions. Later on, we will see how this denomination has an erroneous influence, confusing something real with something virtual, as if the latter were artificial or a non-existent reality.

c   Greater concept of "psychic reality"

When psychoanalysts refer to the content of ideas and emotions of their patients, they speak of psychic reality, differentiating it from material reality. The analysts know that what the patient expresses to us is a version of reality that he/she brings to a session and, when sincere, is what he/she has in the forefront of his/her mind. No analyst considers the material arising from the patient as something virtual due to its lack of clear connection to material reality. In fact, that which the patient brings to the session and that which the analysts perceive from it is denominated as "material"; given that it is considered as a reality which is taking place in the session. Oftentimes, the analyst, in order to be able to understand something coming from the patient which is not so familiar, must situate him/herself within the patient. This is an imaginary game that momentarily implies "being" the patient, although later returning to being the analyst. This is done so that the analyst can gain an acute perception of what the patient feels and thinks (Zac, 1972), and from which *base logic* to process what the patient has expressed.

Barring exceptions, in general it is observed that on the virtual level one supposes to have an ontological knowledge or at least a basic conceptual idea of the subject, when in fact only an empirical contact has been made, perhaps supported in the concept of physics which states that images shown in the mirror are virtual. However, beyond an elementary treatment of optics, many would respond: "Whenever I brush my hair, I always believe that I am looking at myself, I do not think that I am brushing the hair of a virtual image of myself."

A photograph represents a scenic reality that was present at another time and place. It is the reproduction of a fleeting second of the past which becomes "present" at the time of being observed. Nevertheless, it is an image printed on paper or digitally projected on a screen. It is the result of a process of virtualization of the moment in which the photograph was taken from which an optical-chemical-physical process—currently, a digital process—has occurred and transformed it into a photographic image. It is "the present" of "the real" photographed instant upon which a virtualization process has occurred. As an object *per se*, the photograph is also a real object: it is an image printed on a paper or projected on a screen.

Impressionism is based on the concept that one must not paint on the canvas the exact drawing and colours perceived in reality, but rather those that, once the light strikes the canvas, create in the retina of the observer the image that the painter wanted to achieve. Supposing that this goal is effectively accomplished, is the object perceived real or virtual? If we follow the argument as presented thus far, we should say that there are two realities interconnected by a virtualization process. The first reality is what is painted on the canvas, and the second reality is what is perceived by the person who looks at it. This second reality is "the present", subsequent to the process of virtualization made by rays of light affecting the shapes and colours on a surface or screen and which causes an optical-neuronal process in the retina. The impressionism of the painting, as we have seen, is based on the premise of the image constructed in the mind of the person that perceives it. The mind is a constructor of psychic realities, those that very frequently resemble material reality.

2 Subjectivity, socio-cultural transformations, and technological advances

From the dawn of time, the evolutionary phenomena of the human species have always included an inventive search for the production and the use of technological resources. The beginning of the evolutionary development of the species is associated with the creation and use of elementary tools and with the discovery of how to produce and conserve fire. These are clear milestones in the early days of human development. The technologies at this initial stage consisted of instruments that complemented manual abilities and harnessed the power which stemmed from the skill, the dexterity, and the muscular force of humans. From that point on, instrumental intermediation has slowly yet steadily increased, going through all the stages of development known thus far.

In the field of medicine, distance communication instruments of *non-verbal* nature abound. In surgery that is carried out for diagnostic purposes, the surgeon uses techniques in order to explore the body of the patient without cutting the skin. The electrocardiogram and the electroencephalogram are means of monitoring the electrical activity of the heart and the brain from a distance. A visual radiological test observed directly on the screen or that undertaken through the use of simple or complex radiographs (x-rays) provide information with direct images and even with cuts (although no sharp instrument is used) of the surface or the interior of a certain organ. The injection of a radioactive substance allows for the scanning of part or all of the surface and internal areas of the body in order to detect images that contribute to a diagnosis. The updated techniques of ultrasound allow one to see images of the foetus, some of them three-dimensional and in colour. These images are of almost photographic quality. Most recently, we have had access to video images that show the movements of the foetus. These new perceptive realities are modifying babies' date of birth. Furthermore, we can already know the baby's sex and face and give him/her a name well before the day of delivery.

Well known are the operations conducted inside the body using micro-cameras that convey on a television screen what they "perceive". Multiplying this initial possibility, these images can be simultaneously sent to distant places in order to acquire another diagnostic opinion and, sometimes, even for the purpose of surgical manipulation through the use of remote control devices.

The arrival of new technology places socially active and integrated people in a situation of having to operate in a different subjectivity than what they had previously known. Technological advances have an impact on social structure and dynamics. No particular adjective can be assigned to them. It is in the hands of the human—a political animal—to decide how to apply these technological advances. The discovery and industrial application of electricity led to the conception of hundreds of thousands of new possibilities, both industrial and domestic, that had previously been unimaginable. Each new element multiplies the emergence of other new conceptions and applications. The inauguration of a communicational nexus, for example the telephone, between two cities that are many kilometres and several travelling hours apart, changes the perception of distance in both cities, thereby increasing the preconception and the reality of the exchange. The availability of the internet increases this phenomenon exponentially.

Tools are useful, although not by themselves. Training is required for those that handle them. By training, we refer to the capacity to develop the potential applications of these tools. To this we must add the orientation given to their use. In this operation, the dexterity of the person that uses the tool is combined with the intrinsic qualities of the tool itself. Let us take the knife as an example. No matter how good the knife's steel or how sharp the blade, the instrument does not cut by itself. The proper handling of the knife by a competent operator is necessary in order to obtain the objective.

The nostalgic expression, *things aren't as they used to be* is well known. On the other hand, from time to time, we are amazed by a new product that makes its predecessor obsolete. During the last quarter of a century, technological advances occurring in our culture, added to socio-political and economic changes, have shaken the conceptual and operative foundations in which *base logic* was supported and with which reality was observed, contemplated, and operated upon.

Towards the end of the 20th century, Negroponte (1995) in his book *Being Digital* contributed data about the exponential multiplication that computer science offers. In the field of telecommunications, the comparison between the operational speed of a person and that of a technological device also shows exponential differences. While computer science transmits information at the speed of light, the human voice does so at the speed of sound.

Modern communicational possibilities have brought to life what had always been considered inconceivable or supernatural: locating the same experience at the same time in two different places. In fact, in this new communicational culture, it is conceivable that people, institutions, or nations can be connected and immediately share common experiences, despite the great distance between them. The worldwide broadcasting of a televised spectacle is an example. The term *communication* stems from the situation of making a common experience of two elements located in different places. When we put them in communicative connection, a sensation of simultaneity and proximity takes place. Even the reading of a written piece produced in another place and another time transmits this feeling, which has affected the classic concept of presence.

3   The advent of the "global village"

The term "global village" was coined by Herbert Marshall McLuhan. It was he who predicted that with the increase of intercommunicative facilities among people, companies, societies, and nations, the world would lose its borders and would be transformed into a great village. This allows for and even promotes a massive sharing of experiences, similar to what happens in a small village in which everyone knows everything about his/her neighbour and the villagers are always connected to each other's activities. Internet programs such as Facebook, MySpace, Twitter, and others are a present example of this in that they allow us to locate and communicate with other people. The internet has not only promoted what today we know as "globalization" (a term originally applied to industry and commerce), but it is also producing an increasing mixture and/or cultural integration with transforming effects on the mental paradigms that existed prior to this integration. This is a socio-economic-political and mental phenomenon. The thinking of McLuhan regarding globalization, despite not witnessing the massive use of the internet or the computer science revolution, was prophetic. Technological transformations, especially those in the field of communication, allow and simultaneously promote a human attachment of a magnitude never seen before.

This technological and cultural movement, when considered from the social perspective, finds its counterpart in the minds of the population when it introduces new and revolutionary conceptions of operational communication. The interaction of cultures amalgamates and creates new cultures and a "new mind" that implies not only a linear advance but often a great leap, given the contribution of a framework of new logical premises and new factual conceptions that are created from preconceptions or unprecedented starting points. In this new mind, new possibilities as well as new values and ideals (that are now attainable) give shape to another way of living life, allowing for new whims and ideals which were erstwhile inconceivable. Present-day society is going through a process that is gradually taking it towards a socio-cultural metamorphosis that transforms not only habits and customs but also the way of thinking, producing knowledge, and sharing it with other human beings. Berenstein and Grinfeld (2009), when discussing these phenomena and their mental repercussions, denominate them as a *"cultural change of the mind"* highlighting the repercussions that they bring in psychoanalysis, in that they create a "new psychoanalytic culture" which creates the potential for other conceptions of the clinical implementation of psychoanalysis by legitimately qualifying the changes in the traditional framework.

4   Digital natives, digital immigrants

Both terms are insolubly linked to Marc Prensky (2001). "Digital natives" would include young students and those who have recently graduated from university. They grew up immersed in an electronic world that provided them with electronic-digital devices, video games, electronic dictionaries, cellular phones, videophones, and digital cameras, among others. They studied to the rhythm of the computer, which has been entering their *base logic* since the very beginning of their lives. Clearly, there is a great distance between the functions of a slide rule and that of an electronic calculator, which can also be downloaded from the internet. Personal computers and more recently smaller devices such as net books and even pocket-size computers form part of their daily lives. Between these computerized tools and the minds of each of their users, a new kind of mind, which is the product of the amalgam of artificial and natural intelligence, has been born. This young generation has reached a level of ability that would allow us to consider them as experts in the handling and application of this technology. In comparing this situation with that of today's adults, many of whom have difficulty keeping up with the younger generation, Marc Prensky coined the term "digital immigrants". The difference between these two groups has formed a generational gap which has opened abruptly, thereby constituting a qualitative jump that has no connecting bridge. The solution lies in adhering to the conceptual paradigm that these resources provide. The speed and multiplicity of informational searches, as well as the possibilities of publication and communication that the correct use of the internet provides, opens the doors to a world of knowledge, communication, and interaction that was unheard of before the advent of the internet. The difference is so great that it defies comparison.

For "digital natives" the possibilities of such access provided by technology are essential, given their conceptual structure of feeling, living, and operating with themselves and within their social connections. Their way of being is criss-crossed by technological systems whose multiple functions and applications form part of common everyday usage. From these parameters, the way of connecting oneself socially has changed. New ways of social connection based on technology are added to previous ones, creating a new means of social encounter in which it is no longer necessary to be a metre away in order to be with someone. Thus, a comparative question arises, asking whether this new form of encounter is superior or inferior to the previous one. A general answer would be that the context and the purpose of the encounter are subjective and can only be evaluated by those involved in the exchange. However, this solution that I have just left up to the free will of its protagonists deserves further comment. When facing these subjects, I adopt the premise that each person absorbs and incorporates from his/her generational culture whatever he/she wants, while rejecting those aspects of the culture that he/she does not care for. However, it is well known that socio-cultural influences makes it difficult to reject the paradigms of one's generation. We know that the constants of the present time are influenced by the product of the mutations coming from previous habits. The rapid advances in present communication technology put within our reach an infinite degree of information coming from places that were previously inaccessible. Globalization has transformed "our" place into a common place for all those included in it, only differing in regional accent or expression. Less and less space is assigned to the singular and the specific, while more and more space is assigned to the general. The supply of information is so great that it is impossible to digest it. Therefore, one can only absorb a part of it. This means that as we become more similar, we also become more different, based on what part of this great plate of custom and information each one of us takes.

In their qualitative-quantitative wealth, these technological contributions to modern culture have not only generated changes in the individual co-inhabitants of globalization, but they are also indefinite, given that they are subject to future modifications. The cultural intertwining of intra and inter—within itself and among different generations—causes such a great repercussion that it provokes significant (and usually permanent) changes in "digital immigrants".

Technology, as it has such a great influence on both the cultural qualities of society and on the humans that live in it, promotes the establishing of new models of observation, understanding, and action. The idea of a "new paradigm" is directed to those who have a previous one. For those who are born immersed in the current paradigm, it will be their original one and therefore be a "logical and natural" starting point. This should not lead one to think that these young practitioners of the present culture of communication do not know how to distinguish between a contact involving corporal proximity and one involving the use of technology. Nevertheless, it is very probable that for them it has a meaning—and above all—a specific importance which is different from that which "digital immigrants" can give it.

CHAPTER THREE

Communication technology and its articulation with clinical psychoanalysis

B y way of introduction to this chapter, it is important to include some discussions on the subject carried out at the 46th International Congress of Psychoanalysis (IPA), held in July of 2009 in Chicago.

Estrada Palma presented a survey carried out by email and directed to 60 psychoanalysts in Latin America who are engaged in the field of teaching. Thirty-two of these psychoanalysts, that is to say, more than 50%, responded. The survey asked these analysts whether they had added communication technology to their habitual framework. The following are the most significant data.

The results of this survey are quite interesting. Of the 32 surveyed analysts, 25 answered that it is possible to carry out distance psychoanalytic psychotherapy, and 24 of them have had experience in sessions of this type. Twenty-three analysts—72% of the sample—said that they would accept continuing psychoanalytic psychotherapy by telephone, but only after it had begun in the psychoanalyst's office. Fifteen analysts—47% of the total—answered that they would accept continuing psychoanalytic treatment by telephone. On the other hand, only 33%—11 analysts—said they would accept that the analysis be conducted by telephone from the very beginning. It is relevant that only 53.3% of those contacted responded to this survey. These answers can be considered to be quite frank. Furthermore, they have a proportional importance to the professional stature of those surveyed, given that all of them are engaged in the field of teaching and in training analysis. In Chapter Seven, we will see the answers referring to the incorporation of analytic dialogue through written chat and email.

At the same IPA Congress, Savege Scharff (2009) reported that IPA issued a new policy on analysis by telephone or Skype. It may be accepted as valid to the extent of the formation of candidates, clarifying that this type of analysis would only be admitted in exceptional circumstances in which its classic implementation is very difficult. It was established that the experimental character of this treatment must be explicitly recognized by the analyst, and that it must be periodically put to the consultants for consideration as to whether the candidates to be analysed can fulfil the institutionally expected norms.

1   About communication technology

We have already seen that technological advances constitute one of the main factors that modify established social habits—whatever the culture or the era. Given that the advances of the last quarter of a century have been so significant, both in quantity and in quality, they must be discussed thoroughly. Communication technology constitutes a fundamental element in the development of life and in the exchanges among countries, institutions, and companies, and in personal contact of all imaginable type and magnitude. The present communication facilities promote greater and simultaneous integration among relatives, friends, and professionals. Currently, telephone or internet contact is extremely habitual. Communicating by SMS, Skype, chat, or email is practical and very economical. These communication facilities are promoting what can be conceived as a type of clinical psychoanalysis using some of them. The use of the telephone answering machine as a way of leaving messages is mentioned by Sharon Zalusky (2003) and is also included in the afore-mentioned survey. It was not common that analysts of the first decades of the last century would receive the request for a first interview by telephone, given that this means of communication was not common. As this means of communication became more common, it was used as a nexus for arranging the first interview. Currently, email is also being used for this purpose. It can be observed that text messaging is used to communicate a precise message that does not require a complex answer. These new habits are a faithful testimony of the adoption of these technological advances in the framework of analytic work.

New communication technology contributes not only to individual development, but also to that of the species. Its application to the field of psychoanalysis can be conceived as a technical resource that increases the operational range of its implementation. The type of life led by many of the people who undergo psychoanalysis shows that the unforeseeable and the "irregular" occur with a certain frequency. The possibility of communication between sessions by means of SMS, email, or voice message facilitates the notification of any difficulty regarding routine programming arising subsequent to the previous session. We must not ignore, however, that this means of non-synchronous communication can also facilitate resistance to programmed routines.

a   Necessary skills for the managing of communication technology

Psychoanalysis conducted through communication technology requires technical knowledge of the device being used. It is for that reason that only a device that both analyst and patient can manage well must be used. If the analyst were to fail in his/her technical implementation of the device being used, it would cause a negative impact on the patient, not only as an example of technological inefficiency of the method, but also as a flaw in both the clinical system applied and in the analyst, given that the proper operation of the line and the device being used constitute part of the analytic framework. If one wishes to preserve the asymmetry of the bond (Etchegoyen, 1986, 1991) it is necessary to bear this in mind. In extreme cases the roles will be inverted, and the patient may end up teaching and advising the analyst as to the technological handling of the method being used, somewhat affecting the transferential bond. This technological flaw will cause repercussions in the *analytic situation* and, therefore, in the elaborative work. The analyst will surely suffer the effect in his/her free-floating attention and the patient will feel a sensation of discomfort and surprise that will interfere in his/her free association. The defects of the means being used as well as the awkwardness arising at the time will make the patient feel uncomfortable, which may interfere with the analytic dialogue. If this were to occur in both participants in the analysis it would produce a confusing dialogue due to the overload of communicational difficulty.

It is important to highlight that telephone communication carries the advantage of extreme ease for both participants in the analysis. Furthermore, neither sophisticated devices nor deep technical knowledge is required. It is an invaluable merit of telephone technology that it can instantaneously transport the human voice from its place of origin to its place of reception. The simplicity with which it can be used assures good communication. On several occasions and among different patients it has been observed that it becomes necessary to speak from a physical place which is different from the habitual one. At the moment of having to do so, they can also count on the possibility of using the telephone.

Communicating from computer to computer by Skype nullifies the cost of the call, enables the use of a webcam, and has the guarantee of privacy. It does, however, increase the complexity of the device. The telephone is at a great disadvantage in that it deprives the analyst of the corporal image of the patient and vice-versa. However, some analysts, after changing the analytical dialogue from the setting of the psychoanalyst's office to that of the telephone, have been surprised to find that some patients will spontaneously begin to discuss intimate feelings related to their physical aspect (pride, rivalries, and sexual topics) that in the psychoanalyst's office sessions did not appear.

It has been observed that many people feel that their computer or Palm, cellular telephone, Blackberry, iPod, iPhone, etc. are like an extension of their own bodies and in fact their own minds. For them it works almost like an indivisible part of their ego. On this matter John Suler (2003) claims that "computers and so-called cyberspace can be experienced by some people as a 'transitional space', as an extension of the intrapsychic world". Mayans i Planells (2003) defined cyberspace as "a reticular space without centre, where everything and everyone are far and near at the same time. This is something quite new for us and we have no previous experience at the social level, given that we have always lived based on the parameters of Euclidean or physical geography."

The style of writing on the internet is unique. The use of emoticons and special symbols written with the keyboard itself is a kind of digital shorthand that simplifies and abbreviates the writing. Its generalized use constitutes a specific graphic language that complements habitual written language. Furthermore, one needs to have a minimum capacity to express oneself through written language in order to be able to express and understand ideas and feelings with clarity. Both participants in the communication must a have certain capacity to locate the other in the circumstances that surround the production of the text that has been sent. The writing has the characteristic of "speaking" by what it says and, sometimes, by what it omits. Producing a written text that *suggests* instead of *accurately enunciating*—in a transferential situation—can be its defect (due to the confusion caused) or its virtue (due to the wealth of interpretative virtualization that it offers). Its power to codify meaning opens a spectrum of possibilities of making contact with unconscious content. When its implementation and decoding are adequate, they contribute to good psychoanalytic communication.

b   Preconceived ideas about the function and use of the telephone

For many people, especially those who belong to the pre-digital era, the use of the telephone is related to the concrete and synthetic transmission and reception of data, in the sense that it would be appropriate to find an answer to a question. This being the case, when the telephone rings, it is understood that it must be answered immediately. Almost without exception, everyone answers the telephone—even when he/she is with another person. This *a priori* position operates as a preconception that promotes a particular attitude when speaking by telephone, which is that the conversation must be short and concise. Speaking for a long time can be surprising, tiring, or even boring. Well known is the image of a person who moves the telephone away from his ear in the middle of a conversation without caring about what the other person says, while providing him/her with mere monosyllabic responses. In social or professional life, it is justified to speak by telephone if specific information is required, likewise to greet others or comply with other social obligations.

The arrival of the telephone—as a technological novelty—is anachronistic for all today's living generations. Gradually, all the preconceptions mentioned above have been losing validity. For example, "speaking for the mere sake of speaking" is currently justified among family members or among friends. It is also common in reference to matters of the heart, in which lovers will confess their love, their differences, and their anger. Those who have relatives living thousands of kilometres away will say with a certain tone of astonishment: "How is it possible that, through the use of the telephone, we can still share daily experiences although we live on opposite sides of the world?"

Some bonds among relatives or friends continue being updated through the use of weekly or even daily telephone calls in which what is discussed exceeds the simple intention of transmitting information. This possibility of telephone connection is experienced as an opportunity for an encounter adapted to circumstances. It makes it possible to include different types of reflections and even share the daily minutia that sometimes occurs during the very conversation. In professional intra- or inter-company dialogue one observes the same type of classic preconception. The latter can also be sustained by using an online connection of permanent availability called the intranet, which allows for both written and verbal communication.

c   Structure of the transmission of voice by telephone

α   Realism through telephone dialogue

The voice is the result of a sonorous vibration of the vocal cords. The person who speaks has injected into this activity not only a concrete sonorous content, but also a symbolic one, which is the meaning of the word. In the case of telephone communications without the use of a camera, although the body of the other cannot be seen, it is possible to indirectly perceive some of the signals contained in the tone and inflexion of the voice, as well as in the content of the speech. Sometimes the listener can perceive a change in the distance between the mouth of the speaker and the telephone receiver, which gives some indication of movement. In a telephone session, due to the fact that the gestures of the speaker are not visible, the patient and analyst gain specific training for listening to and decoding the different nuances of speech much more acutely—similar to what happens among the blind. It can also be observed from time to time—whether it be in a direct dialogue or in telephone dialogue—that one of the participants in the analysis will close his/her eyes in order to listen more accurately and avoid the distraction of visual stimuli.

Analysis by telephone will inevitably lead to the need to develop new abilities. The infrastructure involved in the encounter is no longer the classic office of the analyst, but rather the technological link used as support for the colloquial connection that transmits ideas, affection, and behaviours. At each end of the line there is a specific place and a singular and different material reality. Between them, there is a shared common space—the *Inter* of the session—whose location, although lacking geographic enclosure, has a place in time (a predetermined day and hour) that serves as the setting for the session.

β "The real" and "the virtual" of the voice

When one speaks by telephone, the voice comes off the vocal cords of the speaker and establishes itself on both sides of the telephone line. This voice—as a physical phenomenon—is both a real and a virtual object due to its potential to decode the idiomatic meaning found in the *manifest content*. This can also undergo a second decoding when the analyst infers that what has been said entails unconscious meaning: thereby the latent content attributed to the material. In the exchange found in the dialogue, the voices, in addition to being a container, are simultaneously a transporting vehicle of the ideas and the affection that are established in the transferential environment. The voice contains its sonorous vibration as a physical substratum. The symbolic is given by that which the words represent. Due to these two qualities, the analyst takes the two aspects of the patient's words as the material and symbolic substratum that come to him/her for psychoanalytic elaboration. In this operation, transference and countertransference, the manifest and the latent, inferred by the analyst and elaborated by both the analyst and the patient, are conjugated together. As a permanent background, it plays an extremely important role—imperceptible when it works correctly—which is that of the proper functioning of the line and the clarity of the messages that are emitted and received. It should also be emphasized here that it is essential to exercise good pronunciation in order to adapt to a dialogue that is devoid of the visual perception of the other participant.

With this type of setting that the analysis session offers, both participants manage to be present in the *Inter space*, which offers the chance of creating a structured conceptual receptivity in an ethical climate of reserve and privacy. The interplay between ideas and affection involved there contributes to the formation of an analytical process which is in permanent reconfiguration.

γ The ubiquitous location of the voice

Telephone communication manages to place the voice at both ends of the line. Its transmission occurs so quickly that the time delay becomes insignificant. In this way, the voice manages to be on both sides of the line simultaneously, that is to say, in one ubiquitous location.

The birthplace of an idea in the mind is what Bion (1965) would denominate as the "O" origin, to which one can attribute a "real" aspect due to its condition of "being", and a "virtual" one due to its possibility of "becoming" in a virtualization process. It becomes feasible to describe several stations of *updating* of the material emitted by the patient: the "O" origin, as a "real" object, would "yearn" to arrive as such at the mind of its interlocutor. However, it is not possible to do so in the way that it was originally generated, due to the series of transformations that have occurred along the way. Let us remember that in the process of virtualization, upon arriving at the "present" pole a certain ontological transformation has taken place. Next, we shall describe the mechanism, the route, and the various stations of physical transformation (*updates*) through which the voice crosses on its way from the mind of the emitter to that of the person at the other end of the telephone line.

δ   Transformation and technological transmission of the voice

At the moment of its technological transmission, the voice undergoes a series of reversible mutations between its emission and its radio-telephone reception. The following description will illustrate the different steps found in the virtualization process that takes place in telephone communication.

a. ***First transformation:*** The amalgam that emerges from the feeling and thinking generated in the mind—the "O" origin—is a first link which, as such, is its *real* aspect, which in itself is also a *virtual* aspect, due to the transformation that must take place in order to include the interlocutor. The virtualization process begins with the passage of "O" to the words of the language being spoken in order to be thought consciously: first "present" moment of this process of virtualization.

b. ***Second transformation:*** The container offered by the words that are syntactically ordered as "thought" is transformed into a voice that is constituted as a discursive message. That is to say, it is transformed from an abstract thought to one which is formatted in the language being used, thus being a second "real" state of the thought as well as the second "present" moment.

c. *Third transformation*: The spoken word, as a physical phenomenon, is the product of sound waves emitted by the vibration of the vocal cords that, in turn, cause the vibration of the membrane of a microphone. This is a physical phenomenon that implies a third "real" aspect and a third "present" moment.

d. *Fourth, fifth, and sixth transformations*: The vibration of this membrane produces electromagnetic waves that are transformed into radio waves that journey through ethereal space or cyberspace. These waves, upon arriving at the receiver's end of the line, are transformed into electromagnetic waves, having given rise to successive "real" aspects and several stations of "the present" in this process of virtualization.

e. *Seventh transformation*: The electromagnetic waves, upon arriving at the receiver's end of the line, stimulate and provoke vibrations in the membrane of the speaker or earpiece, thereby becoming sound waves that are a replica of the original voice. Here we have a new "real" object—the voice that is heard—and a new "present".

f. *Eighth transformation*: The voice emitted at the speaker's end of the line reached to the opposite end in a time that is imperceptible to the human mind. The proof of this is that the movement of the lips of a person on the television screen coincides with the voice that is heard. The vocal cords—the body of the emitter—are present only on the speaker's end of the line. However, the emitted voice can be perceived simultaneously at both ends of the line, which allows for *a ubiquitous and synchronous location of the voice*. The sound waves arriving stimulate the membrane of the eardrum, thereby allowing the voice to be heard. The *virtualization* process does not finish here, given that one last update must take place so that the message can be located in the mind of the receiver.

g. *Ninth transformation*: Upon being heard and processed, the mind attributes a meaning, a process that adds a different *virtualizing* transformation, this time of a semantic nature.

ε   The semantic process

In all these transformations, the process of attributing meaning to what had been perceived cannot be considered to be universal. One cannot even be sure that the same message will be perceived in the same way at all times and in all circumstances. As we have just seen, analytic dialogue carried out by telephone contains elements pertaining to the field of physics and to the field of semantics. A good telephone connection transmits the physical aspect of the voice by means of a phono-radio-electromagnetic reproduction that, when arriving at the receiving end, allows the significant aspect of the message (as originally emitted) to remain intact. The semantic aspect of communication, which allows for meaning, depends on the elaborative work carried out by the minds of its protagonists.

The voice contains words consented to by a common and shared language, put together syntactically and expressed with a pronunciation and tone of voice that is unique to each person, thereby granting identity to the speaker. In each emission it will be observed whether the intonation used coincides with the topic being discussed. In this we must consider the meaning intended by the emitter and his/her own mood and state of mind. Each of these elements, considered either separately or as a whole, constitutes semiological material of an immense wealth, especially if the analyst is well versed in the art of decoding it. Any obstacle that interferes with suitable perception, such as deficient clarity in pronunciation, the improper positioning of the mouth in relation to the microphone, and/or the presence of noises that impede good hearing, make it difficult or even impossible for the two participants in the analysis to have a good analytic performance. When this takes place for more than a fleeting moment, it must be corrected. When it affects a word, and the analyst lets the moment pass so as not to interrupt, it is not always clear whether it was a key word or whether it was insignificant and had no particular bearing on the central part of the message.

Finally, we must ask ourselves: in analytic dialogue carried out by telephone, where should we place the real and the virtual? Communication per se is undoubtedly "*real*". This is the case inasmuch as the participants of the conversation consider that both are aware of what is discussed. If some commitment is made by telephone, the obligation is to fulfil it. As we have seen, from the very birthplace of the idea and the feeling of the emitter—the "O" origin—until the arrival at the mind of the receiver, a series of phenomena takes place, which contain both a *real* and a *virtual* aspect located in all the "stations" of the message, those that constitute the "present" link of the *virtualization* process. Words that arrive by means of the earpiece, either those pronounced by the person or those reproduced electronically—as a physical phenomenon—are real. The emitted concepts also contain a *real* aspect—the word or sentence as a signifier—and their *virtual* aspect, as its signified. Once the message arrives, assuming the sound is clear, the interlocutor perceives the signifier that the emitted idea implies as *real* and decodes the *virtual* aspect of the message, thus assigning its signifier both the manifest signified and the latent signified that he/she interprets.

Regarding analytic dialogue occurring in the analyst's office, similar processes involving real and virtual aspects can be conceived, except for the arrival of the voice to the interlocutor by means of the technological process described.

d   Inclusion of a television camera: uses and implications

The analyst must evaluate the importance that the employment of a television camera can have when deciding whether or not to add it to the telephone communication. This resource requires thorough analysis. Its use will depend on whether the necessary technological means are available and how prepared the participants in the analysis are to use them. One must also consider what the analyst deems as suitable in each specific case. In this decision, the analyst must consider whether he/she should be seen by the patient. Nevertheless, there are specific situations in which the patient needs to see and/or be seen by the analyst, due to the belief that it improves the connection.

The inclusion of a television camera requires the possession of more complex technological equipment than that of a simple telephone. Nevertheless, computers, cellular telephones, videophones, and other similar means are more and more within the reach of the general public. With this camera it is possible to see the other participant's face and the expressive messages that it projects, as well as general body language and the background of the place from which the other participant is speaking. By this means it is possible to decipher sign language, which qualifies psychoanalysts trained in this language to treat deaf-mute patients.

In analysis conducted in the analyst's office, there is a mutual visual perception at the time of the encounter and of the greeting. Afterwards, the patient lies down on the couch and no longer sees the analyst, although he/she senses the analyst's bodily proximity and has the fresh image of him/her in the retina. The patient will only be able to visually appreciate some derivatives or "extensions" of the body and personality of the analyst, coming from the elements of the office that are sensorially perceived: sight, sound, smell, touch, and also the proprioceptive sensation derived from the recent greeting and the bodily contact with the couch. This contiguous presence of the analyst is perceived by the sonorous emanations of the voice and the movements and sounds coming from his/her body: clearing of the throat, coughing, moving in the armchair, etc. If we compared this to what can be perceived on a television screen, many differences would be evident. However, any attempt to make this comparison is inadequate. From each reality one can only perceptively extract that which reality can offer. Whatever this reality may be, it will only be possible to catch that which circumstances allow and which the intellect can perceive. Silent movies are an example of this. At its time, silent cinema was a great success, although it was not theatre and the actors were not present. Given these deficiencies, the creators displayed a cinematographic sequence in which their actors performed and highlighted their mimic expressiveness, at times accompanied by a written text. On the other side of the screen, the spectators had to forego the sensorial elements offered by theatrical plays, to which they were accustomed, and adapt to the new system. In this type of cinema, Charlie Chaplin, for example, came to be known as one of the greatest actors in the history of the art form.

I raise this concept because it exemplifies what I believe should be a basic position when facing a kind of psychoanalysis that is different from that to which we are accustomed. The analytic dyad works with what a certain framework offers. The analyst must ask him/herself whether he/she is taking full advantage of everything that the method *per se* is capable of offering and, if so, evaluate whether it is possible to psychoanalyse a particular patient, taking into account all the pros and cons of the framework in question. In each analytic setting, the two participants in the analysis examine the situation in order to find the resources that can be taken from the communicative system itself. Many current cultural situations can be taken as examples. Cinema, radio, and television achieved success by having looked for the expressive and communicative possibilities that exist within their own systems. Readers of letters, emails, or chat dialogues have also searched for and withdrawn the expressive and communicative possibilities that exist within their own systems. The author of a good novel will use the written word in order to transmit ideas, passions, and even images as if they were real. It is for this reason that the use or non-use of the camera must be left up to the criteria of the two participants in the analysis. Nevertheless, the analyst is responsible for the conditions upon which an analytic process must work, and therefore it is he/she who must have the last word as to this or any other matter.

Is it possible to conceive of the use of a camera as equivalent to a treatment conducted face to face? There may be some similarities, although the question is inadequate and therefore objectionable. It is necessary to conceive of its use as a resource that, assuming it starts up, will reach its true potential and depend not only on itself, but also on the profit that each participant in the analysis is able to gain from it. The internal relation with the communication method being used also influences to the degree that it contributes or disturbs, which is unfailingly transferred to the analytic dialogue. The incorporation of a TV camera in the analytic dialogue should not be decided with the intention of replacing near and direct perception, but rather be based on the necessities that each distance analytic treatment requires.

Visual on-screen transmission can be carried out in two-way form, in one-way form, or be left up to the particular necessity arising from specific sessions, which will be agreed with each patient. Maintaining a dialogue with this system throughout the session requires the analyst to take certain precautions because the heat of the dialogue generally makes him/her forget that it is being filmed.

Should we consider what is perceived by means of the TV camera to be authentic?

To this question, we must add another, which is of both an introductory and complementary nature. Is it possible to realistically perceive anything by means of a TV camera? One could say yes, within the general limits that imply understanding reality. In this sense, Kant declares that it is impossible to know a thing in itself, although it is possible to make contact with its manifestations. If there are no technical problems, the images that are taken at the camera's end and transmitted correctly to the TV screen are considered as *real* objects—just like a television programme. It is important to mention that one perceives everything that has gone through the appropriate mental process. This is the case for both visual and audio messages, depending on the attention and the interest of the person receiving the transmission. However, unlike common television programmes, the communication involved in synchronic distance psychoanalysis is interactive, and therefore it is possible to ask one's interlocutor to repeat or clarify what he/she has said.

Some body expressions are the direct result of emotions that the very emitter was not aware of. The television camera makes it possible for the interlocutor at the other end to have access to the information that a facial expression can reveal. These facial expressions can minimize, increase, or completely contradict what has been expressed verbally. The camera also catches body movements or positions that sometimes offer some information—such as *rocking*—or certain corporal movements that denote anxiety.

2   New clinical conceptions: do they promote new theories?

The issue of validity regarding the clinical implementation of psychoanalysis is still under discussion within psychoanalytic institutions. In addition to scientific criteria, there are other factors involved in this disagreement. Among these, one can find non-epistemological factors in which sometimes personal or professional interest, as well as professional rivalry and the struggle for ideological/institutional power may intervene (Aryan & Carlino, 2010). Leaving this issue aside, these analytic institutions should prepare seminars in order to train their members in the practice of distance analysis. The next step would be to include this practice in the study programmes of theory of technique, which are developed in the institutes of psychoanalysis of psychoanalytic associations so that analysts, when attending patients by means of telephone or Skype can operate with better preparation than those of us who initiated this practice and did so more by means of intuition and trial and error.

Analysis carried out by any of the modern means of communication technology is still officially considered to be something special and even a matter of exception. It is only considered to be a valid alternative when classic analysis becomes impossible to carry out. That is to say, it has not yet gained the status of being a new kind of analysis that can stand on its own. However, once these new formats of systematic practice become more widespread, some classic concepts of analysis will adapt and specifically construct whatever new concepts are needed for better implementation. The practice accompanied by systematic research will bring forth the specific subjects that need to be considered in order to make way for this not-so-new *analytic situation*. Although it could be considered useful for us to standardize a means of psychoanalysis with a framework adapted to the type of distance method used, the matter does not end here. In fact, the method of implementation must be reopened, taking into account changing social reality, the reality of the patients, and also the changing panorama of psychoanalysis which is brought about by advances in neuroscience. In this sense, it is erroneous to superimpose the custom of how psychoanalysis should be implemented, thereby confusing it with its theory. At this point, we can answer the question as to whether we are trying to create a new *modus operandi* for classic psychoanalysis or whether we are trying to construct a new psychotherapeutic theory. The latter will only become reality if it is considered that in adapting psychoanalysis to this new form of implementation, its essential principles, in accordance with its desired objectives, have been altered. It would be prudent to observe and to think about the conceptual gaps that appear when assigning a new format to the classic analytic setting. One must also look for its possible answers and test them to see whether they are of a psychoanalytic nature.

a   Influence of the arrival of new paradigms

Anything new taking place in the social field not only requires that psychoanalysis take on new forms of implementation, but also offers new technological tools for psychoanalysis and those who are interested in it. These are people with a social and operative mentality which is in line with the current *base logic*, including the habits and customs promoted by new technological possibilities that before were difficult to obtain or were non-existent.

Treatments carried out through communication technology yearn for legitimacy. For this reason they are trying to structure themselves within a theory with the specific elements that are necessary for each type of implementation, which helps not only to give them identity, but to differentiate them as well. These classic and consecrated conceptions will be enriched by the impact of new scientific discoveries, which in turn will add more elements and greater complexity to our conceptual doctrine. With regard to other scientific advances, above and beyond those being applied in distance psychoanalysis, I would like to make a specific reference to new discoveries contributed by neuroscience regarding unconscious communication among beings of the same species. It has to do with the role of mirror neurons. It is necessary to research their role in telephone intercommunication (only auditory) and in videoconferencing (auditory-visual) in which it is reasonable to suppose that they could be playing some specific role in the understanding of distance treatment.

b   "Mirror neurons": interaction and inter-effect of their roles

Mirror neurons are very specialized cells. They have a double possible function: emitter and receiver. They have the capacity to stimulate and to catch those signals emitted by another. This double quality means that a person in connection with another can perceive and reproduce the acts of the other, thus imitating them. Inversely, it is also possible to provoke these actions in the other by operating with the receptive function of the mirror neurons. These cells, when put into operation, promote conduct or acts of imitation. They can also produce neuronal stimuli of a similar nature although the act is not carried out. Furthermore, they produce a psychological effect, although its action mechanism depends on the biological resource that these cells offer to the subject.

If we take into consideration all the hominid species, it would seem that, in the phylogenetic development of the species, the resource offered by these cells has been put into action to perpetuate the identifying characteristics that make them feel "similar". Another possibility, although not very acceptable, would be that this was the product of an accidental evolutionary event. These cells produce an intercommunication that, although including the sensorial apparatus, precedes the attempt to consciously inform the receiving and effecting subjects of their actions. Their activity produces effects such as cellular activation, with or without a behavioural consequence that often even exceeds the will and/or the decision to do something. The operation of these neurons assures a "coming and going" of a biological nature. This way they would assure a "gregarious instinct", which makes them feel that each one has something in common with the rest of the species, thus the annotation of "similarity". It is assumed that autistic people have a functional deficit of these neurons. These primitive mechanisms of intercommunication are also observed in the human relationship with pets.

The evolutionary history of this discovery, like so many others, was the result of a coincidental event. It was also the fruit of the acute perception and scientific curiosity of Rizzolatti, Fogassi, and Gallese (2001)—researchers from the University of Parma, Italy—who accidentally discovered an imitative neuronal reaction in a monkey that had electrodes placed on its frontal cortex. Although the original purpose of this experiment was to study the movement of the monkey's hand, one of the researchers coincidentally took an object in the presence of the ape and detected that this action provoked the activation of certain motor neurons in the monkey although no actual movement was perceived. He repeated the experience, this time with the curiosity typical of a researcher, and the phenomenon was repeated. These nerve cells are located in the cortex, the inferior frontal gyrus, and the parietal lobe.

This is how mirror neurons were discovered. These researchers gave the neurons this name because they have the quality of reproducing behaviours in imitative form. That is to say, they activate in the "subject" when the "object" carries out an action or, to the contrary, they activate in the "object" when the "subject" emits a gesture or a signal. This stimulation of coming and going caused by its double function— motor and sensory—was also an important discovery within the realm of neurology. These cells have connections with areas linked to emotion and language. Due to this function of imitating what is perceived of the other and provoking the other to respond to stimuli has led many to think that these cells act in the complex process of identification and empathy.

Before this observation, we analysts in our understanding of identification managed the classic concepts of this principle (identification), as a first form of love for an object. We could say that Freud in his acute observation of human conduct was not mistaken, because this conception *per se* has not changed. With the discovery of the functioning of these cells we can observe a more complex mechanism. It is possible to suppose that these neurons, as they are located in the prefrontal area of the brain, have to do with the process of learning to speak and decoding the motivations of human conduct. This highly neuronal interconnection is also observed when feeling and emitting emotions, and therefore would allow us to understand those of our interlocutor whenever engaging in a colloquial exchange during a psychoanalytic session. These extremely specific functions lead one to believe that these neurons, due to their function, form the neurological base in the process of empathetic connection, in order both to influence and be influenced by different moods.

The question arises as to whether it will be possible, from the clinical perspective, to take advantage of the information contained in this imitation-provoking stimulus sent by the patient. We could also presume that in the radiation of those neuronal stimuli their intentions and emotions are encrypted. If the analyst learns to decode this information, he/she would bring about better understanding of the mechanisms put into play when including this psycho-neuronal quality.

Notwithstanding what has been stated, from the practice of psychoanalysis analysts have had access to these phenomena for some time now, from the conceptualizations made regarding transference, countertransference, projective identification, and projective counter-identification, to mention the most developed—all of which were carried out without the support that neuroscience offers us today. Adding this new research opens an interesting panorama.

The research in human beings was carried out with EEG (electroencephalography), later complemented by the arrival of FMRI (functional magnetic resonance image) and TMS (transcranial magnetic stimulus).

It is well known that when listening to someone by telephone, one automatically tends to make an imaginary representation of who is speaking. One can suppose that when doing so, these mirror neurons can play a major role in the sense of imaginarily representing the other and giving him/her an empathetic and/or imitative identification. These discoveries open us to the possibility of finding some foundation in the mechanisms by which we try to get to know others. In any case, this phenomenon is not so unknown, given that this way of knowing others has been denominated as "intuition" or "empathy", without this current neuro-scientific base. Due to the location in the cerebral cortex, in the inferior frontal gyrus, it is possible to think, as a deductive inference, that these neurons could have played some role in the evolutionary development that allowed primitive gestural communication to be transformed into spoken language. If this affirmation were to find scientific support, it would allow us to apply inverse reasoning and suppose that through spoken language, one could establish contact (albeit precariously) with gestures of the other speaker although they are not visible. This would be the scenario of a telephone conversation. In fact this is something that is presumed in the routine practice of telephone speech. It would constitute an experience promoted by the learning that the interactions of mirror cells have left in each one of us. On this matter, a colleague once commented that during a telephone session, her secretary silently entered the place where she treats her patients by telephone and handed her a note written in gigantic letters so that it could be read easily. In this note, she informed her that once the session was finished, she should contact the family of a psychically decompensated patient. The analyst, at the moment the door was opened, was listening to the patient with the telephone receiver on her desk and the speaker on. Upon noticing that her secretary was approaching her with a note to be read, she made hand gestures instructing the secretary to leave the note on the desk and then exit the room. At the same moment the analyst turned her head to see who was entering the closed room, the patient on the telephone line abruptly interrupted his speaking and only continued once the secretary had left the room.

Pier Ferrari (2005), of the Department of Neuroscience of the University of Parma, is an avant-garde researcher of this subject. He has long studied the operation of "mirror cells" in primates. These studies are an important contribution to the neuropsychology of behaviour. Based on these discoveries, Geoff Anderson (2009), at the 46th IPA Congress held in Chicago, in his contributing address to the panel on the topic of psychoanalysis carried out by telephone and by Skype, mentioned the experiences of this researcher and expressed his interest in finding in the operation of "mirror neurons" a neuro-physiological explanation as to how auditory stimuli may produce representations of body movements in telephone psychoanalysis. The idea was to understand the correlation of certain neuronal phenomena that occur in the brain when a voice is listened to on the telephone, as well as the representational stimulus that this implies. It is assumed that this type of neuron contributes to the process of discernment of a peer's behaviour.

Notwithstanding what has been discussed here, some researchers in the field of neuroscience are dubious about the idea that the operation of mirror neurons can explain the phenomenon of empathy. In any case, above and beyond the concurrent or controversial result of scientific research, the phenomenon of empathy, like that of identification, has always been observable. Well-trained analysts tend to have countertransferential ideas that are thoughts born in their minds but which reflect what the other feels at that moment.

If we can take advantage of all of the positive aspects of innovation, several achievements would be reached—one of them specific to our doctrinaire heritage: the expansion of the theoretical-technical bases.

3   Critical opinions: a brief history

If we were to search for some remote precedent of distance psychoanalysis, we would find the epistolary self-analysis carried out by Freud. He was very open and bold in his thoughts. The procedures and guidelines of his time were based primarily on "straightforward" conceptions. Nevertheless, he could observe a varied terrain that others did not see. Within the context of his possibilities and the reality of his era, Freud tried to approach a creative search, anchored in his ability to free himself of any distortive prejudice.

In the newsletter "Insight", published by the IPA (June 2003), seven psychoanalysts approach the subject of psychoanalysis by telephone. In that edition a couple of central questions arise. When for any particular reason a patient cannot continue going to the analyst's office, is it valid and effective to adopt the telephone method of distance analysis? And, if so, does that treatment continue being psychoanalytic or does it become psychoanalytic psychotherapy, or therapy of still a different nature? The objections to telephone analysis rest in the belief that any attempt to change to another form of implementation constitutes a resistance of the two participants in recognizing that an obstacle has arisen which makes the analysis impossible. Continuing the analysis by telephone was considered by some as a negation denial of the fact that the two were facing a situation of mourning and therefore must accept the reality judgement that if it is impossible for the patient to visit the analyst's office, the analytical treatment with that analyst is impossible; and therefore it would be necessary to analyse the loss of the relation with the analyst and of this analysis. Other articles in that same publication, however, justify that the setting be modified and agree that analysis by telephone be implemented in order to continue with the treatment.

Some of the basic notions included in the opinions of those who oppose distance psychoanalysis could be refuted. In fact, based on their criteria, the blind would not be able to read because they cannot perceive the written letters and the Braille alphabet would be a non-genuine substitute for those letters. Something similar would occur with sign language, which allows the deaf and the mute to communicate. Helen Keller became deaf and blind at 19 months of age. An ingenious and creative teacher, Anne Sullivan, put all her will and perseverance to the service of enabling her little disciple to communicate by insisting that she could "hear" in another way. To this end, the sense of touch was used. Her teacher spoke to her and she made her "hear" through means of vibrations. However, these vibrations, instead of impacting on her sense of hearing, did so on her sense of touch. This method also helped her to learn to speak. In addition, she learned to write and eventually graduated from university. As we see, by different means, it is possible to achieve goals that are similar or equivalent, although not identical. Obviously, one needs creative imagination and will to reach the proposed objective.

The psychoanalytic bibliography contains articles, some of them quite old, in which experiences and opinions were published about telephone psychoanalysis.

An example of the "new" shaking the foundation of the "old" can be found in the mid-20th century. The post-war period, a time of political and social restructuring, greatly affected the paradigms of personal behaviour as well as the criteria of industrial and economic procedures. Simultaneously, a "disarming" of established habits and customs occurred in order to give rise to a new reconstructive context. What had earlier been considered obvious became less clear. In fact, it could even be considered inadequate or erroneous.

In the field of psychoanalysis, Heinrich Racker (1948) in Argentina and Paula Heimann (1949, 1950) in Zurich, at an IPA Congress, presented their ideas about "counter-transference" almost simultaneously. The conceptual commotion and the malaise that these ideas produced among colleagues are well known and for this reason it is not necessary to discuss the topic in detail.

A few years later, Kurt Eissler (1953) published his work on *Technical Parameters* in which he tried to psychoanalyse in a non-classic format in order to adapt the analysis to a certain type of patients who presented a deficit in the "ego". As it is seen, during times of social commotion there is a repercussion in the practice of psychoanalysis. Concepts that had previously been held as inherent to the fundamental structure of clinical psychoanalysis begin to be considered as simple formalities that are open to modification and even substitution. These social commotions produce a shaking-up of concepts and principles that await an answer in the field of analytic theory and analytic technique.

In the mid-20th century, Leon J. Saul (1951), an analyst from Philadelphia, published the idea that psychoanalysis could be transacted through sessions conducted by telephone. Another analyst, John A. Lindon, in 1988, presented in a Menninger Clinic publication his accumulated experience throughout 24 years—beginning in 1964—of telephone treatments for patients who, for different reasons, could not reach his office.

Precedents similar to these, also previous to the digital era, are registered in well-reputed publications. This information was not spread widely due to the scant repercussion of that time, given the slight practical importance that they promised. At that time it was difficult to establish telephone communication and the cost of maintaining it during the length of the session was a serious obstacle. It is also true that the present paradigm that globalization has impressed upon distance communication was non-existent. Another reason for its slight use could be that little communication about the subject was forthcoming, so as not to risk being subjected to severe criticism.

Another analyst, Mark Leffert, when in 2003 he presented his ideas on the subject in the *American Journal of Psychoanalysis*, commented that he had already been practising analysis by telephone for more than 20 years and that it had become his habitual method of psychoanalysis. The unique aspect of this revelation is that it is he who proposes this form of analysis to his patients due to the fact that he does not reside permanently in any one place. This is not exactly anecdotal if we consider how many professional opportunities are avoided by analysts simply because they would require being away from their office for a length of time. The idea of travelling to different places in the middle of the working year is quite difficult, given that it would imply suspending the sessions at his/her office. A framework that contemplates the possibility of telephone sessions would offer the analyst a different kind of professional life. From the point of view of the patients, it would allow them to undergo analysis with a suitable degree of frequency and consistency despite any possible question of distance or instability of residence.

In a publication of the pre-digital era—from the 1970s—reference is made to psychoanalytic supervision by means of recording sessions on tape. Although certainly not of the same nature as that of a distance session, I include it as an example of how the phenomenon of globalization also began to enter into the professional field of psychoanalysis. In this it is possible to see the need for active intercommunication among analysts from different parts of the world. One important work dates back to 1972 and includes very reputable analysts, such as J. A. Lindon, B. D. Lewin, M. Ballint, J. Fleming, M. Gill, L. Grinberg, H. F. Searles, I. M. Josselling, and R. S. Wallerstein. Some analysts of international prestige who are currently required as supervisors as a result of their specific knowledge in a certain line of psychoanalysis or a particular psychoanalytic school receive the material beforehand by encrypted email and supervise the material by telephone or video-conference.

In my professional experience on the subject, I presented my first publication on telephone psychoanalysis in Buenos Aires. The commentary about this professional practice that was heard in the corridors of the institution was favourable and had a nuanced content. Some analysts showed astonishment and others, while offering their comments in a low voice, as if confessing a secret, said: "I attend a patient by telephone", and finally, another group of colleagues took the practice for granted and it was therefore not a novelty for them.

4   Distance as a critical element

G utiérrez Maldonado (2002) took notice years ago of a conceptual reality that every day is perceived as more concrete. He stated that the massive use of the internet made the global village an irreversible fact. He said that there would no longer be multiple spaces, but rather a great single space. It would no longer be necessary to travel from place to place in order to undertake common activities with other people.

Clinical psychoanalysis in one of its formal aspects has always been structured as an interpersonal encounter in the analyst's office. In this situation, the unveiling of the unconscious is nourished by what arises from the communication of verbal messages to the framework. To this we can add the visual perception of the analyst at the moment of greeting or even within the session itself. The "Little Hans" from Freud's case histories is an exception that confirms the rule. Furthermore, it reminds us to entertain the possibility of other means of implementation when the circumstances require.

When one considers an analysis to be "distance", one tends to localize it in a specific conceptual "place". For some analysts, the distance is a limit of the method. Nevertheless, when this limit is surpassed it is not invalidated, but rather given the label of "psychoanalytic psychotherapy". If this qualification is processed from a conceptual bandwidth, from one of its edges it can be justified as precise and unquestionable. As the observation moves towards the other edge of the band, it is possible to find the panorama of all that has already been discussed and written in round tables, workshops, etc. on the subject of psychotherapy and psychoanalysis, and therefore is not necessary to repeat here.

Due to their perceptive visual limitation, many analysts conceive these treatments as a non-genuine or "handicapped" form of psychoanalysis. For those who are more critical, it is a conduct which is devoid of ethics and thereby malpractice. They claim that the practice is claiming to be something that it is not. A third position can be found in those analysts who do not hesitate to validate this practice as ethical as long as it is carried out by an analyst with a good and solid psychoanalytic background. They only consider it valid as a psychoanalytic attempt at the time of having to accept or contraindicate distance treatment by fitting its criteria to each individual case.

a   Possibilities offered by communication technology

The first attempts at any new procedure must go through a period of experimentation that, methodologically, should be evaluated *ad referendum* to its results. Analyses carried out through communication technology, from the academic point of view, are somewhere between the first stage of experimental implementation and the following one (which we can call intermediate), based on the experience contributed by present-day professional analysts training in this method. There are even some psychoanalysts who already have a solid and proven experience based on years of practice, although their publications are not widespread in the academic media.

In treatments carried out by means of communication technology it is observed that certain patients can establish a sincere and transparent bond with greater facility and with a lower degree of dissociation. They achieve a greater integration in their spontaneous speech due to the effect of disinhibition that is produced by not having the person of the analyst by their side. On the contrary, they feel that the analyst is "all ears" and otherwise would feel some obstacles in the production of their free and spontaneous expression. Despite the effect of disinhibition produced by this type of communication, when necessary it should be taken advantage of in order to show the patient that he needs to separate the person of the analyst from his/her personal qualities, to be able to have good contact with him/her. Certain patients taking advantage of this situation become somewhat daring and even shameless when communicating by telephone or in writing (chat or email). This is often not the case when they carry out their analysis face to face. It is to be expected that this lack of inhibition helps the patient to analyse deeply the—generally unconscious—reasons that provoke his inhibition.

Psychoanalysis with this type of framework can and must be conceived as an instrumental resource that extends the field of application of psychoanalysis and, presently, also offers the opportunity to explore a road that still has an important stretch to traverse, both in its theoretical conception and in the field of technical theory.

b   Communication technology in psychoanalytic treatment

The use of the internet is associated with the need to obtain a precise answer for any informational search in the blink of an eye. Undertaking psychoanalysis by means of a modern apparatus of communication can be influenced by the pace of everyday life. Nevertheless, in psychoanalytic dialogue carried out by telephone, it is necessary to contemplate the answer psychoanalytically before answering it. This can cause uncertainty if it is assumed that a prolonged silence is due to an interruption in the connection. The need for a fast answer that the use of the telephone inspires is common in many people due to the way in which they are accustomed to managing this device. This must be taken into account in psychoanalytic dialogue carried about by telephone given the possible preformed transference (Meltzer, 1967) with the habitual use of the telephone. The imperative sensation of being in a situation that requires concise messages and quick answers leaves little space for contemplation or the production of reflective dialogue taking place at a calm pace. The fact that communicating by telephone must fit into the space that an analytic session of analysis offers can help to assign that dialogue a proper identity and achieve the pace that is required to speak and listen with *analytic attitude* (Etchegoyen, 1986, 2005). This encourages the establishing of a suitable ambience for elaborative thought. The patient will begin to understand that he/she has a 50-minute session which serves as a space to express his/her spontaneous communication, his/her associations, and give room for the interventions of the analyst. As time goes by, the patient will understand that silence in a session is not due to "technical difficulty", "distraction of the analyst", or "wasted time". In general it is observed that little by little the patient begins to understand that this is a reflective conversation and he/she begins to accept silence as a resource and not as an alteration or failure. This comprehensive evolution of the method referred to the patient finds a parallel in the evolution of psychoanalysis and psychoanalysts. In effect, clinical psychoanalysis is not immune to the transformational social phenomenology that places the human being in the situation around him, or as Ortega y Gasset (1914) would say: "*Yo soy yo y mi circunstancia*" (I am myself and my circumstance). If the practice of our profession were not directed in this way, little by little it would lose ground and be recommendable for fewer and fewer people. In the evolutionary history of psychoanalysis, one can observe a permanent updating as well as a constant and appropriate adjustment process to the changing demands of humanity. It has surpassed its original conceptions and also its initial boundary, which was to treat patients diagnosed as neurotic.

5   Warnings and recommendations

It is also important to indicate that in analyses carried out by modern communication technology, especially those undertaken through the use of deferred dialogue (as is the case of email) it is necessary to pay attention not only to the exact speech of the patient's, but also to the degree of coherence and credibility that exists among the different messages sent over time. It is also important not to block the perception of anything new that can arise in the patient as a product of his/her psychic change and his/her mental growth.

One of the reasons for this publication stems from the desire to promote a work of reflection as to the type of conceptual *predisposition* that analysts with experience in distance psychoanalysis have towards new digital techniques. In contrast to this, as we have already seen, young analysts or those still being trained have been educated in the digital era and therefore have a disposition and a familiarity with the use of modern communication technology. Therefore, at the time of accepting the method, they will not consider the means being used as something novel, but rather as something natural, and well within their habitual paradigms of observation and action. Many of them, when beginning as psychoanalysts, are already experts in engaging in dialogue through the use of the computer (especially with written chat) and often even without having seen their interlocutor's face.

Something similar occurred before the appearance of present-day communication devices. Many anxious young people established contact with pen-pals in distant places through the use of conventional postal mail. From this epistemological contact, many of them formed valuable friendships where intimacies and the possibility of an eventual personal encounter existed.

Encounters established through the internet entail *a priori* doubts as to the genuine sincerity of the interlocutor at the other end of the line. The idea of a broken or deformed contact is always latent (Levis, 2005). Each of the participants knows how sincere his/her communication is, but is not sure about that of the other. Therefore these dialogues carry the weight of *preformed transference*, which would possibly operate as a factor of distrust, thereby sometimes generating a semantic distortion (Liberman, 1970). However, unconscious breaking away, deliberate hiding, deforming, or even lying is something typical of every patient, just like in classic analysis. It is for that reason that at the time of indicating distance analysis, the analyst must bear this in mind and decide on a case-by-case basis whether the proposed means of communication is suitable. Also, although in an inverse sense, vignettes 3 and 4 of Chapter Six illustrate the possibility of greater and more effective sincerity on the part of the patient, promoted by the lack of physical presence of the analyst.

CHAPTER FOUR

Theory of the technique of distance psychoanalysis

The basic component of clinical psychoanalysis is the analytic dialogue between the analyst and the patient during the analysis session. The words exposed there are inextricably linked to feelings, gestures, attitudes, and to a way of being which give information about the two protagonists of the analysis and the bond between them. This dialogue is both a path and an instrument of ideo-affective exchange between its protagonists. The words uttered there are influenced by the affective quality contained in the transference-countertransference, which will have an influence on the degree of collaboration and/or resistance, as well as in the interpretative work. In the flow of these words, the following components of effective semantic value can be identified:

a. Verbal: words emitted and connected in a particular syntax.
b. Para-verbal: intonation given to the words.
c. Extra-verbal: gestures, expressions, conduct, laughter, tears, clothes, and any other corporal manifestation that accompanies the speech. In distance psychoanalysis, we are only concerned with those components that can be captured by the perceptive senses in action, which will depend on the method and means being used.

a. **Verbal component:** *words emitted and connected in a certain syntax*		
Dialogue in the psychoanalyst's office	*Dialogue conducted through video-chat*	*Dialogue by telephone*
One engages in a dialogue with the subjective sensation and the evidence of objective certainty that the emitted message arrives at the interlocutor.	Similar to psychoanalyst's office dialogue. Technological problems (although uncommon) can provoke moments of uncertainty when they occur, due to the imagination that is promoted. This sensation tends to be mitigated and can eventually disappear once one becomes accustomed to this means of communication.	Technological problems can create moments of confusion and/or uncertainty due to the impossibility of seeing the other. It is mitigated once one becomes accustomed to this type of session.
b. **Para-verbal component:** intonation given to the words		
In addition to the degree of attention and interest placed in the dialogue, the detection of these components depends on the training and auditory skill of the listener.	Assuming that reception is clear, the video images and audio appear clearly at the other end, much as they would in the consultation room.	Assuming that reception is clear, it depends on the sharpness and auditory skill of the listener. With the practice of this type of session, the skill to discern specific semiological shades of words is developed. This is so because of the need to compensate for the lack of visual contact.

c. Extra-verbal component: gestures, expressions, conduct, laughter, tears, clothes, and any other corporal manifestation that accompanies the speech		
There is direct visual access. The fact that the patient is lying on the couch causes certain elements of the extra-verbal component in line with this body position to be produced. Furthermore, the analyst is not always attentive to them and can be careless or lose his/her perception. In fact, the analyst often closes his/her eyes or directs his/her gaze on a fixed point so that the line of vision will not disturb the possibility of concentrating on the ideas and affection emanated there, as well as in his/her own countertransference.	There is direct visual access, although limited to what the camera focuses on. One has rather good access to that involving gesture and conduct. Although limited, it bears a certain resemblance to what can be sensed in a situation of corporal proximity.	There is never direct access. Indirect signals can be tracked or one can take into account what a patient specifies as to what he consciously perceives of himself. Some hints of the para-verbal, such as a breaking voice, moans, and pauses can be detected. In reference to corporal performance, one can detect added noises, silences, distance of the voice from the telephone, etc., which suggest some body movement or allude to other extra-verbal elements which are captured through sonorous nuances. Countertransference contributes a suitable instrument of interpretative registry.
d. Characteristics of the contact: given by the analytical situation, the sign of the transference and countertransference, the degree of resistance, and the interpretative work		
In these three types of analytic setting, there are not differences worthy of comment.		

Below we can observe a chart comparing the characteristics of three types of dialogue: that which is conducted in the analyst's office, that which is conducted through video-chat, and that which is conducted by telephone.

The following scheme describes in detail the specificities that characterize dialogue conducted through the use of communication technology. It emphasizes some of the similarities and differences between this type of dialogue and that which takes place in the analyst's office. The basic ideas of this chart, which are presented here in more detail, were taken from the presentation of the Latin American group participating in the Panel on "Telephone Analysis" of the 46th International Psychoanalytic Congress, Chicago in July–August of 2009. The Latin American group was consisted of: A. Aryan, S. P. de Berenstein, R. Carlino, P. Grinfeld, and J. Lutenberg.

Similarities and differences between distance psychoanalysis and analysis performed in the analyst's office

A SIMILARITIES

Theoretical

One operates with the conceptual baggage that comes from the fundamental concepts of psychoanalysis, adding the theoretical currents to which each analyst adheres:

- All of Freudian meta-psychology, expressed in a stratified psychic apparatus in instances; the theory of repression and that of psychosexual development in its economic, topical, and dynamic aspects.
- The theory of the unconscious and its derivatives: the analysis of the dreams, oneiric symbology, and Freudian slips.
- Repressed infantile sexuality, the Oedipus complex.
- Theories regarding identification.

Technical

a. One works with an analytical contract that includes a framework that circumscribes the dialogue within a session. Elements such as: "Fundamental Rule", "free association", "free-floating attention", "transference", and "countertransference" are viable in synchronous distance psychoanalysis. In the asynchronous analyses, such as email, the "Fundamental Rule", and the "free association" take on a special characteristic that will be discussed in Chapter Seven.

b. The first perceptive station hits the sensory organs that the applied technological means allows for. In any case, the sensory apparatus being used perceives what the complex preparation within the mind of the analyst has made available for perception. The saying "he who knows, sees" illustrates this. From that complex perceptive preparation the analyst observes: whether the patient calls at the agreed time, the ideo-affective and behavioural material of the beginning of the session, and the response given to the interpretations. Free-floating attention is the suitable way of catching what is inferred as "the latent content of the material". When the analyst deems it advisable, he/she interprets and then is attentive to the answer given to his/her interpretation. He/she perceives the patient not only in his/her speech but also in any omissions from this speech. The analyst observes the qualities of the ambience of the session, as well the silences, and what these can say or suggest. In synthesis, the analyst perceives the complete performance of the patient; not only through the sounds and images that reach him/her by means of the technology being used, but also from the mental processing of everything that happens during the session.

Ethical

a. The analyst must acquire a specific and specialized preparation in order to inform the patient about the still experimental nature of distance treatment, unless there are specific reasons not to do so.

b. The analyst must be well oriented in his/her indication and periodically research the latest uses and applications.

B DIFFERENCES

Theoretical

It is necessary to include within psychoanalytic theory a re-conceptualization of the traditional use given to the terms *real* and *virtual*. Given that language is transmitted through a means of communication technology which would commonly be denominated as *virtual*, one can permanently debate whether this dialogue is real or virtual. It is necessary to define this considering the following:

The first three elements that are discussed below [a., b., and c.], legitimately include distance analytic dialogue in the category of *real dialogue* (non-virtual). In fact, from the points of view taken into account, one observes no difference with dialogue carried out in the analyst's office.

a. Distance analytical dialogue can only occur in a session arranged for a specific time on a specific day.
b. It is hoped that it will produce effects that will contribute to the analytic process.
c. It is an act carried out with professional responsibility and subject to legal and tax regulation. The patient pays and the analyst charges for the service.
d. In the distance framework, the idea of *presence* is separated from the need to be in front of the other person. It acquires an abstract and symbolic conception. The *presence*, when separating it from the need for a direct physical meeting, is bound to the idea of *contact* and *encounter* between the analyst and patient. The quality achieved through these multiple elements will have a result in parallel to the depth and penetration that can be obtained in the colloquial exchange of the session.
e. Geographic distance is taken into account basically with the aim of determining how to establish analytic dialogue. It is measured from communicational parameters of time: *milliseconds* and not in patterns of geographic distance measured in the metric system.

Techniques

The analytic setting brought about by means of technology circumscribes each person in his/her own atmosphere. This will influence the terms and scope of the contract and the framework, referring to schedules, fees, the holidays of each specific country, etc.

The deprivation of the use of some of the senses is supplanted by a suitable training applied at the time of semiologically decoding the nuances of the voice, the material of written chat, or the image of the web camera.

In the material that arrives to the earpiece, it is possible to distinguish and to decode the manifestations of the libidinal body which frequently emerges in the content of the ideas and feelings that the words transmit, whether it be through the meaning of the words, the tone and inflexion of the voice, the gestures perceived (when using video-telephone) and/ or in the kind of typing used in written chat. In synthesis, in distance treatments the *in toto* performance carried out by the patient during the session is taken into account. In reference to the implementation of analyses by means of communication technology, it is required that the analyst be well versed in the specific details of this type of approach, and that he/she have certain skills in the technological handling of the devices being used.

In order to orientate distance dialogue in the proper direction, it must take place in the conditions marked by a specific analytic technique that provides inclusion and support. It must be undertaken by a psychoanalyst who is well versed in the latest theoretical-technical aspects of the method. It is essential that the analyst have the experience of having shared the content of his/her clinical work in supervision sessions, clinical discussions, and other areas of theoretical and technical exchange where he/she can receive feedback from colleagues (Helman, 2006). That is to say, it is essential the analyst not be professionally isolated.

On this matter and with the purpose of deepening the legitimacy of distance analysis, it is important to mention M. Baranger and W. Baranger (1961), who maintain that analytic dialogue is structured on the basis of the construction of an unconscious fantasy shaped by both participants during the session. This conception should be framed in the functional concept of the analytic session, conceived as a dynamic field.

1 Conceptual spaces in which the analytic dialogue and process take place

Distance psychoanalytic dialogue and what occurs in the analyst's office both take place in a session and their content is exposed in the *Inter space* in which verbal communication mixes and circulates with elaborative objectives. This common space operates like a container that includes the conjunction between the behaviours and the ideological and emotional expressions of each one of the participants in the analysis. The two interlocutors of this dialogue speak to each other—in the *Inter space*—but also do so with themselves—in the *Intra space*—thereby structuring a multiple dialogue that contributes to the possibility of analytically processing what is spoken (Cantis-Carlino & Carlino, 1987). In the space where the analytical dialogue takes place, schematically considered, one can visualize several zones of different kinds in which the multiple dialogues take place.

a. The session of distance analysis offers a place that is circumscribed to a period, a space, of time: the analysis session. There the ideas, emotions, and behaviours of both protagonists intersect.

b. The *Inter space* is a transference area of an abstract and conceptual nature. Just as the Fundamental Rule requests, the patient communicates his occurrences. These, for reasons of interpretation, are taken by the analyst based on content, form, and opportunity. The analyst will analytically process what he/she listens to and then offers his/her interpretation in the *Inter space*.

Metaphorically, it works as a kind of game table covered by a mat on which the game is played. There the cards are thrown and establish themselves as communication. These contain a state of mind and conceptual "value" that engage in a dialogue with those of the other. The dialogue takes place from the manifest content in rational and logical form, and it is interpreted including what is inferred as latent content, within an atmosphere that, instead of being filled with smoke, is filled with transference and countertransference.

c. The *Intra space* corresponds to the mind of each one of the protagonists. It is one of the places where what is said in the session is processed, and as the analysis continues, the analytic process develops. Although it occurs in every session, it takes place in the mind of the patient and that of the analyst, who acts as a contributor to that process. As we see, the analytic process does not take place either in the analyst's office or on the telephone line but rather comes to light due to what is specifically occurring in the mind of the patient and, in a greater sense, in the mind of the analyst, where the experience spawns professional growth (Carlino & Torregiani, 1987). This explanation highlights the precise location and hierarchy that must be assigned to the setting as a place for transit and exchange, thereby differentiating it from what is happening in the mind of each of the participants in the analysis.

d. So-called cyberspace corresponds to an area of an abstract nature, without exact space, around which the messages circulate within a net of electronic waves from their point of emission to that of their arrival. It is not a linear or direct route but rather one that is formed by a grouping of computer networks that belongs to the electronic system of communication.

We are considering different methods of psychoanalytic approach which, although different, certainly have similarities and/or equivalences. In distance treatments, the language must be adapted to the method implemented. The distance between the interlocutors should not always be the decisive point which makes the treatment possible or impossible. In analytic dialogue, there should be an encounter between the material contributed by the patient and the catching of that material, using the free-floating attention of the analyst for its specific elaboration. During the first century of analytic practice, this procedure took place in the psychoanalyst's office. That is to say, it was transformed into a habit that seems immutable, although it must not be considered essential for analytic work. The "psychoanalytic encounter" must not be construed to be a situation in which the analyst and the patient have the obligation of shaking hands from a metre's distance before engaging in dialogue.

Classic analytic dialogue is made up of a verbal language with intonations that contribute some connotation to the signified. It is complemented with extra-verbal signs, some unconscious, and all with the possibility of being registered. In distance treatments, extra-verbal signals are obviously excluded, except when a web camera is used, due to the fact that it allows access to facial expressions, gestures, and movements of the patient—any of which may contribute some significant signs. In the use of written chat, one may include emoticons, capital letters for emphasis, and stenographic signs, all of which serve as a rich and complex language.

In distance analytic dialogue, what circulates in the *Inter space*? Words originating at both poles which, in themselves, are physical phenomena from which a signifier and its corresponding signified emanate.

Of all the manifest content of the emitted verbal material, obviously the analyst will only consider that which he/she can register. What then will become of the emitted content that cannot be perceived due to the limitations of the method? In principle, it is necessary to consider it as lost, unless the emitter believes that it was not registered and therefore repeats it. However, he/she will only repeat what corresponds to his/her conscious area. This will not be enough due to the fact that the analyst is very interested in connecting with the unconscious of that material. The patient will not be able to help in this matter because he/she is not aware of it. However, we know that the unconscious wants to come out and that if it is not registered in a session, perhaps it will find another opportunity to arise and thus reach the analyst. It is also conceivable that some sign of the unconscious will never reach the analyst, because the method being used does not allow him/her to register it. This will constitute a limit of the used method.

2   Analytic dialogue from different surroundings

Distance psychoanalysis must construct a suitable framework for its operative necessity. Each of the two participants in the analysis is immersed in a complex contextual situation which is different from that of the other. This can have an influence on the logic of the feeling and thinking of both participants. In the classic framework, some of the elements of the surrounding reality, as they are common to both participants, can produce stimuli and awaken an interest and a valuation that can be analogous, different, or perhaps controversial. Puget and Wender (1982), in an original article entitled "*Mundos Superpuestos*" (Superimposed Worlds), described in detail this influence which produces analogous or different subjective reactions.

Based on the premise that *the context makes the text* I will refer to how distance analytic dialogue is affected by everything that happens unilaterally in the surrounding world of each of its actors. I denominate it specifically as a *proper and different context*. I refer to the relationship that is established between "the being and his/her circumstances" in which both members of the analytical couple are immersed. The amalgamation of the two with the "being" also puts into play the norms, customs, values, and paradigms that comprise the *base logic* of each one. When these differences are put into play, without clear awareness of the divergence from that of the other, a conceptual shock of misunderstandings will take place and will affect the colloquial exchange and the elaborative process (Carlino, 2000). Ignoring that one undertakes dialogue from different paradigmatic logic will influence the way of thinking of each one and limit the fulfilment of some formal aspects of the analytic contract.

At the beginning of the analysis the patient may not understand from where the analyst deduces his/her interpretative intervention. He/she does not know of the existence of a conceptual approach that supposes a latent content of the manifested material. He/she does not know that when the analyst remains in silence it is not because he/she is providing a bad service, is distracted, or is showing disrespect. Furthermore, in reference to telephone analysis, the silence does not mean that the line has been cut. Sooner or later the patient will begin to understand that the different understanding that the analyst has of what is being said to him/her is due to the interpretative aspect of his/her role as analyst. The analyst could make an erroneous processing of the material or the behaviour of the patient if he/she were not familiar with some guideline that enters the general logic of his/her place of residence. It is for that reason that when a performance seems odd or is not clear with a certain patient, it is better to do further research instead of insisting upon a particular interpretative content.

In the patient's place of residence, specific events regarding climatic and environmental conditions, or those of a political, economic, or social origin may be taking place. The analyst must bear these phenomena in mind. As the prevailing values and cultural customs in a country may be very different from those of the other, these elements must be taken into account when deciding on the analytic contract. For example, the fees, patient absences to sessions, different national holidays, and annual vacations of the patient at a time of the year different from those of the analyst are all matters for discussion. We are now far away from the guidelines which emanated from the classic work of Karl Menninger (1958) on the analytical contract, in which he stated that the patient did not have vacations from his analysis but that it was the analyst who interrupted the treatment in order to take his/her vacations. Instead of judging his criterion, I will simply highlight that the statement was based a social context of values which are different from our present ones. In reference to contextual differences, I tend to set up a clock that gives the time at the patient's place of residence. With the Skype system, this is not necessary since the screen shows the local time of the place where the phone call was made. When I look at the clock during a session, I become more aware of the time difference with the patient and therefore of the different circumstances of the place in which he/she is located.

3   Specificities arising from the different aspects of each applied method

These different possible ways of practising clinical psychoanalysis open questions and new issues to consider. If the issue is one of continuing treatment from long distance, upon changing the framework the quality of the interpersonal relationship will inevitably go through some transformation, which in some cases warrants that some pre-established technical and clinical criteria of the diagnosis be adjusted to each particular situation. It is inherent in the adoption of any distance method to accept that, as it is held at a physical location in which the analyst is not present and therefore cannot witness the environment in which the patient is inserted, one must accept the unknown and/or accidents resulting from this framework and let these play their role, processing them as material. Approaching the time of the meeting, the analyst awaits the communication through the agreed-upon means. Neither of the two participants in the analysis knows the physical space in which the other is located, unless it is explicit. For the patient, this may lead to deductive inferences and/or fantasies influenced by transference feelings.

In treatments carried out without video images, it will not be possible to perceive the corporal aspects of the patient, nor the area from which he/she is speaking or engaging in written chat. One cannot know about the degree of light, the influence of temperature, whether the patient is alone or accompanied, or anything about his/her body language, gestures, clothing, etc. Neither of the two participants in the analysis has the visible access to verify whether the other is fully focused on the dialogue or distracted by something else. Neither knows whether the other is wearing appropriate clothing for a professional meeting. Furthermore, in these circumstances it is not possible to know whether the patient eats or drinks, takes notes or records the session, or simultaneously watches television or a computer screen. Keep in mind that questions of this nature, to a greater or lesser degree, may also be in the patient's mind about his analyst. In any case, the material reaches the telephone receiver and although it does not perceive the patient's body, it may instead receive and decode the manifestations of the libidinal body that emerges from the content of ideas and feelings that the patient's words convey by way of perceiving the tone and inflection of the patient's voice throughout the session. Additionally, the analyst has his/her countertransference register. The concepts and comments made in the previous chapter on "mirror neurons" become quite relevant here.

Some analysts, when experiencing unannounced "absences" to the meeting, develop experiences that are different from those which arise in treatment in the consultation room. The amount of uncertainty created by the geographical distance can be felt differently and raise some concerns, due to the number of uncommon environmental circumstances. These circumstances are much greater than those of common analysis, as a result of *different contexts*. When the patient's call does not come, the first question that arises is whether he/she is trying to call and the connection cannot be established. Each analyst will make an evaluation based on the established habits of the patient. The analyst may also feel a sense of uncertainty such as: "Did he/she try to call but wasn't able?" "Could it be my phone, or because there is difficulty with the line?" "Could it be that he/she didn't want to call or simply forgot?" With some patients the analyst may even think: "Will he/she never call again?" Several factors could lead the analyst to be concerned about the possibility of the patient's desertion. One worth mentioning is the fact that the two participants in the analysis are physically located in a large common area of many millions of square kilometres, which may subjectively create the feeling of the need for a higher degree of adherence to the connection and the treatment. However, this feeling deserves to be thought of as an occurrence that emits a countertransference signal related to the state that the analytical process is undergoing. Another factor would be promoted by the fact that patients, as they contribute 50 per cent of the physical elements of the framework, show their degree of belonging to the link with the input contributed at each meeting, which (as stated) is half of the framework material. The expectation of a firm performance of the contractual provisions would also be connected to the lack of concrete materials that these frameworks contain. The arrival of the call on the agreed day and time, coupled with the dialogue in the session, are all that give materiality to the analytic relationship. The only material element of the link is the payment. Presumably, something similar is also necessary for the patient regarding the compliance of the analyst.

With reference to the stipulation of contractual rules before beginning treatment, several different opinions should be considered, although some of them are conflicting. A universally acceptable principle is founded on the idea that the contract should contain very basic terms which, if not met, would make it difficult or impossible for the treatment to take place. In the different norms for each method proposed, it is expected that the analyst have an analytic attitude which is clear and precise regarding the technical formulations and the proposed contractual terms. However, it is necessary that he/she maintain an attitude of understanding towards different points of view, as well as towards the possible inability of the patient to respond to the contract properly.

In the distance setting, the patient is deprived of the semantics that emanate from the ambience that an analyst's office provides, with its iconic couch and the analyst's university degree on the wall, which in some way determine the "places" and qualities of each of the roles. The establishing of a climate of analytical work will therefore depend on the analyst's attitude from his/her internal *framework* and the appropriate interpretations with which he/she is able to process the material. Importance is given to the intonation used when speaking, as well as the good management of the space given to the patient so that he/she can express him/herself verbally. If the dialogue were to be carried out by written chat, the proper use of the language codes used in this style of writing gains utmost importance. The more finely tuned the technological instruments chosen to communicate are, and the greater the skill in handling these instrument is, the more easily the task can be carried out. If there are no difficulties in this, what then becomes basic and fundamental is that the analysis be conducted by an analyst who has a solid theoretical and technical training and an attitude committed to the vicissitudes arising from the transference-countertransference.

Regarding the performance of the patient, it is expected that he/she be responsible for the material, intellectual, emotional, and behavioural engagement that any analysis demands. What distance treatment adds to this equation is whether the initial motivation for undergoing distance analysis endures and is perceived as the successful establishment and development of an analytic process through the setting employed. On the latter point, a position of observation and specific research becomes an expectation. A micro test taken on a trial basis for a short period of treatment might be enough, depending on the perspective that the analyst has when establishing the agreed method of distance treatment. It would be an agreement *ad referendum* to the reality of implementation and whose results would soon come to light.

Some analysts, motivated by the responsibility that comes with the launching of a new way of analysing, adopt a cautious approach when deciding its implementation. They propose and articulate a framework in which it is stated, from the very beginning, that the analyst will meet with the patient in the analyst's office with a predetermined frequency in order to take stock of the results being obtained with the distance method implemented. In this regard J. Lutenberg (2009) basing his statements on the premise that telephone psychoanalytic treatment is still at an experimental stage, informs patients that "the first months can be taken as a trial period." The analyst additionally tells the patient that he/she has must also observe the process carefully in terms of the coherence and sense that the method acquires. This principle is what the analyst refers to as the "audit performed by the patient". This indication is aimed at the "adult side" and is symmetrical with the analyst. It is valid to rely on the "audit performed by the patient", but the analyst must unfailingly take into account that it is not always possible to have this collaboration. Beyond this, in order to ensure an adequate indication for treatment, as well as its correct implementation and development, the analyst in charge must endeavour to undertake a very professional performance in its theoretical, technical, and ethical aspects.

Another approach would be not to propose the "trial period" so as not to provoke initial "doubts" and, if eventually necessary, as in any classical psychoanalyst's office treatment, carry out an assessment process on the progress and performance of the method employed. If such an assessment were imposed *per se* and the analyst were to overlook it, two possibilities could arise: one could be that both would ignore this phenomenon in a sort of denial pact (Kaës, 1989), and the other could be that the analyst may eventually encounter a suggestion from the patient promoted and pursued from an *adult* position of spontaneous "audit".

It is advisable, from the beginning, to guide the dialogue by giving it the structure, sense, and pace that any session of analysis requires, depending on each particular treatment. The analyst must be receptive and attentive at all times in order to avoid occupying the role of a non-specific interlocutor—not analytic—since the analytic methods used (telephone, computer chat, etc.) are themselves charged with multiple semantics given their established family and commercial use.

It is also necessary to observe how each one grants or usurps space to/ from the other: especially due to the fact that they are giving each other space, not only for speaking, but also for thinking. As we see, there are several elements of behavioural observation in the way of articulating the dialogue, which provide a signifier edge added to the observation and elaboration of material loaded with signified. Some patients who undergo analysis by phone constantly talk during the session and leave no space for the analyst's intervention. When the analyst tries several times to "shyly" say something and the patient continues talking without even hearing him/her, the analyst, having listened carefully, realizes that this is evacuative speaking. The interpretation of this intervention of the patient can no longer cover only the content of ideas of the material, but is inextricably attached to the way it was delivered.

4   Initial interviews

In the initial interviews, the analyst focuses his/her attention on the apparent reason for the consultation and makes some guesses about what latent elements might be underlying. This process includes the motivation that may lead to the choice of a distance analysis. This is the appropriate time for the analyst to learn the reason for the consultation, ask about any historical items that the patient is willing to discuss, track symptoms and defences that are close to the patient's consciousness, and detect the structure of linking configurations with family and those closest to the patient. During this first contact the analyst observes the performance and the transference- countertransference affect that this experience produces. All this enables the analyst to gain orientation as to the symptoms, as well as the situational and psychopathological diagnosis of the potential patient. Last but not least, the analyst assesses and decides whether he/she can and wants to work analytically with the interviewee via a distance method, whether this format be requested by the patient or not.

From an opposite perspective, in the interviews the patient should take the opportunity to decide whether to accept the analyst and the analytic contract suggested, including the recommendation about the technological means to be used. Nowadays, these interviews, in most cases, are performed in the analyst's office. Presumably, as this method becomes more widespread and more institutionally formalized, the initial interviews, when the material reality of the distance merits the case, would also be carried out by the same long distance method that the prospective patient expects for his/her analysis. This issue, which is currently controversial, is developed in different pages of the book, according to the subject being discussed.

a   The "analytic contract"

Although I have only devoted a brief space to the topic of interviews, I will dwell on some considerations that I believe are important to highlight regarding the analytic contract. Some of the points developed do not entirely agree with the classical form in which the analytic contract is proposed and implemented. Indeed, a certain concept and way of being expressed here carry singularities that in some ways make it very different from what has been previously established.

Before proposing an analytic contract, it is necessary to have a fairly solid idea of for whom it will be formulated. Taking into account the concepts presented earlier in this chapter referring to the dissimilar contexts in which the two participants in the analysis are placed, I denominated this situation as "proper and different context". We have already seen that by the end of the diagnostic interviews, the analyst has formed an idea about the interviewee, as well as about the why and wherefore of his consultation. Furthermore, the prospects of what type of analytic work could be discerned given the method of distance analysis to be used have been weighed. With reference to commitment to the analysis, one of the criteria that needs to be fulfilled, at least superficially, has to do with the ego and the material resources that the prospective patient possesses, as well as whether he/she has a sufficient sense of responsibility so as to enable the patient to be responsible for that role. Why do we ask this question with regard to the beginning of distance analysis? One reason is that the prospective patient will be responsible for half of the material infrastructure of the framework, as he/she will be responsible for establishing and maintaining good communication equipment, and to rent, if available at his/her place of residence, a good public communication line. Moreover, the geographic distance over which these treatments take place requires some ego resources for possible self-containment in distressing or critical situations. Should this not be the case, it will be necessary to establish a framework that includes a psychiatrist and a general practitioner in the patient's place of residence.

From this point on, it is necessary to see whether the analytic contract agrees with both generally accepted premises and provisions, and with others that are more specific to each particular situation. This will lead us to consider and eventually decide whether they are to be admitted in their present form or whether it is necessary to reconsider them in order to make them acceptable to both parties. Each would become obligated, from his/her role, to carry out the task of psychoanalysis: the analyst must analyse the patient and the patient, at least formally, must work towards this goal of successful psychoanalysis by being responsible for his/her role. David Liberman, a prominent Argentine psychoanalyst, in a professional seminar there has said that "the analytical dyad consists of two people who speak about just one of them." R. H. Etchegoyen (1986, 2005), when referring to the tasks that make each a participant of the analytic dyad, said it "consists in the exploration of the unconscious of one of them, with the technical participation of the other".

The statement that contains the analytic contract gives us explicit indications as to the rules at work in the relationship between the protagonists. This will undoubtedly affect the logic of thinking which will be established as the *base logic* at different moments of dialogue in the sessions. This is one reason why it is necessary to seek an agreement and then make it explicit. Some of the points mentioned are "as is" and cannot be otherwise. On the other hand, there are certain elements that may have some particular aspect or undergo some adjustment once they are implemented and as the treatment develops. When necessary, new points can be created and the agreed-upon points can be modified, thus taking the form of new contractual premises. There are some patients with certain legal and commercial training who raise the objection that the *analytic contract* is a "standard form contract", a term coined in their professional jargon. They claim that it limits the patient to accepting it as they would accept a commercial contract. This objection can be answered with the conviction that what is stated is not only compulsory for the patient, but simultaneously, in his/her complementary role, for the analyst as well. For example, if it is agreed that the meetings will take place on pre-determined days and at pre-determined times, the analyst assumes the same obligation as the patient. The analyst knows that when he/she accepts a patient's commitment, he/she is simultaneously committed to exercising his/her role as an analyst and never otherwise. In summary, it is expected that both will assume their role in the analytic work. Experience shows that every so often there will be a flaw in compliance and the so-called "contract" will serve as a guide for processing this deviation and bringing things back to the correct path. In fact, one should be guided by the spirit of the provisions of the contract, more than by the letter of the contract.

It is a deeply rooted belief that, at the time of closing a contractual agreement, both parties should be face-to-face, eye-to-eye, and shaking hands. This figurative description corresponds to the emblematic image of two people in the act of agreeing to something.

In treatments whose beginning interview is also conducted at a distance, this emblematic and representative image of making a commitment, both concrete and symbolic, must find a minimal equivalent in order to convince both parties that the commitment has been established. If necessary, it could be replaced with another kind of symbolic act. On the other hand, one could simply wait until the signs of the commitment and the bond gradually appear. After all, "the proof is in the pudding". In fact, looking each other in the eye and shaking hands does not guarantee that the commitment will be fulfilled. Whenever formulating a contract for distance analysis, one should articulate an appropriate and credible type of commitment which can be both assumed and fulfilled. Otherwise, this contract risks becoming iatrogenic, given that the analyst assumes that the commitment cannot be fulfilled.

For some patients, the need to perceive the analyst at less than a distance of a metre may be important, and this must be taken into account when indicating the type of treatment. Situations such as these could occur in patients who are very regressive, some teenagers, and others who are limited in their capacity for symbolization. Although the voice can be conceived as an expression of what is psychic-corporal, it cannot completely replace the body's ability to emit certain signs that may be necessary for certain patients, as well as the analyst. As a "halfway" solution, in the case where the matter of distance were to make it difficult to meet several times a week, it would be advisable to mix sessions at the psychoanalyst's office with distance sessions. Another element that would help would be the use of a videophone. These considerations should bear in mind that some people have acute abilities regarding one of their five senses and therefore prioritize the use of that sense over the rest. For example, for those prospective patients who have a highly developed sense of hearing, telephone analysis is often recommended. It is important to consider these comments when choosing the distance method.

With regard to what is being considered, it is important to stop and think once more about the role played by the analyst's body in the analysis session. This role will have significant differences when treating children, adolescents, or adults. In principle, I see an opportunity for distance analysis for neurotic adult patients and for some adolescents who may be able to profit from it. Psychopathic patients and those in their childhood years must be excluded. Regarding psychotic patients, there may be situations involving a change in the country of residence of the patient. In such a situation, it may be appropriate to evaluate on a case-by-case basis whether it is better to change analysts or to use distance analysis in order to continue with the same one. In these cases it is necessary, as previously pointed out, that in the new place of residence there be a psychiatrist to prescribe medication if necessary and a general practitioner to monitor the patient's overall health. With adolescents one must be very careful when giving indications, accepting that although they come from a very suitable age group for the use of the latest communication technologies—especially written chat—their familiarity with this type of communication does not automatically enable them to undergo distance psychoanalysis. Teenagers need, for their own development and social inclusion, to interact with others in direct physical form. They need to test themselves to see what it is like and to see what is expected of their performance when face-to-face with another person. If the analysis is performed in a direct exchange, without technological intervention, they may appreciate it as more realistic than if it were preformed from long distance. This drawback could be mitigated by interspersing sessions in the psychoanalyst's office with sessions carried out by a distance method. Thus, this kind of combination analysis would provide an opportunity to analyse the tendency of defensive isolation in the world of ideas and words and/or computer use while offering the adolescent the possibility of psychoanalysis. This is especially suitable in the case of a teenager who lives in a remote place and therefore cannot travel often to the psychoanalyst's office. Furthermore, this could even help the adolescent in making a foray into the world of social reality.

b   Purposes of the analytic contract

The analytic contract must contain the basic clauses necessary in order to articulate the analytical work. It should be clear that the contract is between two people—the analyst and the patient. It should be proposed, not in order to analyse an ideal patient, but rather in order to offer the best possible treatment for a specific patient. In other words, the Procrustean bed trap must be avoided at all costs. This Procrustean bed must also not be applied to the analytic performance of the analyst, no matter what ideas the patient may propose—or impose—with reference to his/her treatment. The analytic contract sets out the rules of the game and structures the commitment that each one must have, from the scope of his/her role. The analyst has an ethical commitment to the patient, to him/herself as a person, and to the society that has let him/her practise the profession. In each analytical act, he/she feels a loyalty both to the improvement and/or welfare of the patient and to the proper use of the theoretical and technical psychoanalytic tools used for achieving those goals. The success will depend on his/her skill in implementing this with the "art and science" that the patient demands, while executing a correct analytical operation in each intervention.

The patient comes in search of psychological help. Some use the term "psychoanalysis" to refer to any non-specific psychological treatment. Others, however, are well aware of what psychoanalysis is. However, during the sessions, at the time of expressing him/herself in his/her role, the patient does so according to what he/she is like as a real person. It is supposed that it was his/her adult part that formed the agreement with the analyst and the only pressure involved was what stemmed from the need to agree to the contractual provisions set forth by the analyst. Logically, these provisions were set forth with the aim of undertaking successful psychoanalysis.

On one occasion, at the moment in which I was explaining the Fundamental Rule to a patient, he informed me that there was something very important about which he could not speak, and that he would begin his analysis only if I accepted this condition. My response was aimed at showing him that, as long as this impediment endured, his proposal was more a contractual clause than a temporary condition. I then explained to him that I could not accept this, but that I would agree to begin the analysis so that we could gradually see how the situation of his initial difficulty would develop.

Notwithstanding these considerations, it is important to make clear that the "adhesion" nature of this contract required of the patient has a similar and parallel counterpart for the analyst, given that they are *sine qua non* provisions for successful psychoanalysis. They do not stem from the needs, desires, or whimsical ways of the analyst. One of the conceptual premises to bear in mind is the following: one should not apply standards that are far from accepted—and much less applied—by rowing against the current of social consensus unless there is a clear conviction on the part of the patient and a strong possibility of frank agreement.

c   "Assent"

In the act of assenting, one accepts as true or advisable that which a person claims and/or proposes, given the sincerity and/or authority of the person in the area in which the agreement is to be reached. In this case it is assumed that those who seek analysis, in principle, recognize the analyst as an expert in his/her profession. We have already seen that at the conclusion of the last diagnostic interview, the analyst makes a proposal to the prospective patient about what rules would be applied for analytic treatment. The patient cannot be put in a position of having to decide to respond on what he/she is not technically prepared, although he/she can be made responsible for accepting or not accepting the conditions of treatment proposed by an expert in psychoanalysis. In the case of accepting these conditions, the patient approves what the analyst proposes. I mention this to highlight the patient's recognition of the analyst's authority and therefore his/her trust in what the analyst proposes. This trust stems from the institutional authority of both the state and the psychoanalytic society that support and enable the analyst to work professionally. This is often coupled with the recommendation of a friend and the positive impression that the analyst produces by the end of the initial interviews. This dual institutional authority granted to the analyst involves an ethical commitment to these institutions, in addition to the analyst's commitment with him/herself and with the patient.

d   "Consent"

Etymologically, "consent" means to "sense" or "feel" with others. It differs from the act of assenting in that, although the final result is one of approval, it was achieved despite the initial existence of different positions. Once exposed and discussed, they have been transformed into contractual agreement. In fact, when the patient has an objection to a proposal made by the analyst, it opens a space for discussion. If the patient's objection comes from the adult part of his/her personality, and both the patient and the analyst discuss the objected proposal, any agreement reached will be the product of consenting to new contractual terms. What is discussed and eventually agreed to may not contradict or disturb any of the essential and necessary elements for the implementation of psychoanalysis.

e "Dissent"

The question that arises naturally and spontaneously is what may occur if it is not possible to reach agreement on the initial contract. Can one begin analysis despite dissent in the contract? The answer will depend on what the analyst considers to be the chance of addressing this dissent whenever it might arise. The premise upon which this lack of agreement took place must be included as a *variable* and not a *constant* of the analytic contract (Bleger, 1967; Zac, 1971), i.e.—as a part of the process rather than part of the framework of the analysis. If the analyst assumes that there is a prospect for further development, he/she is not only giving an opportunity to the patient, but is simultaneously opening a window for mutual enrichment, given the learning experience that this approach could bring about.

In the case that there are points of disagreement and that these are the result of the most neurotic aspects of the patient, the analyst must assess the prospect of beginning analysis in this way. It may be necessary to wait for some of these symptoms to be mitigated in order to reach the kind of agreement that is not possible at this early stage. Many times certain preformed transferences, an initial distrust, or a general attitude of stubbornness may impede progress in the contractual agreement. If the analyst perceives that analysis can begin, he/she does so knowing that there are no guarantees of a mitigation of these symptoms. In such cases, it must be explained to the interviewee that there is no agreement on all items proposed. The fact that the interviewee asserts his/her position in order to begin the treatment does not mean that the analyst has declined his/her position, but rather that he/she has simply agreed to begin the treatment despite those points of difference. The analyst is responsible for the technical management of the treatment and therefore, whenever he/she deems appropriate, may reiterate what was not agreed to at the beginning. However, this must always be done with the tone of trying to reach a mutually consented agreement—never one of imposing that agreement. This does not imply the expectation of an immediate solution. The patient's sustaining of that initial point of disagreement may come from a symptomatic aspect which is temporarily inapproachable, or from a simple unwillingness on the part of patient: what Baranger (1961) would denominate as a *"baluarte"* (bulwark). He defines it as a shelter full of powerful unconscious fantasies of omnipotence. The patient feels that if he/she were to change his/her position on this point of disagreement and allow it to enter the psychoanalytic session, it would leave him/her defenceless. For some patients, for example, anything that smacks of asymmetry in the contract is tantamount to submitting to the will of the analyst. The mere fact of putting into question the foundation on which his/her pride and self-esteem rest leads this patient to continue resisting any possibility of elaborative revision. When dissent is based on this, it is a resistance in which the patient wants to impose his framework upon the analyst without having even considered what has been proposed by the analyst. This suggests that this analysis would begin with what Bion (1963) developed conceptually as "reversible perspective", which is one of the forms of resistance that attempts to paralyze the dynamic aspect of psychoanalysis. When this occurs at the beginning of analysis, it becomes very difficult to establish the analytic process.

So then, what approach should we take when we come across prospective patients who dissent in one or more terms of the proposed contract but, nevertheless, express a willingness to be analysed, albeit with the imposition of certain conditions? Some of them come to seek help and others come for unknown reasons, but they all insist on undergoing treatment "their way". There is no single answer, unless one assumes that analysis under these circumstances will not only be very difficult, but in fact impossible. In that case, one cannot promise to begin the analysis, not only for technical reasons, but also for ethical ones. The decision also touches on private aspects of the analyst—primarily his/her degree of interest in analysing a patient who promises little chance of success. This is a point that requires some consideration. We have already seen that some people seeking an interview with a specialist in "psychoanalysis" often do so without taking this as a specific term but rather as a generic name that encompasses any treatment of a psychological nature. They have the belief that they will undergo analysis in order to see what is happening in their lives but primarily to confirm "almost all" of the impressions that they already have of themselves. In cases like this, one possible way of beginning the treatment is to execute it with a framework of psychotherapy, but leaving aside the element of psychoanalytic understanding. It is important to observe the degree of care (or neglect) placed in the analysis regarding the patient's attendance and his/her performance in responding to the content that emerges in the sessions. Special emphasis must be placed on how the patient bonds with the analyst's interventions and how he/she behaves when arriving at a situation in which the "topic" on which no contractual agreement could be reached, finally emerges. The patient may need first to build up certain narcissistic support before abandoning what he/she has built as a stronghold. We must bear in mind that in the field of clinical experience we psychoanalysts have had surprises in two different directions—sometimes disappointment and sometimes unforeseen encouraging discovery. If it is perceived that the treatment could gradually be directed towards psychoanalysis, the analyst cannot be sure that the point of disagreement can be redirected. The analyst must keep in mind that his/her initial position was that of the toleration of dissent, which allowed him/her to "play this difficult game". The evolution of the epistemological history of psychoanalysis has shown us that analysts must "leave one space blank" in order to gain specific experience from a patient's dissent. Sometimes we have learned that we were wrong when we wanted to apply a particular premise to a given patient. When did we realize that we had learned? We had learned after having got to know the patient better. We must not forget that ultimately, every analytic treatment is unique. I referred to this premise somewhat earlier when I said that dissent may "open a possibility for mutual enrichment, given the learning experience that this approach could bring about". It is only contraindicated if it is assumed that one or both of the participants would run the risk of harm in the implementation or continuation of the experience.

f   Mutually agreed commitment

As we have already seen, a mutually agreed commitment covers contractual agreements linked to some formal aspects that are necessary to reach an agreement, given the real possibilities of each of the participants. It deals with issues related to the *amount and form of payment* as well as the *days and times of the meetings*. This entails different possible methods, which obviously must be agreed to before beginning the analysis.

The analyst may stipulate his/her preferences from the very beginning. Another approach would be to consider the economic possibilities of a prospective patient when determining the amount of the fee, as well as the day of the month on which to make the payment. For those living in other countries, one must also take into account the way in which payments are typically made: weekly, biweekly, monthly, etc. In fact, an ad hoc agreement between the two parties is advisable. Generally speaking, these formal elements, whenever possible, should be agreed to in advance, except in the case of very apprehensive patients who may become anxious or frightened with so many stipulations and therefore may decide not to begin the analysis.

There is no doubt that on this issue, especially when the question of distance is involved, the degree of trust/mistrust that can develop between the analyst and the patient will have an influence on the agreement. In this, one should consider the difference between patients who are already known to the analyst or who have been referred by a trustworthy source, and those who have no prior acquaintance or connection upon which to base trust.

There are several questions that arise: in distance treatments, when there is no established trust—would it be correct to charge in advance? Although it is impossible to set a fixed rule, there are different systems of implementation that can be applied at the discretion of each analyst. Some professionals who provide psychotherapy services through internet portals charge in advance. They are structured in the format of a "consultation of psychological orientation", and some advertise that they have psychoanalytic orientation. They offer packages of several interviews that will continue until the particular topic of the consultation has been dealt with.

In these media there are prepayment systems that, schematically considered, implicitly contain this message: pay first, and then take my services. Although this stance is not entirely objectionable, it contains some potential objections. The analyst charges in advance for a package of several telephone or written chat sessions or for sending and receiving several emails. Several systems are implemented. Each will have a reasoning that the therapist will consider valid. However, even if the patient accepts this *modus operandi*, he/she may attribute some added signified to the mode of payment requested, which adds a certain ambivalence to the quality of acceptance that should be taken into account. Money is requested based on *a priori* trust, which only those analysts with a high level of public prestige could expect to have.

Some patients agree, but feel that they grant the solicited "trust" only because it is demanded of them. However, this trust has not yet been genuinely established. This type of bond will certainly operate in the content of the dialogue because it is included in the "ambience" or basic layout established in the transference relationship.

Another point of the contract that could fall into the category of *assent* or *consent* is the amount of the fees. It is known that the cost of a session may vary in the countries of residence of the two participants in the analysis. One must also take into account that, with the passing of time, the exchange rate between the currencies used in the respective countries may also vary. These considerations must be addressed with care and detail, especially considering that this is an area in which objections may arise in the process of reaching a final agreement. When inflation in the patient's country of residence is less than in that of the analyst, the situation requires that the analyst, when attempting to update the value of his/her fees, consider how this change will affect the patient regarding the value of his/her national currency.

One must also specify how to proceed with regard to possible differences in time zone between the analyst and the patient, as well as differences in national holidays and typical vacation periods. Guidelines must be established regarding these issues. For example, at certain times of the year, some countries move their clocks ahead or back in accordance with changing seasons (winter and summer) while others do not. This will bring about a periodical need to renegotiate agreements. For this reason, it needs to be considered a "constant" of the framework with predetermined periodic modifications which therefore do not fall into the category of "variable".

Let us take one last, but very important look at the contract. Throughout the history of psychoanalysis it has been observed that some of the formal applications that were conceived as intrinsic to and inseparable from the method could not be applied for several different reasons. When this occurred, it was proved that the omission of these applications did not remove psychoanalytical validity from the substitute means of clinical implementation.

Oftentimes, a means of implementation of psychoanalysis can be confused with the basic and indispensable elements of its theory. The formal image of an office in which an analyst sits behind a patient who is lying on a couch tends to be confused with the ontogenetic element of psychoanalysis, when, in fact, it is only a form of implementation.

Other legal aspects of the contract are analysed in Chapter Eight.

5   The analytic situation

H. Etchegoyen (1986, 2005) states that the etymological origin of the word "situation" refers to the "site" in which a dialogue will take place.

When considering the term "site" or "place" in distance psychoanalysis, one must think in a broader, somewhat more abstract sense and accept the metaphorical extension of the term. In analysis carried out through simultaneous communication, the analytic situation is set in a synchronous time axis. Its most relevant characteristics are:

a. Regarding physical location, the answer is possible in the form of a comment because it is not possible to do so with a word that indicates place. In principle, we find two separate physical locations that correspond to each of the protagonists of the analytic dialogue.
b. If the "site" is considered in terms of space occupied in time, the analysis takes place between a starting time and an ending time, i.e. during the analysis session.
c. From the perspective of locating the "place" in which the messages reach each of the participants, this would be the *Inter space* of the dialogue. This is the "area" for the *encounter* and serves for processing the patient's material and the analyst's interpretative intervention.
d. Regarding the electronic aspect of communication, the dialogue flows throughout so-called cyberspace.

In analysis carried out with asynchronous communication, a different configuration takes place and its unique aspects will be addressed in Chapter Seven.

a   Framework

The formality of the analytic dialogue is set within a framework that organizes and coordinates the participation of the two protagonists through the guidelines which are stipulated as "operating rules" and are set forth in the analytic contract. Patient and analyst utilize the framework as a regulatory guide for their actions, aimed at the realization of sense and the objective of the conversational encounter. A difference between distance treatment and its more classic form of implementation comes from the logistics of the instrument being used. This includes the technological means of the instrument and the responsibility for establishing a public line of communication (telephone or broadband). This responsibility is shared equally by the analyst and the patient.

b Process

As the sessions progress diachronically, the *analytic process* will be established in both minds—the *Intra space* of the dialogue. The subsequent analytic work carried out in each of the sessions is the substratum which is necessary for its formation.

J. Bleger (1967) notes that when one of the "constants" of the framework becomes a "variable", it becomes part of the process and is therefore analysable. For example, when a patient who has attended at the psychoanalyst's office requests to be treated at a distance, some of the elements that form part of the "constant"—for example, the physical location and direct communication involved in the analysis—move to the status of "variables" and temporarily form part of the analytical process. It is therefore opportune to analyse the conscious and unconscious motivations and expectations for the change of framework. Once the framework is agreed to and implemented, the new elements that are now part of it will become part of the "constants" of the analytical process.

c The Fundamental Rule

"Free Association"—"Free-Floating Attention".

One of the pillars of conversational exchange that contributes to the richness of psychoanalytic sessions lies in the principles of "free association"—"free-floating attention". Freud (1923a) includes the "free association" principle as part of the Fundamental Rule which suggests that the patient communicate everything that he/she thinks and feels without selecting or filtering anything, no matter how negative the content may seem to be.

Laplanche and Pontalis (1973) in *The Language of Psycho-Analysis* indicate that the Fundamental Rule does not invite the patient to say incoherent things but rather to not make coherence part of his selection criteria. It is well known that when this attitude is put to work in the session, it contributes to the revelation of unconscious representations. It is also known that the attitude gives rise to mechanisms of resistance. The patient is also somewhat aware of this and his/her resistance to comply with what is asked of him/her is because he/she is not always willing to let this or that issue come out. However, the Fundamental Rule has a chance of materializing throughout the session, notwithstanding the patient's wishes. His/her speech, whether it be profound or insignificant, complemented by the analyst's suspended attention, forms one of the basic structures of psychoanalytic dialogue. This becomes a finely tuned instrument for overall perception that at some point allows the analyst to clearly configure some of the content of the patient's speech, while allowing the rest to blur into the background. The sensory pathway is the first link which picks up the conveyed stimulus, and therefore serves as a gateway to the mind. It is precisely with this that the analyst processes the content of the material and all that occurs in the session. The analyst processes in his/her mind—the *Intra space*—everything that he/she perceives from the patient, not only the words, but also the omissions, the pace of speech, the presence or absence of silences, the presence or absence of associative work—any of these, conscious or unconscious. These are all semiotic elements that give information about the patient. In summary, the analyst permanently perceives and processes the entire performance of the patient throughout the session. This process involves both the science of the analyst and his/her subjectivity, which is found in his/her countertransference. At times the analyst's own prejudices and errors may also play a part. It is therefore important that the analyst understand that his/her interpretative interventions are hypotheses that must go through the process carried out by the patient in order to continue being elaborated.

Some of the patient's ideas arise in the flow of his/her words in the session, either through *lapsus linguae* or included in the description of a dream, and manage to overcome the barrier of censorship, allowing for the emergence of material for the "primary process". This process, which is vital for a psychoanalyst, has to be implemented with the specific skills required for the setting in which the analysis takes place. At this point, the patient who undergoes analysis "from a distance", especially at the beginning of the analytic process (Carlino, 1991), is likely to assign the manifest content a direct and specific signified, resisting to accept that what he/she says may contain a latent meaning. He/she transfers to the analytic dialogue the sense that is given to a normal phone conversation. When listening, he/she encounters difficulty and may even become angry for not understanding the interpretative sense of the analyst's involvement. When this occurs, it is because the patient operates with the same paradigm that he/she would apply to an ordinary telephone conversation. Changing this way of giving meaning can sometimes be difficult and painstaking when the patient confuses the dialogue of a session with that of a telephone conversation. When it is difficult to achieve the proper analysis session ambience, the dialogue must be given a content that makes reference to the fact that a session of analysis is being undertaken and that the content may have an unconscious symbolic meaning that can refer to something that deserves to be interpreted. This conversational exchange must acquire the typical identity of psychoanalytic *dialogue in session*. To achieve this, it is important to be careful with the framework, which marks the differentiation from ordinary telephone conversations.

When the analyst can rely on the previously acquired analytical training of the patient, compliance with the stated objectives is somewhat easier, although not everything depends on it. The transference set in the "here and now" is very important. A story illustrates this. An analyst brought to her supervision session the case of a patient who had begun her analysis by telephone a few months beforehand. She had undergone psychoanalysis with another analyst a couple of decades back. Her mother had died approximately five years ago. She dreamt that her mother had in fact not died, and she blamed her father, who was still alive, for having made her believe that she was dead. Behind this discovery was also the joy she felt when she thought her mother had returned to life. The analyst considered that it was a transference feeling stemming from the analytic link in which the patient felt that the maternal role of carer "was not dead". She felt she had found this bond with the analyst. She had recovered the possibility of having someone to whom she could tell all her troubles and problems. When the analyst gave her this interpretation, she was surprised to hear the patient say emphatically, "You know … I thought of that … " and even show her joy at having arrived at the same interpretation. When the patient was awake, she did not deny that her mother was dead. Her joy came from the fact that at times she felt that the maternal function felt in transference had present effects that were comparable with her past.

Bion (1967) advocated listening to material with free-floating attention while adopting a mindset devoid of *memory, desire, and understanding*. This involves a jump in the receiving and elaborating of analytic listening. This position, taken from the philosophy of Zen Buddhism, is very different and even somewhat alien to our usual Western way of perceiving, thinking, and forming opinions about reality. Bion strives to free the mind of the prejudices inherent in the usual sense given to the perception of reality. He suggests avoiding both the search for rational understanding, and the temptation to form coincidental relationships among different elements. In essence, he proposes the acquisition of knowledge which is more intuitive. This position offers more possibilities to learn from the new elements that arise in each material. Evoking active discussions from previous sessions would be motivated by the habit of linking previous reasoning to the new, posing obstacles to that other way of thinking, and allowing oneself the chance of being surprised by what is to come as thought, beyond any coincidence imposed by reason.

The very fact that the protagonists are not in the same room could facilitate the analyst's *suspended attention* and perhaps even the *absence of memory, desire, and understanding* that Bion (1967) advised. In this distance setting some analysts say that they feel free and less restrained by not having the patient near.

6   Transference-countertransference

Beyond whether analysis takes place in a psychoanalyst's office or by means of communication technology, the dialogue takes its structure from the patient's *free association* and the analyst's *free-floating attention*. Distance treatments must be coupled with an exploratory research in order to assess the potential for development, acquisition, and implementation of the transference-countertransference in the analytic dyad despite the lack of physical proximity.

The production and registration of affective manifestations in the transference relationship is an inherent phenomenon of the clinical situation. When the bond is carried out by means of communication technology, the possibility for the production and emergence of transference fantasies is potentially expanded. The participation of the analyst from another physical location may also facilitate this phenomenon. The patient, by not having the analyst by his side, may more readily separate him/herself from the anchorage of concrete reality. Once again, I can attribute to this a functional similarity to the situation of a patient lying on the couch. Due to the fact that the analyst is out of his/her visual perception, thus not having this effect as an anchor to material reality, certain values and existing inhibitions in social exchanges have less impact, enabling the patient to feel, think, and talk within the premises of the Fundamental Rule. Here are a couple of clinical stories that illustrate this.

A patient lying on the couch thought he heard certain noises coming from behind him, which were very similar to those made by leather, which his father used to use. He then thought that the analyst was entertaining himself with this material while he listened to what he was saying. The patient suddenly turned around and saw that none of this was happening. It was a hallucinatory way of using transference to feel the analyst as if he were his father. In a session carried out by Skype something quite similar occurred. In an apartment adjacent to where the analyst was speaking by telephone, masonry work was taking place, and the patient overheard some of the resulting noises. The patient, a metal worker's son, began to change the pace of his speech and eventually began to speak hesitantly. The analyst asked about the reason for the change in his speech and he, with a faltering voice, replied that he believed he was speaking from a body shop due to the pounding he heard. The pounding was a trigger of childhood memories of frustration that involved his father's behaviour towards him.

The analyst, who also has limited use of sensory capacity, cannot perceive the physical appearance of the patient or the environment in which he/she is located. If there were belching, rumbling, and even flatulence that provided meaning to the material, he could not perceive them. This puts him in a position of adding imaginary deductions and/ or inferences, either by including the non-existent or excluding the present. From time to time, it is also possible that a situation may surprise and impact both the participants at once, and therefore each must carry out a mental elaboration in his/her *Intra space* in order for it later to be elaborated in the *Inter space* of the analytic dialogue.

Having briefly reviewed some of the manifestations that occur as clinical phenomena and the limits of their perception in distance methods, we shall now see the possibilities of perception that this type of analysis does offer.

The transference-countertransference is crossed by all phenomena occurring in the established analytic setting. When there is an analytic process underway, the patient perceives the analyst with different meaning that he/she attributes, often amalgamating the real with the subjectivity that he/she applies to it. These transference feelings emerge amid the ambience proposed by the analytic setting. To this we must add the impact of "the real" that the analyst offers. The degree of accuracy and appropriateness of his/her interventions and the human quality of that link play an important role. Linguistically, the proper implementation of complementary style (Liberman, 1962) that should occur according to the timing of each session is also vital. The theories with which the analyst proceeds will only illuminate his/her understanding if they are properly applied. It should also be said that when they are not, the analyst's understanding will be blinded and the progress of the process will be disrupted.

The differences between physical proximity and distance have a significance that should not be overlooked. It is known that the analyst, when in his/her office, is not constantly looking at the signs that the patient's body emits. An analyst treating a patient by telephone, although deprived of perceiving the visual images transmitted from the other end of the line, can perceive countertransference signals of him/herself, including those coming from his/her own body, which is constituted as a possibility of contact with the patient's libidinal body. When he/she recognizes some noteworthy signifier, he/she wonders whether this is an occurrence or a countertransference reaction (Racker, 1959) which gives some information about the patient. Certain bodily sensations felt by the analyst during the session can give indications as to what the patient is feeling at that moment. Regarding this, I once received a phone call from a patient using his cellular phone. He spoke while walking down the street towards my office. He wanted to tell me that he felt dizzy and somewhat sweaty. At that moment I felt a sudden shooting pain in my lower chest/upper stomach area, which went away very quickly. In an act of introspection I scrutinized myself and thought it could be a countertransference message that, due to projective identification, had an affect on my own body. I instructed the patient not to come to the meeting, but rather to go to a medical emergency room. Upon seeing the doctor, he was diagnosed with a chest angina and the threat of heart attack (myocardial infarction), which was avoided due to the haste with which he was treated. A couple of days later a stent (internal vascular prosthesis) was placed in a coronary artery that was becoming blocked. In analytic dialogue carried out by telephone, the transference connection operates as such, allowing for the production of emotions or physical symptoms of a countertransference nature. Free-floating attention takes what was perceived within a global complexity.

Regarding the patient's performance during the session, the analyst takes into account the time of the call, the greeting, and how the session begins, noting whether it is similar to or different from the usual. As for the audible, he/she watches and listens to the patient, observing whether he/she allows for an alternation in the dialogue or overlaps with the speech of the analyst. The analyst also takes into account the silences and their meanings and pays attention to the manifest content of the message and the variations in tone, pitch, and pace of the voice. Comparing this with previous meetings, he/she will see what similarities or differences arise from that which appears regularly.

7   Session ambience

It is important to consider, just like in traditional treatments, the ambience of the sessions and its influence on their dynamics. It is comprised of a set of elements that are, one might say, "floating in the environment". It is perceived by the way the session begins and whether the same tone continues over its course. The circumstances surrounding each session also bring their share of influence. One can eventually add accidental elements such as the sound of a doorbell or telephone, or the meowing or barking of a pet as an influence on the beginning ambience of the session. Thus the ambience of the session is structured with a complexity that increases its capacity for emotional radiation, operating on the psychic will of both partners in that dialogue, which will influence its content and direction. It can promote distraction, enthusiasm, or disappointment. In this regard, during a telephone session, a five-year-old son of a patient abruptly entered the room where he was speaking and demanded his attention. There was a brief interruption in the session. The patient then spoke at length about the emotional state prevailing in his house just before the session began. He explained that he thought his son was trying to figure out what his father was up to, which led him to make associations with episodes from his own childhood. He recalled that, as a child of divorced parents, these were questions he would often contemplate when his own father would speak to his mother on the phone. This material also refers to the patient's need to know what the analyst is up to when they are not in session, and it may even refer to the analyst's activities during the session itself. The same can occur with the impression caused by an interpretation that was carried out adequately and in a timely way. The stimulus caused by the words might cause some joy in the patient by raising his/her awareness of him/herself. On the other hand, the learning of this aspect may cause the patient frustration or pain.

The analytic situation is constituted by the place, time, and circumstances under which the analytic dialogue is established. These three components are included in a session operating as the physical, emotional, and social ambience. It does not always prevail only as a context, but also provides the words for the text of the session, whether these are registered consciously or not.

The ambience of the session, in itself, can be considered as a message stating something that emerges from the session, either from its inception due to the pre-disposition of the patient or by something emanating from the elaborative work. The ambience itself will provide richer meaning if there exists disagreement between the manifest content of what is being said and what is radiated and felt.

8   About the "silences"

An ordinary telephone call takes place in order to request information or as a means of social contact. This form of communication requires engaging in speech and listening to what the other says. In this situation, the "talking" forms part of the substance that gives meaning to the telephone conversation. If we compare the silences with those that take place in the psychoanalyst's office, in analytic telephone dialogue they are shorter and less frequent due to the "logic" inherent in the use of this device in non-analytical situations. This logic operates unconsciously as preformed transference (Meltzer, 2000), and has an influence on this type of sessions. In the analytic sessions carried out by telephone, silence is a constituent part of the rhythm of conversational exchange, and it is just as important as the words pronounced. They are also necessary in order to allow space for reflective moments, albeit established within a coherence which harmonizes with the natural use of the telephone. A comparative illustration will serve to show the semantic difference implicit in silence during analytic telephone dialogue if one does not take into account the means of communication in which it is established. In an office it may happen that a patient arrives, greets the analyst, lies down, and remains in silence for several minutes. In an analytic telephone dialogue, a long silence immediately after the greeting would be much denser than in the previous case. Calling by phone, greeting, and then saying nothing runs the risk of being interpreted as a malfunction of the telephone line, an unwillingness to engage in dialogue, or perhaps even a serious problem of the patient. Such is the case that the fact of being connected is often called "talking on the phone". In analytical dialogue taking place in the psychoanalyst's office, being "silent" is not tantamount to "not speaking" or "not communicating". In fact, in order to release his/her thoughts (as dictated by the Fundamental Rule) and in order to think and make interpretations, sometimes it is necessary not to talk. The same happens with the analyst. Both need silence in order to enter the internal dialogue of his/her own *Intra space*. Silence has an active role in phonic discourse in that it limits, administrates, and offers a place for reflection. Many times, in the midst of an ambience of unrest or violence, silence can establish calm and allow for more reflective thinking. It can sometimes be used to mark a before and after, giving the sensation of "So far, we've seen this …, but from now on …".

As can be seen, when properly administered, silence is a useful and valuable tool. However, we must take care not to make it a refuge. It is only valid as a tool if it carries out a role in the development process. Its usefulness will vary according to the personality and style of each member of the analytic duo, as well as the transference phase that the bond is undergoing. The alleged "management" of silence is sometimes the responsibility of the defence mechanisms of the patient and sometimes even of the analyst him/herself. One can be silent and very present or, conversely, continue speaking and prevent a space of silence that might have been productive. The "presence" of the analyst becomes evident through his/her satisfactory way of establishing contact and making interpretations, above and beyond the amount of words and silences that he/she introduces into the session.

When the listening time of the analyst becomes long, a sense of uncertainty and anxiety arises due to the fact that the patient does not know whether the analyst is present, whether he/she is distracted, or whether the line of communication has been cut. When facing this situation, some patients ask: "Are you there?" or "Can you hear me?" Others test the current state of communication by saying "Hello, hello?" This uncertainty in communication, although sometimes provoked by a prolonging of the silence, can often increase the patient's anxiety.

At the beginning of treatment, the spans of silence are subjectively much more suggestive and require a somewhat more explicit justification than those which take place in dialogue conducted in the psychoanalyst's office. This is due to the fact that, even without words, it is assumed that the analyst is there. In telephone sessions, the conversation must find its own structure and coherence, which will be different from both a normal telephone conversation and from an analytic dialogue carried out in the psychoanalyst's office. The silence on the line can be disturbing when it is not justified or when it is interpreted erroneously. Sometimes it may be occur that one of the two continues talking without realizing the actual interruption in telephone communication. This part of the dialogue is reduced not even to a monologue, but in fact to a simple soliloquy that leaves the displeasure of having been shot into space.

a   The patient's silence

Towards the beginning of the analysis it is necessary to evaluate the tolerance and adherence of the patient to silence and to research its motivations, given that these will be the criteria for determining the meaning attributed to it. Generally the sense that it contains is more important than its duration, except in telephone treatment or chat without video—situations in which the importance increases. Although silence is the absence of speech, in its content one must distinguish semiological qualities, trying to appreciate the signifier nuances given by the factors that promote it. Conceptually they can be summarized into three groups: silence due to action, silence due to reaction, and silence due to omission.

There may be multiple motivations:

- For maintaining an active attitude of "being in silence", whether it be as a contribution to the dialogue, or as resistance.
- For maintaining silence in order to listen and/or think, as a space for reflection.
- For being included in the session with a schizoid attitude (non-participating observer) (Liberman, 1970).
- Out of paranoid suspicion.
- For adopting an active attitude, although carried out by a dependent person: trying to provoke the intervention of the analyst from a position of passive listening.
- For being a product of intense dubious hesitation that is manifested as paralysis of speech.

- For expressing a lack of motivation or interest.
- For being the manifestation of a moment of bewilderment and/or confusion stemming from an emotional state produced by the analytic work. It is the equivalent of "I don't know what to say".

The absence of words does not always imply absence of analytic work. Refraining from talking when it is more appropriate to think means that one is working in the session. Conversely, talking nonsense, or talking when it is not called for is tantamount to absence or disturbance of the analytic work. Above and beyond this list of the different motivations that can lead to silence, when an extended silence occurs in analytic telephone dialogue, one must always face the lurking question of whether the pause in speech is due to a malfunction of the telephone communication.

Silence can be a space of the session taken by the patient in order to perceive and develop in his/her mind what will soon appear as free association, which will help him/her understand the meaning of what has been occurring. The intervention of the analyst asking, "What is he thinking about?" is not always necessary or justified. This action is only valid if the analyst is questioning that silence in the belief that it is a tactic for avoiding compliance with the Fundamental Rule.

b   The analyst's silence

Depending on when it occurs, there will be different types of silence. Each session begins with the analyst silently waiting for the patient to speak. This silence offers a space for the patient to speak according to his/her occurrences in compliance with the Fundamental Rule. When the silences are longer than those typical of a particular patient, the analyst may intervene compulsively with the intention of demonstrating that he is still on the line and attentive. This is intended to be an alert about the looming possibility of a verbal acting-out of the analyst, in which his/her speaking could become mere noise which clogs fertile silences. It is not always easy to decide when and how to intervene in the middle of a silence.

9   About privacy

Communicating by means of technology involves crossing a public space, whether it be through the use of a simple telephone line, a cell phone, broadband videophones, or through satellite communications. Privacy has a statutory importance for the elaborative work of the sessions.

How then can one acquire the necessary privacy when speaking in a public space with people nearby? In everyday life, one approaches the other's ear and speaks in a low voice. When one speaks by telephone connection, at the moment of discussing intimate or even secret things, there is a fear that it could be overheard by third parties on the line. The same applies to email communication. When they reach a high degree of privacy, they are transmitted only through encrypted messages or through the use of a password which is necessary to open the document.

One cannot exercise free association or suspended attention in the session if it is felt that the means of communication does not guarantee absolute privacy. The same occurs if there is a fear that the session could be recorded. The same security is required of emails or messages sent via written chat. There must be no record of the dialogue available to anyone other than the addressee. It is also important to bear in mind the similarities and differences that exist between privacy and intimacy. While the former is linked to and is a necessary condition of the latter, it is not sufficient. The climate of intimacy is achieved to the extent that the analytical dyad feels that it is able to create its own micro-climate which is suitable for analytic dialogue. The analytic setting is precisely what promotes an analytic attitude in each of the participants. Another important factor for the maintenance of this ambience of privacy-intimacy is the trust that is provoked by the good performance of the analyst, as well as the appropriate emotional ambience provided by the patient. These elements are very important in distance analysis because the lack of physical proximity makes it necessary to find elements of containment and presence from other factors. I have had sessions in which the patient was speaking to me from a table in a café, amid the chatter of the other patrons sitting at their tables. Therefore the desired atmosphere of privacy and intimacy was not achieved. One must recognize, however, that in such situations this goal is quite difficult. However, it is important to note that the session with these characteristics bore fruitful results for the patient. The motivation for speaking with me from a café was prompted by his interest in having a session that would not disrupt his weekly routine. The same situation, if it were to take place with an attitude lacking in motivation, could be seen as resistant acting-out.

a   Minimum conditions of privacy

In the analysis that take place at the psychoanalyst's office, the setting itself offers not only the necessary atmosphere of intimacy, but also a safe and sufficient guarantee of privacy. For this to be so, it is required that the office be sound-tight and that the ethical and legal status of "professional secrecy" be maintained.

In distance sessions, the words spoken in the session cannot be kept private by the ethical conduct of the analyst alone. Not all technological means of communication can guarantee absolute privacy, although some do because of the security built into them. Speaking by means of telephone systems that use broadband can avoid interference in the communication. The responsibility for maintaining the privacy of the dialogue in the session does not lie only in the analyst and his commitment to "professional secrecy" but also in the patient, although not to the same extent. If the patient were to tell someone what is spoken in the sessions, except in the case of an emergency or one of genuine and legitimate intimacy, it could be an acting-out that deserves to be interpreted and elaborated.

The possible lack of any of the basic conditions for privacy produces some type of resonance that must be addressed. When the cause is unknown it leads to assumptions, deductions, or simply groundless fantasies which, when manifested by the patient, can serve as a contribution to the analysis. The appearance of a noise in the middle of the session may lead one to assume that the other member is not alone or that he/she is distracted by the reading of something, amusing him/herself with a game, reading something on the computer screen, etc. The perception of what seems to be an added noise operates only as a trigger for the imagination and does not produce any certainty. It is therefore often not expressed or explicitly included. When this imagined element appears in the mind of the patient but is not mentioned by him/her, the analyst can perceive a change in the pace of speech, leading the analyst to ask the patient: "What is happening?" or what is he/she thinking about? Something similar can happen in a psychoanalyst's office. On one occasion, a patient lying on the couch assumed that the analyst took notes. When he turned around to see that it was true, he accused the analyst of using his session time for writing things that had nothing to do with him. It never occurred to him that he could be taking notes on what was occurring in that very patient's session.

From the analyst's side, sometimes it is he/she who imagines that at the meeting there is no guarantee of privacy. In such cases it is expected that he/she can differentiate between the real and the imagined. In the latter case, the fantasy can be processed as countertransference occurrence (Racker, 1957).

In the sessions in which communication is written—chat, email—it is possible to save and file the dialogue. Thus this material becomes readily accessible to others unless, as mentioned before, it contains some form of built-in security. This is a fundamental issue to consider in this type of therapeutic practice.

Email and written chat dialogue are easily "hackable". In the case of treatment performed by chat, if the patient's identity is not authenticated, one cannot know with certainty who is at the other end. Therefore a mechanism of authentication is necessary. Video chat systems dispel any difficulty in identifying the caller and telephone communication allows for voice recognition, which helps to facilitate identification.

It is necessary to bear this type of situation in mind at the moment of undertaking distance therapeutic practice. It entails the need to include in the analytic contract recommendations to carry out extreme precautions in order to ensure privacy. The fact that the analyst recommends this does not imply that the patient will always comply. In these cases, as we have seen, when one of the "constants" of the framework (such as the guarding of privacy) is not met, it becomes a "variable" and therefore can be analysed in the analytic process.

b   Electronic recording of the sessions

Modern recording technology trumps the preconception of inviolable privacy. This possibility, per se, could cause inhibition or even a sensation of persecution in the patient at the moment of exercising the Fundamental Rule and the ability to associate freely. Concomitantly, it may disrupt the analyst's suspended attention, given that his/her mind must be free of any and all worries and disturbances that could interrupt his/her attention or frazzle his/her mind. If this apprehension arises frequently, one must reconsider the means of communication implemented and evaluate the opportunity of changing it.

Does this hypothetical possibility of the patient recording the sessions mean that the analyst must always be very careful with what he/she says? The first answer that follows is that under conditions of mistrust and insecurity, the only necessary and urgent matter to analyse is just that: the mistrust and insecurity. Another general and comprehensive response would be to evaluate each case individually.

10 Technological provisions for adequate communication

In the case of video chat or written chat treatments, the analytical dyad communicates by computer or cell phone with image transmission. However, as in a classic analysis, the meeting will take place only at the scheduled times of the sessions. In written chat without video, although this norm increases the level of authentication of each of the dyad's identities, it does not suffice. It is important to establish a complementary method for ensuring the patient's identity.

As already noted, the material needs for the setting are provided equally and symmetrically by both members of the duo. For this reason, prior to adopting a particular technological means, the analyst must be sure that the patient has expertise in the handling of the device and can install a high-quality public line of communication.

It may be possible to take precautions and sign a written agreement which states the technological specifications of the method to be used, as well as other aspects of a legal nature. However, if a distance psychoanalytic treatment is devoid of trust at the beginning stage, it will be difficult, although not impossible, to implement it. If the patient were to perceive the analyst working in a climate of mistrust, some negative effect would operate permanently, unless the patient were to consider that he/she is not worthy of trust, and therefore accept that the analyst has good perception.

11 Conceptual evolution of the idea of "presence"

The term "presence" is connected with the word "present", which means being in front of …, or in sight. "Present" is the verb tense that indicates simultaneity with a moment in which something occurs. *Presently* means *now, at this moment*. Notice that "presently", "now", and "at this moment" indicate a place in time, which also allows for the consideration of distance in terms of time. It is also applied to indicate that someone is physically present in a place. *Presenting* oneself before someone implies being physically in front of that person. When someone meets another person for the first time, he/she says: "Nice to meet you." That is to say, the expression refers to a *meeting*. The word "present" is used for a gift that is given with the intention that the receiver of the gift have the giver "present" in his/her mind every time he/she sees it.

The general notion we have of the term *presence* is associated with the idea of being located in a common geographic space that physically and concomitantly includes two or more persons. These persons, who are *present* in the location, can be mutually perceived by sensorial means, without the need for technology.

It is logical that from a long time ago and until relatively recently people have thought in this way. Spoken communication between or among people had to be exercised in a small and adequate space. However, we know very well that the means of distance communication become more and more advanced with each passing day. Milliseconds suffice in order to establish contact. This means that one can undertake a private dialogue by employing communication technology, assuming the proper precautions have been taken.

The consequences of the creation and widespread use of these communication technologies have given rise to the so-called global village, a term that has been coined precisely because of the fact that it has gained recognition in "the real" and possesses its own body of existence.

A new communications space called cyberspace, which is accessed via the internet, has transformed all the infinite micro-spaces existing erstwhile into a single locus of communication. This common area allows people to be connected experientially, with real possibilities of interaction and exchange, regardless of the geographic distance between them.

a   The idea of "presence" in distance treatments

The fact that the existing technological means of communication offer immediacy, privacy, and easy access has encouraged the idea that geographical distance is no longer of great importance. Prior to this new communicational reality, it was absolutely necessary that the analyst and the analysand be located in an intimate and closed environment, such as the analyst's office, in order to be *present* and establish an analytic dialogue. The possibilities offered by these media have brought about a new notion of communicative possibilities in which the concept of distance, previously measured in terms of metres or kilometres, is now being measured in terms of time. In fact, as this time is measured in microseconds, it could easily be considered to be instantaneous. With this new concept, the idea of *presence* will no longer be linked inextricably to physical proximity.

From the smoke signals of yesteryear to the cellular and satellite technology of today, a logic—both subjective and objective—has contributed to communicative possibilities and to the idea of *presence* and *distance*. This logic has helped to redefine the scope of these two concepts. The speed and effectiveness of communication technology, coupled with its widespread use, has created communicative spaces that have no consideration for territorial distance. This allows—and encourages—people who are geographically distant to feel closer to those who are within easy reach of communication. This includes those who were once considered remote or even inaccessible. Currently, two people who are geographically distant, when communicating by phone or chat, may feel that both are "there". Where is "there" and what scope does being "there" have? "There" is the specific location of the meeting. When the paradigmatic perspective of consideration is changed, that "there", although technically an adverb of place, is no longer conceived geographically. "There" is the space of the "encounter". In this regard, at the beginning of this chapter, we considered in detail the non-geographic "places" where analytic dialogue occurs.

The experiential dimension that can be achieved between the participants in the analysis is directly related to the psychoanalytic quality of the dialogue. When one achieves a certain or honest feeling of proximity in the "contact" and closeness in the "encounter", it is the result of the psychoanalytic depth that operates by minimizing or decoupling the significance and importance of the possible effect of geographical distance.

b   Communicative presence

Four spaces were described earlier in this chapter: the session, the *Inter space*, the *Intra space*, and cyberspace, which together offer the potential for building a new concept to give recognition to a new reality which

I have named "communicative presence". This is the feeling of presence in a situation of distance communication. Far from being a mere subjective sensation, it is clear to say that those that participate in the dialogue are actually "there" at the moment of properly filling the four spaces that begin to work automatically at the beginning of each session, regardless of geographic distance. To justify this claim I will take several elements into account.

The feeling that the participants in a distance analytic dialogue have during the session and what they have afterwards are open to debate. The degree of belonging and relevance of ideas and emotions poured into the dialogue and the quantum of achievement in the communicative contact and encounter will influence the construction of a reality that makes the analytical dyad feel a sense of *communicative presence*.

When carrying out analytic dialogue, one should be attentive to the development of a fundamental objective: the promotion of an adequate communicative "contact" and "encounter". The feelings of the participants in the session and the objective marks that the elaborative work produces will be the witnesses of the quantum of "presence" that took place during the communicative encounter. A third element would be that of assessing the degree of proximity or distance that was experienced at different moments of the session. If we stop to consider these concepts, we see that we have used terms that refer to space, such as: "contact", "meeting", and "presence"—all evaluated in reference to the proximity or distance that was felt in the communication. It was also noted that subjectivity played an important role in "communicative presence", whether it takes place at a distance of one metre or by means of a telephone connection.

I have consistently emphasized the necessity for contact and encounter in "communicative presence". This is due to the relationship that one has with very early experiences of contact of the baby's skin with his/her mother, of the baby's mouth searching for his/her mother's breast, and the mother's voice in the baby's ear. When analytic dialogue allows for the re-creation of these basic and foundational experiences that make a bond we should consider that a "contact" and "communicative meeting" have taken place. This would be an ideal condition that does not find permanent accomplishment. Distance analysis, as a method in itself, has greater need of a contact and a deep transferential encounter so that there will be a libidinal encounter with the other, which is what significantly contributes to the sensation of presence. Another type of permanent contact in an analytical relationship is established in the mind of the patient all day long while he/she is "walking the pathway of life", and from time to time, is connected to an imaginary transferential dialogue with his/her analyst.

The sense of reality and its anchorage in analytic dialogue are found in the concrete elements and facts that are described below:

a. The fact that the dialogue between the analyst and the patient is performed in a session of analysis. This is a temporal reality carried out at a time and date previously agreed upon.
b. The professional work done by the analyst implies not only the devotion of his/her time with the patient, but also a concomitant concern and professional responsibility.
c. The maintenance of an ethical stance is an inseparable aspect of psychoanalytic work. However, sometimes this can increase the work effort of the analyst.
d. The payment of fees by the patient obliges the analyst to a professional responsibility before the law.
e. As expectable goals are reached, there is a true mental growth in the patient and professional achievement in the analyst.

Given all the considerations expressed regarding distance and instantaneous communication, as well as the degree of reality involved in analytic dialogue, the idea of *presence* is clearly detached from the absolute need for a mutual physical presence of both participants in the dialogue. It acquires a more abstract and symbolic conception, linked inextricably to the idea of *communicative contact* and *encounter*.

The extreme antipodes and the intermediate range between them in which conversational contact and encounter can be located will enrich or impoverish the communicative presence.

a. "Contact": much↔little; close↔distant; reception↔rejection;
          close↔far; union↔separation; attach↔separate
b. "Encounter": opportune↔inopportune; enthusiastic⇔↔indifferent,
          patient↔impatient; pertinent↔inappropriate;
          congruous↔ incongruous

In treatments that take place with synchronous dialogue, this distinction in the different possibilities of contact and encounter occurs at the same time in which the communication takes place. In the case of asynchronous sessions—by email—as the analysis session offers no particular space, the mentioned possibilities occur at the moment of writing and reading the messages that are sent and received with ulterior transcendence. One can similarly categorize all the evocative moments taking place in imaginary dialogues that involve no real contact with the other and are influenced by the transference experienced at each moment.

In patients who find it difficult to symbolize, the inclusion of a webcam can further contribute to the sensation of presence, similar to when in-office analysis is practised face-to-face, as opposed having the patient lie on the couch.

The conceptual and emotional qualities developed in analytic dialogue depend on the input that is given to them. While it is expected that the greater the number of weekly sessions, the greater the chance of contact, if it is not accompanied by a sense of closeness in ideological and emotional contact, and of effectiveness in the elaborative encounter, neither the analyst nor the analysis will have great presence in the patient's life. This can also occur in treatments conducted in the psychoanalyst's office.

12   Role of the body in the psychoanalytic session

The absence of physical proximity is the first major difference that tends to be compared with classic analysis. To understand what influence this has, it is necessary to define the role that the bodies of the analyst and patient play in conversational exchange. This difference can not be ignored. In order to address this issue conceptually, it is necessary to have attended patients through at least one of the means of distance technology. Only having gained the experience of this kind of analysis can one pass proper judgement.

The clinical task is performed based on the patient's ideas and spontaneous emotions to which one adds more reflective thoughts and feelings produced by their mood. In the analyses performed by telephone, these elements are "packaged" in the format of: words with intonation; silences; haste; overlapping with the words of the other; relevant or senseless interventions that do not provide coherence, but rather disperse, etc. The discourse is rooted in a syntax that gives coherence when put together within the grammatical rules of the language used.

When this does not occur in he/she who has or had the capacity to do so, one must research the latent content of the emitted material. Given that the paraverbal component of the discourse emits audible signals that give meaning, it is expected that the analyst "at a distance" is trained to perceive the thorough, instantaneous, and sometimes complex and enlightening meanings. The extra-verbal component would not be entirely excluded, as discussed in Chapter Three regarding mirror neurons.

The body can manifest itself when the speaker chews, drinks, smokes, or moves away from the microphone. If one perceives the noise caused by typing on a keyboard or something similar, it is inferred that the patient is writing or touching something. Other sounds or noises can indicate whether the patient is accompanied by another person, whether the room door is open or whether the patient is speaking from a public or private space. Notwithstanding the above, it must be accepted that many of the body signals emitted cannot be perceived.

In treatments carried out in the analyst's office, the communicative role of the body is considered to be a natural and obvious situation. The added semantic gestures made by speech are included in the signified of the spoken messages. It is important to note this because in the past two decades the importance of the body in the session has been gradually increasing due to the fact that many analytic treatments are conducted face-to-face. This includes the incorporation of a histrionic or scenic component in the analytic dialogue in which the signals coming from the analyst's body also take part. It is so spontaneous and so natural that specific reference is rarely made to the decoding of this signifier, perhaps because it is taken into account intuitively or irrationally. This way of conducting dialogue includes in the speech a series of gestures that the intended receiver, while listening, simultaneously captures visually. *Mutatis mutandis*, when the speaker knows that he/she is being seen by the receiver of the message, a mechanism, which is sometimes conscious and other times comes automatically, produces a verbal language which is as graphic and understandable as possible.

After more than 100 years of psychoanalytic practice, there is a slow and gradual transformation in some of the procedures of the analyst and patient in the session. As already seen, analysts have generally been accepting, in parallel with new social conceptions and the maturation of the profession as such, some changes in the basic and proven conceptual complex consecrated in traditional psychoanalytic technique.

There has been a review in the application of certain formal models that operated continuously as *constants* of the framework. This revision and transformation is the result, in general, of the search for a harmonious meeting with new social paradigms or "frameworks", and in particular to the decision to tailor the framework appropriately to fit each individual patient. In another social time, not so long ago, in Buenos Aires, an article (Popovsky de Berenstein & Sor de Fondevila, 1989) addressed the issues of whether one could use informal speech in analytic dialogue, and whether the analyst and the patient could decide together whether the patient should sit or lie down. However, in the article mentioned and in the general concerns and questions at that time, one could see changes in general social interaction that begged to be included as an update to the formalities existing between patient and analyst.

More recently, Mantykow de Sola (2007) raises these issues in the attempt to establish an appropriate framework for treating today's adolescents. She focuses her work on the analytic situation, showing great interest in building it up without ignoring the social situation that operates as a macro-context in which the analytic dyad must locate (and relocate) themselves. Apparently the author understands well how to distinguish the figure from the background. That is to say, she conceives the need to permanently reformat the formal, adapting it to existing social values and customs, without abandoning the basic tenets of psychoanalysis.

13   Consequences of the blocking of visual perception

The reasoning and deductions inserted here tend to appreciate differences from the preconceptions and logic emanating from the practice of treatment in the psychoanalyst's office. It is not common that the sessions which take place in the office take permanently into account whatever is perceived visually from the patient, except in the case of information which is out of the ordinary. In the classic setting, the visual perception of the patient is inherent to the method itself. Its absence is not even imaginable except in the case of a blackout during an evening session or in the case of an analyst who is blind. In this regard, it is worth remembering a fact that is historical, truthful, and transcendent.

In the 1960s, there was a story floating about among college students that a blind student was denied the university's degree that would enable him to practise professionally despite having passed all the subjects of his psychology major. In its place, the student was only offered a certificate of having passed the subjects taught in that major. The decision was based on the belief that a blind man could not practise as a psychologist.

As an additional and controversial idea, I would like to present another fact, also taken from reality. Juan Carlos Álvarez, who was an elementary school teacher and director of the National School for the Blind in Argentina, once commented that during a fluent dialogue with a blind student, her son, who was five or six years old, was playing near her. In the middle of that conversation, the mother turned her head towards her son and said: "How many times do I have to tell you not to pick your nose!" Incredible! would be the most normal reaction to this exclamation. On another occasion, this teacher commented that some blind people could create a sculpture of a person's face simply by touching it. It was even more incredible to hear that the blind could play soccer with a ball that contained a rattle that they could hear. Certain biases may operate as if they were a source of complete and irrevocable right, thereby excluding certain procedures which, when considered from another perspective, may be absolutely feasible. Prejudice can operate as a discriminatory instrument. It can often lead to institutional detriment in that it blocks the entry of novel contributions as well as hitherto unexplored ideas in the constant evolution of psychoanalytic concepts. An obstructing prejudice would be the assumption that psychoanalysis has found its final identity and application technique. Any innovation is considered *a priori* as an ontogenetic deviation. This position produces a strong iterative and oppositional effect in one who operates with functional deafness. It is irrational and closed to any possibility of revision. In dialogue, it is instrumented as if it had absolute power of reason, inhibiting any such opportunity.

In psychoanalytic institutions, there are moments of conceptual discussion in which the institutions face a paradigm that values as right and proper that which has already been established. In this environment, the desire is that the discussion will bring about a result based on a uniformity of values and criteria. The mere idea of having a different or even discordant opinion deeply affects the sense of identity and institutional belonging of the one who expresses this thought. In the creation of this climate of unrest, one can find prejudices and interests of an unscientific nature (those linked to power) as well as feelings based on irrational convictions that have been elevated to the status of obvious and unquestionable. The fact of being trained in an analytic institution which allows for this type of discussion implies a strong characteristic of psychoanalytic identity that leads to the need for being accepted as a worthy member of the institution.

Psychoanalysis which is carried out verbally but without visual contact needs to be assessed in terms of results. It is necessary to research and publish clinical material. It is very important to understand the difference between a personal decision to conduct distance analysis with a given patient and a generalized conceptualization that endorses this type of implementation and includes it as part of psychoanalytical theory.

If the spirit of research is based on the idea that in an analysis session it is possible to forego the chance of visual perception of the patient, the analyst, in carrying out the experience, will be paying attention in order to observe the possibilities and limitations of the method. The analyst will focus on observing how psychoanalysis is carried out without seeing the patient and therefore without processing the signals emanating from his/her body. The story of the blind mother scolding her child is an example taken from reality, which shows that a blind person can perceive signals, which, for a non-blind person would require the use of sight. It is true that this lady was the mother of the child, and she was only a couple of metres away from him. In this situation of our hypothetical research we would be changing one of the *constants* of the framework if we added the possibility of visual perception by using a webcam. This would bring us to place analytical attention on the consequent result of allowing the analytical dyad to perceive and be perceived visually throughout the session. A third situation in this imagined experimental research would be to allow only for unilateral vision throughout the session, with the exception of the greeting at the beginning and end of the session. Except for these two moments, only the analyst would be given the benefit of visual perception.

After making or even imagining these three possibilities, we must evaluate each of the experiences from the perspective of cost-benefit, as well as *what* and *how much* is demanded, added, and/or taken away from the role of each member of the analytical dyad in each of the variables introduced. We must remember as added cost the inclusion of broadband and a telephone with on-screen vision or a computer with a webcam in order to carry out distance analysis with visual content.

In this inquiry, it is very important to distinguish between the visual functions of seeing or not seeing and looking or not looking. Looking is an act driven by the decision to put special and directional attention on the act of seeing. For example, when the eyes of the analyst, instead of simply *seeing*, *look* at some part of the patient's body, from his/her status as subject of an action the analyst will ask: "Why am I staring at that part of the patient's body or his/her clothes?" From his/her status as the object reacting to an alleged action of the subject patient, he/she will ask: "What is it about the patient that provokes this compulsion of mine to look?"

The sensation of *seeing* is not always limited to vision in the sensorial sense. In everyday speech, upon listening to an explanation of a difficult and complex nature, one can confirm understanding by saying "I see", which is equivalent to "I understand". These expressions are related to a subject that, although at one time difficult to understand, has now been illuminated and therefore "seen". These expressions come from the ability to perceive qualities of the object that could only be carried out through the sense of sight. Here the verb "see" is used as a synonym for "understand". This metaphorical appreciation is installed in the mind as a matrix that generates judgement experienced as obvious, and therefore not changeable. With this I would like to highlight that there is a certain bias dictating that it is necessary and perhaps even essential to have a functioning sense of sight in order to "know" or "understand". This is exemplified in the phrase, "seeing is believing". However, this does not always imply the need to perceive visually. When someone says that he/she "sees" a problem or "sees" a solution to it, he/she is referring to a mental operation. In comic books, when someone has an original idea, a light bulb is drawn above his head. The concept of clinical eye attributed to the wisdom of a doctor refers specifically to the "vision" of someone who is reliable due to his/her profuse and disciplined experience.

Let us now consider more specifically the dialogue of telephone sessions with the following question: what is the sight of the participants in psychoanalysis typically fixed on? It is not always voluntarily focused on a certain point. In fact, as mentioned before, we occasionally close our eyes intentionally in order not to become distracted. It is an act of mental retraction and abstraction carried out in order to facilitate the connection with the heart of the idea in question. There are gazes that go into space, others to a fixed point on the wall with the intention of "not seeing" in order to focus attention on a specific idea. When listening to the other, it is sometimes necessary to "imagine" (creating pictures about) what the speech suggests. At any meeting at the analyst's office or via web camera, the process of free-floating attention automatically cancels many visual stimuli. The same also occurs with the verbal and paraverbal material as befits a free-floating attention. This manner of partially invalidating the sense of sight and using the free-floating method is one of the *constants* of the framework. When the analyst's eyes "wander" to a visual object or he/she listens with close (non-floating) attention, we find ourselves facing a *variable* that becomes part of the *process* that deserves an elaborative work as transference-countertransference material.

When, if necessary, there is a need to assess the development of the patient's physical appearance, so as not to be trapped in subjective and/or distorted information; sending photos and even the including of a web camera are no more than an attenuated means of perception, given that they do not resolve the need to form opinions with a clinical eye. If there is concern about the physical health of the patient, the solution is to design a framework in which the patient must have contact with and, if necessary, be treated by a physician and/or specialist in their place of residence. The analyst should establish a link with a general practitioner in the patent's place of residence so that, if necessary, he/she can be well informed about the state of health of the patient and any pertinent prognosis. If a physical health concern were to appear at the time of the first interview, it should be assessed whether a framework of these characteristics would impede the beginning of analysis. If in doubt, one must search for an answer to each specific situation as it arises.

The visual perception of the patient when he/she arrives at the analyst's office constitutes a significant moment that could be described as the "very first impression". It is an experience of sensory impact—preponderantly (but not exclusively) visual—that stimulates in the analyst a poignant yet fleeting impression at the moment of opening the door and receiving the patient. The impact is caused by the way of greeting, the attitude, the physical presence, and the poise of the patient. In the case of a first interview, the impact differs according to whether the patient comes alone or accompanied. The amalgamation of the impact and the thoughts that arise could offer some allegedly semiological information, whether it be confirmed on that occasion or any other. In the brief moment of the greeting, the arrival of occurrences (logical, sensible, unspeakable, absurd, etc.) in the analyst's consciousness are due to the fact that his/her operative censorship does not work effectively. The patient, with his/her corporal attitude and conduct, also provides signals that are captured by the semiological eye of the analyst. Both types of occurrences will be considered timely if any link associated with verbal material is found.

In treatments conducted via communication technology, it is possible that an analyst with some practice in this type of analysis may develop a specific semiotic perception, paying special attention to signals that arrive at the moment of the greeting, depending on the method used. In general, this method of inquiry only provides useful information when it differs from what is expected.

There are some aspects or some kinds of information that patients omit, either intentionally or unintentionally. In a session which takes place in the office, although not expressed verbally, they often "come up" due to the fact that they become evident in the patient's behaviour during the session.

In this regard, a situation that occurred in the office of a colleague will illustrate this. It was a female patient who felt inhibited whenever men looked at her, especially if she also felt attraction. Once she came to a session more made-up than usual. She wore a pendant of the same colour as the jumper that was below, so that it was almost imperceptible. This drew the attention of the analyst, since the patient was a person who could appreciate colours and their proper combination. The analyst was shocked to open the office door and see her with a necklace of the characteristics described, especially knowing her aesthetic background. The patient began the session by saying that after the session she had a work meeting in which she would surely meet with a colleague, to whom (as already mentioned in a previous session) she felt attracted. Subsequently, she said that she felt cold, given that she had left in a hurry in order to get to the session and had therefore forgotten to put on her wool jacket. The room temperature was not so low as to understand the logic of the comment. Since the analyst knew the patient's ability to combine colours, she pointed to the lack of harmony in the colour combination of the necklace and the jumper. She pointed out that the lack of colour contrast did more to hide the necklace than to allow others to appreciate it. At this point the patient began to make associations with the wool jacket that she had forgotten. She said she used it in order to cover the prominence of her breasts. A first elaboration was that the patient, in forgetting the jacket, was unconsciously rebelling against her own inhibitions and that this forgetfulness prevented her from dissimulating the prominence of her breasts. However, her own repression tricked her by encouraging her to put on a necklace that highlights bad taste, rather than the prominence of her breasts.

The question that arises from this clinical story, which occurred in a psychoanalyst's office is: could this situation have been analysed in a phone session? "Impossible!" would be the only valid response. One of the most important signs of that meeting was visual (the colour of the necklace in contrast to the colour of the jumper that was below). Another element that would not be reproducible is the forgetting of the "jacket". This is so because, in all likelihood, the woman would have taken her session at home—without a jacket, without a necklace, and without having made herself up in order to see the person to whom she felt attracted. As we see an analysis system as a whole, it produces certain phenomena that another, as a whole, does not produce. Therefore the answer would be that the two situations are not comparable. Each session conducted according to the analytical method employed can only be considered in terms of its structure. It will deploy the semantic potential allowed by the analytical method used and lack what the method cannot provide.

John Lindon (1988) refers to the sensory problem presented by the telephone method when he says: " ... the analyst is deprived of the use of *sight, touch,* and *smell.*" Depending on which communication technology is available, the senses in play will not always be the same. It will also be necessary to differentiate and evaluate some specific technical aspects. In this regard, Lindon says his patients are fully aware of this and tend to describe very poignantly any element which they know could not otherwise be perceived by telephone. By communicating verbally what is not otherwise perceptible is the patient's way of showing that he/she is well connected with the analyst and the method used. If the patient were not to communicate this, one would think that he/she is denying whatever goes unsaid or attacking the possibilities that the method offers.

In telephone psychoanalysis, although the bodies are not in each other's view, the mere act of participating in a session implies, in itself, being—in greater or lesser degree—connected to the other because of the link and correspondence that structures the intention and desire of the telephone encounter and the analytic dialogue established. This is succinctly illustrated in the title of a work on telephone analysis by Sharon Zalusky (1998): "Out of sight, but not out of mind".

CHAPTER FIVE

Scope and limits of analysis carried out with communication technology

Freud (1923a) in "Two encyclopaedia articles" defines psychoanalysis very concisely in the first paragraph. In this paragraph, he states what he believes that this term encompasses conceptually:

"Psycho-analysis is the name ...

1. ... of a procedure for the investigation of mental processes which are almost inaccessible in any other way,
2. ... of a method (based upon that investigation) for the treatment of neurotic disorders and,
3. ... of a collection of psychological information obtained along those lines, which is gradually being accumulated into a new scientific discipline."

Laplanche and Pontalis (1967) in *Vocabulaire de la Psychanalyse* (*The Language of Psycho-Analysis*, 1973), based on the contents of the article published by Freud, along with the cumulative criteria in the 45 years following its publication, provide an expanded definition, but without detracting the essence of the original paper of Freud:

"Psycho-Analysis
Discipline founded by Freud, whose example we follow in considering it under three aspects:

1. As a method of investigation which consists essentially in bringing out the unconscious meaning of the words, the actions and the products of the imaginations (dreams, fantasy, delusions) of a particular subject. The method is founded mainly on the subject's free association, which serve as the measuring-rod of the validity of the interpretation. Psycho-analytical interpretation can, however, be extended to human productions where no free associations are available. .
2. As a psychotherapeutic method based on this type of investigation and characterized by the controlled interpretation of resistance, transference and desire. It is in a related sense that the term "psycho-analysis" is used to mean a course of psychoanalytic treatment, as when one speaks of undergoing psycho-analysis (or analysis).
3. As a group of psychological and psychopathological theories which are the systematic expression of the data provided by the psycho-analytic method of investigation and treatment."

These definitions are designed and stratified into three aspects. Any practice that can be recognized and included in any of these statements is considered analytic activity. If we take as an example the clinical work of a psychoanalyst who knows and can operate in a manner that reflects the assumption in section 2 of the definition, we are then facing a clinical operation of a psychoanalytic nature.

1   Framework "Procrustean bed" or according to "analyst-patient-analysis"

The three points of the definition contain basic elements of psychoanalysis. No reference, however, is made to the *how* or to the clinical procedure. Therefore, we see that a treatment should be considered psychoanalytic when it fits the criteria of point 2, which in turn is inseparably connected with points 1 and 3. If we find that a psychoanalytic treatment lacks or exceeds in something that does not contradict or obstruct the essence of these three basic principles, there is no reason for treating it as the mythological bandit Procrustes did. Procrustes tied his prisoners to a bed and either stretched or severed their legs in order to make them fit perfectly into it. In this definition, in point 2 Freud includes only neurotic patients, as could be said in 1922. On the other hand, Lapanche and Pontalis in 1967, in point 1 include delusions among imaginary productions and thereby automatically make room for psychotic aspects of the personality and psychosis. Many are the psychoanalysts that have addressed this topic. Among many others, we can name: Wilfred Bion (1957), Herbert Rosenfeld (1965, 1969, 1978), and Harold Searles (1965, 1980). Among the Argentines it is opportune here to evoke Jorge García Badaracco (2005) and David Rosenfeld (1982, 1992), both eminent psychiatrists and clinical psychoanalysts.

2   Focusing implies broadening one's view by narrowing one's sight

Reaching the *quid* of a definition consists of abstracting the essential qualities from the object, even when running the risk of minimizing other aspects of the object's definition. The goal is to bring about a result which is impervious to ambiguity. It is therefore important to interpret the complexity of the object with a careful and attentive eye. At the moment of clinical definition, an analyst cannot limit him/herself to the narrow focus of a definition, but he/she must also not be unaware of its existence. His/her experience together with a professional code of ethics enables him/her to apply the method in an opportune, satisfactory, and suitable fashion, although it may not concur absolutely with the design of traditional psychoanalytic theories and techniques. The initials "*s.a.*", meaning "secundum artem" or simply execute "at your discretion" are written on medical prescriptions whenever the physician sees fit. This is done to express faith in the art and science of the pharmacist at the moment of carrying out his/her duty.

Since its inception, psychoanalysis has been able to found, instead of "Procrustean beds", new theoretical-technical "bases" due to its daring to experiment outside its known and consolidated borders. This has occurred primarily due to clinical need in the absence of precedent. Whether or not the expected results can be achieved, innovations must always take place in the spirit of research and ethical responsibility. This is how the pioneers of psychoanalysis were able to expand their scope and the pathological spectrum of patients who could benefit from psychoanalysis. Elizabeth Rudinesco (2000), psychoanalyst and historian of psychoanalysis, refers very briefly to this in a newspaper article which has the merit of focusing several specific points of the epistemological evolution of psychoanalysis. She states that "For psychoanalysis to continue being in force, it is necessary to reformulate some of its tenets, without denying the essence of Freud." To accept the scope of this statement, there must be agreement as to what are the essential elements of the *quid* which she considers "essentially Freudian". Surely this essence will be found in more than just a handful of concepts that are fundamental to psychoanalytic theory. However, once one progresses a bit more, one will begin to object with the typical *yes ..., but ....* Here begins the first chapter of disputes, not only in tone, but also in major additions or deletions. Going further into this, we find that the essence of some of the current prestigious and outstanding psychoanalytic movements have elements that add to or conflict with the core of Freud's theory. An illustrative example is found, for example, in the important difference between Freud's Oedipus concept and the early Oedipus theory developed by Melanie Klein (1928). These theoretical or conceptual variations can be conceived of as the result of the ongoing research established in psychoanalytic thought. This statement coincides with two basic premises of Freudian thought: one emanates from his theory and the other corresponds to an attitude of openness towards new knowledge. This is expressed in the heading of Chapter One, which clearly demonstrates the epistemological concept of Freud's as compared to psychoanalysis as an empirical science.

In this age of digital communication, there is a need to open new paths in clinical psychoanalysis. In telephone treatments, although its implementation is no longer so novel, it still lacks recognition in academic psychoanalysis. The clinical material of sessions will be among the most representative elements for critical discussion. They also offer the possibility of processing the methodology of technique as well as simultaneously discussing whether new theoretical conceptualizations are required.

In the aforementioned 1922 article, Freud refers to several key points of the theory and technique of psychoanalysis. Among them he mentioned Freudian slips, dreams as the *via regia* to the unconscious, symbolism, the Oedipus complex, the doctrine of resistance and repression, the interpretative task, etc. On these points, we can not tolerate any modification or deletion due to the mere fact of applying a new method of approach. One must add the influence of the transference that has been preformed depending on the domestic or business application of the technological devices used, the influence of the lack of visual perception, the physical distance, and the amount of reality actually achieved with a method commonly referred to as virtual. One must research, for example, the degree of influence incurred by the lack of a period of time otherwise existing both prior to the beginning of a session and after its conclusion. In classic sessions there is always a geographic distance to cover between the patient and the analyst's office. As it takes time to cover this distance, there is always a juxtaposed time before and after the session. One can also consider the fantasies that emerge during this commute as fertile ground for elements that can contribute to the session. Occurrences appear in the form of images or loose ideas that have unconscious content. These can take the form of daydreams that can be unzipped and developed into manifest material with rich latent potential. The same occurs once the patient exits the office. The time spent to arrive at his/her destination contributes to the dissolution of the mental ambience of the session. It takes time for the patient to leave behind the analytic attitude—regressive and reflective—which the analytic situation has shaped and established in the patient. In this time of returning to everyday life, the ego finds a suitable space to return to material and social reality. Both time slots are set up as a part of the "pre" and the "post" session, which form an intrinsic part of the session itself. Wender, Laniado de Cvik, Cvik and Stein (1966) make a thorough conceptual contribution to this topic.

In distance treatments, this time slot before and after the session generally does not appear. The patient simply disconnects from his everyday routine, takes the communication device, and connects to the analyst. When the session is over, the reverse process takes place, and the patient does not have a slot of time in which to readjust.

In the stated article, Freud does not stipulate that treatment should be carried out in the consulting room of the analyst. Neither does he stipulate that analysis should take place a certain number of times per week, or that the patient should lie on a couch with the analyst sitting behind him. One might think that this was understood, and that it was obvious that the sessions should take place in an analyst's office. The question is: is this because clinical psychoanalysis can only work in this way or because this was the custom, which later became an established *modus operandi*? The formal aspect of its application should not be considered as the ontological of psychoanalysis. However, it is known that an established custom can many times eventually take on the force of law. In fact, the image of a patient lying on a couch and an analyst sitting behind him is a symbolic icon representing clinical psychoanalysis. It is also possible to assume that two centuries ago the emblematic image of a traveller could have been represented by a man sitting in the back of a coach driven by a coachman and pulled by horses. If we had not been able to surpass the limits of this iconic figure, we would still be travelling this way. It is said that at the time when tramcars first began being run by electricity (as opposed to being pulled by horses), it was necessary to have a horseman pass by blowing a horn in order to notify the passengers that the tram was coming. There was so much fear that the tram could hit people that until midway through the last century, the trams of Buenos Aires had a device at the front of the vehicle called a "lifesaver". These preventive measures had certain logic because these new electric "cars" exceeded the maximum speed paradigmatically established in the public's mind.

3   Reasons for existence and persistence of distance analysis

The application of communication technology in clinical psychoanalysis has become an important tool for reaching people living in places that are geographically distant from the analyst's office. Concomitantly, this form of implementation is going through a process of seeking its proper place within the "new developments in psychoanalysis". In earlier chapters, we discussed that the birth of distance analysis came about due to the need of some patients to emigrate, which placed them in a position of having to choose between terminating their treatment and undertaking distance analysis. Parallel to this, distance analysis was established as an interim method for the occasions in which the patient could not reach the analyst's office. An exceptional case is that of Mark Leffert (2003) who notes that he has been practising telephone analysis for 20 years because of his lack of a stable residence in one fixed place. After these and numerous other extraordinary experiences spontaneously came to light, one could no longer consider them to be strange. In previous pages, I stated that in April 2005, when I unveiled in Buenos Aires the first report of an experience of this type, some colleagues said in *sotto voce* that I "treat a patient by telephone", while other colleagues took the practice for granted, and it was therefore not a novelty for them. The statistical experience made by Estrada Palma (2009), discussed in Chapter Three, serves as a quantitative graph of these comments.

To the extent that these methods continue to show psychoanalytically satisfactory results and they become more developed theoretically and technically, one can expect that they will occupy their rightful and legitimate place as an accepted option of implementation of clinical psychoanalysis.

Although it may not be a question of great distance, current lifestyles measure the weight or importance of the time it takes to arrive at the analyst's office. If it were necessary to travel an hour or more in order to arrive at the analyst's office and the same amount of time in order to return, it would be necessary to devote three hours per session. Many patients are unable or unwilling to spend almost half a day travelling several times a week in order to undergo analysis.

Some analysts who emigrated from their countries at a young age were trained as such in the countries in which they now reside. When their good or excellent training becomes news and transcends national boundaries, their reputation reaches their countries of origin. As a result, their professional services may eventually be required by their compatriots due to a lack of well-trained local analysts or because the patients choose not to be analysed locally due to fears about having details of their private lives spread to the general public. The advantage for the patient of being treated by this native analyst working "offshore" is that he/she can be treated in his/her native language. A distance psychoanalysis implemented in this way offers the patient a highly trained analyst who speaks the same language and knows the idiosyncrasies of the country from which he/she emigrated. This, in itself, involves the establishing of a significant preformed transference in this bond.

When viewed from the perspective of an analyst who emigrated from his country as a young person and receives a request for treatment from a prospective patient from his/her home town, the analyst has the rewarding experience of helping someone who could have been his/her neighbour. If his migration occurred several decades ago, the analyst may be somewhat outdated in his/her management of certain idiomatic forms of expression. From time to time, the analyst will receive additional information from the social, economic, and political development of his/her native country. These feelings deserve to be observed and self-analysed to discriminate whether they are due to countertransference feelings or are own production and crop.

Some of these feelings can be conceived as "analyst's transferences" (Carlino & Torregiani, 1987), which are not generated by a transference stimulus of the patient, but rather all that the evocations of this dialogue generate in the analyst.

Nowadays, the internet is seen as a tool for consultation on many issues. One of them is related to queries related to the field of mental health. Some people visit such portals with the intention of seeking psychological assistance.

First are those who live in remote areas and therefore find it very costly in time and money to go to a city and see an analyst, especially given the need for continuity in the process. On the other hand, there are those who do so for reasons of their own personality. Such is the case of those who are introverted, either intellectually or emotionally, and therefore have difficulties in social interaction skills and expressing their feelings. Finding an analytic dialogue or simply a psychological consultation carried out through the use of a computer gives them a proper mood for talking about themselves with a certain degree of sincerity. In such cases, distance psychoanalysis would be indicated as a first attempt in introverts, who tend to perform socially with an attitude of withdrawal or with some degree of social anxiety disorder or even with paranoid feelings. The internet offers a means by which they are encouraged to interact with other human beings due to the fact that the connection is "familiar" to them. The internet represents to them a world full of resources that they use in order to reach what they want. They feel that they can "ask for" what they want from this means without having to give an equal share in return. They feel that they can establish a relationship of dependence, much like that of a young child with his/her parents, and request what they want without feeling an *a priori* commitment to giving anything in return for the services they manage to obtain.

In soliciting psychological help through the internet, one expects to have a "medical consultation" and the resulting "prescription" to solve the problem or, at least, the acquiring of a general psychological orientation. It may also be the case of people who feel that talking about their problems involves talking about themselves and they experience it as the equivalent of unveiling themselves. However, *a priori*, they have a different attitude when communicating by the internet. They feel that this may be an appropriate "place" to talk about themselves, their insecurities, their complexes, and in general about their feelings without having to face more than a few words, oral or written. They play with the eventual possibility of being or not being, appearing or disappearing, and the feeling of being able to alternate their communication in a channel which may be tendentious, capricious, or harshly real. Sometimes what is usually classified as a lie, on the internet becomes "legal" as a fictional version of something supposed and expressed as a reality in which the patient expected his/her words and not his/her person to be put into play. These patients avoid physical contact, both literally and metaphorically. This is the case even when the patient gets to the situation in which he/she does not put any personal commitment in the online attempt to find the psychological help that he/she is seeking. For some people, using the internet to ask questions involving psychological matters is as far as their inhibitions or interest will allow them to go. They may expect some kind of immediate response and magical cure. It may occur that after a consultation of these characteristics, the inquirer may establish contact with the complexity of the problem and become aware of how much he is involved in its production and maintenance. If this is achieved, the chances of psychotherapeutic treatment will increase. Its development will indicate whether it can be transformed into psychoanalytic treatment. When this type of query is dealt with by an expert analyst with good management of persecutory anxieties, of defence mechanisms, and of timing, it can help a patient to get in touch with him/herself. Perhaps in this session or a future one, the patient will give him/herself the opportunity to access treatment in a less anonymous way and reveal him/herself before the analyst as a person, and not just as a voice or written text.

a   Extending the possibilities of choice

After accepting the ease of implementation that communication technology provides for clinical psychoanalysis, one realizes that this opens up a range of possibilities of choice. From the patients' perspective, the number of analysts available increases their possibilities of choice. From the analysts' perspective, this may either increase or decrease the range of patients who arrive. This situation, like many others, will be governed by the laws of the market. Some of the central elements of this equation are the professional quality and reputation of the analyst, the financial cost *per se* and its comparative international value due to the fluctuating value of currencies, the possibility of being treated in a particular language, etc.

b   Rationally justified reasons

At the beginning, patients assume that what they are conscious of is the only real reason for looking for an analyst from other latitudes. It is known that there are unconscious motivations that reinforce the initial idea of searching for this type of analysis. Some people will only accept to be analysed by professionals who are willing to provide treatment through communication technology. For them, it is the only treatment eligible. The analyst will evaluate each situation and consider what he/she believes to be appropriate. Some are former patients living in areas far from their analyst and wish to resume the therapeutic contact with him/her. Also among those who demand this type of analysis are people who prefer that the analyst not live in their place of residence because they are well known and worry about the possible exposure of their private lives. Others may do so because they are interested in a particular analyst, either due to recommendation or his/her theoretical line.

c   Various kinds of disabilities

Distance analysis is a useful method in both emergency and permanent situations, either due to travel that may occur in either of the members of the analytic dyad, or due to temporary conditions regarding disease, which may affect the patient's ability to move about. In this regard, Zalusky (1998) mentions this latter circumstance and recommends distance analysis as the method of choice for patients who are temporarily impeded from going to the analyst's office. Some of the situations in which it may be recommended are the following:

- Patients who temporarily need to rest.
- Patients with acquired immunodeficiency syndrome, who must be isolated.
- Patients who are blind. Distance analysis allows the patient to avoid the onerous trip to the office. Of course this does not mean that there is no difference between sessions which take place in the

analyst's office and those that take place outside it. These sessions will have a different framework and the influence caused by the difficulty in arriving will operate in the ambience of the session. In the telephone dialogue, the perception of the analyst will work differently, being put on the same level as that of sighted patients.

- Deaf-mute patients or those who have severe hearing and speech difficulties, such as those who have had their larynx removed. Treatments carried out via written chat or email can also be possible. Furthermore, it is possible to use a videophone and communicate through sign language if the analyst is prepared to communicate in this way.

d   The psychopathological identity of the prospective patient

In addition to the reasons presented, there are others for prescribing distance analysis, which are based on the psychopathological structure of the prospective patient. These are unknown people who formulate their consultation by means of the internet. Some, in principle, feel that anonymity gives them security—a topic that should be analysed in a timely manner so as not to mute the avoidant symptoms and the motivations existing therein. If not, the feeling of confidence and peace of mind that is produced by distance and/or anonymity will only legitimize and strengthen their insecurity regarding direct contact. However, in these patients, distance analysis could be a first step to introspection in its communicative presence with another. At this early stage, it is important to help the patient to consolidate the possibility of sharing his/her own intimate feelings. Once achieved, the patient him/herself will begin to see how to establish the transference link without much distance or shielding, not only with the analyst but also with other possible bonds. However, in such cases it is important to make a good diagnosis before accepting a treatment of this nature.

The registration of personal data (name, age, marital status, gender, address, phone, etc.) is an important issue to consider, especially when not interviewing the patient in the office. In written chat, sometimes a name can be used for either of the two genders. It is therefore important to ask about this before jumping to conclusions. The possible ramifications of the use of a nickname, which is extremely common in anonymous chat, must be considered if the case applies. If a nickname were used for the purpose of ensuring anonymity, eventually some attached latent meaning will be discovered. The permanent existence of this nickname can promote a treatment "as if"—i.e., a treatment that only encompasses the words of a patient and not the person playing the role of patient. The analyst is faced with the decision of accepting (albeit temporarily) the use of a framework that permits nicknames or whether he/she refuses it outright. However, the analyst must also avoid descending into prejudice. For a person accustomed to the internet, the use of a nickname is commonplace. By taking part in treatment initiated through this means, the patient can make us think, in principle, that he/she is showing his/her habits and still has not realized that the analysis cannot be simply "another service" provided online. In such cases the analyst will need to analyse the significance of the nickname for the user, the fantasy that he/she has when proposing it as an identity in the analytic dialogue, and what significance it implies in internet analysis. On the other hand, when a patient goes by a particular nickname or alias on a permanent basis, it is no longer considered anonymous. He/she may feel more identification with the nickname that with his/her legal name. It is one thing to provide a nickname with the purpose of hiding behind it, and another to use it out of habit or because of identification with it. An example of this difference would be in the case of a patient who provides the analyst with his/her full name, but then states his preference for being addressed by the nickname. This does not obligate the analyst to use the nickname, but it does obligate the recognition of its existence.

The dilemma that the analyst faces is whether it is necessary to know the patient's real name. Furthermore, the analyst will have to consider whether it is better to accept not knowing the patient's real name at a beginning stage in order to begin with the analysis in the only way that the patient is able. If the analyst accepts it to be "natural and definitive" it will become one of the *constants* of the framework. On the other hand, if he/she only accepts it as part of the beginning stage, it will become another variable of the process, which requires further analysis.

In Buenos Aires, in treatments performed in the consulting room, the analyst does not verify the patient's identity by examining his/her documentation. There is a widespread custom of asking the patient for his name, address, phone number, and most recently, the email address. The mere fact of having visually perceived and contacted the patient in the office produces the subjective experience of having identified him. In distance treatments, the analyst gives greater importance to the personal data of the patient. In any case, one must keep in mind that from the legal point of view, it is necessary to know the personal data of the patient.

e Economic motivations

The possibility of financial benefit to be obtained by searching for an analyst in another country may be either in the forefront of importance, or simply an additional advantage. We must remember that the cost of treatment is a very important element for the patient. However, if the economic benefit factor was the main reason for choosing an analyst at a distance, the treatment could end up being very expensive. The conscious and unconscious symbolic value of a "cheap" country can contain an initial charge of belittling that can mask the valuable aspects of the analyst and the possible treatment to be carried out with him/her.

f Reasons of time

Another reason for distance analysis, as already mentioned, is the time factor. The use of communication technology eliminates the effort to arrive at the session and allows that time to be used for other purposes. These sessions may be just a few thousand steps or a few hundred or even thousands of kilometres away. The truth is that in distance analysis, the patient only requires a few seconds or minutes in order to drop everything and "enter" the session. By adopting this method, the possible problems caused by the commute to the analyst's office—such as traffic, cost, and adverse weather conditions—shall not affect the effort to arrive on time. On the other hand, we should mention the material disadvantage of the method, which is its vulnerability to technological failure at the moment of or during the connection.

g Instability of residence

Everyday life is gradually moving away from a regular and uniform system. Some people have a daily routine which is different from that of the average population. There are situations, permanent or temporary, that make it difficult for some patients to accept the classic framework of attending sessions in the psychoanalyst's office. In some patients, adopting a method of classically structured treatment could expose him/her to feeling that he/she makes great efforts that will frequently be useless due to the real impossibility of complying with formal requirements. Proposing a framework of treatment that from the very beginning seems very difficult or impossible to accomplish is an error that could amount to iatrogenesis. Keeping this in mind is of paramount importance. One cannot propose anything to the patient whose compliance would be tantamount to an excessive demand within the type of framework to which he/she commits.

h Other determining factors involved in the choice

There are patients with symbolic difficulties, who additionally do not have the option of attending sessions at the analyst's office. In these cases, distance analysis is the only option. In these cases, both the distance and the mentioned symbolic difficulty must be taken into account. From the outset, only a psychotherapeutic treatment is conceivable for them. Communicating by videophone can contribute to the quality of conversational exchange. The combination of audio and visual images gives patients the ability to "feel" the image transmitted by the analyst. Knowing that one can continue analytic treatment from a remote location opens a perspective of continuity to an analytical process, either in real or hypothetical situations of migration.

In preceding pages we noted the advantage for the patient in having the possibility of contact with analysts from his/her place of origin, as a way to anchor him/herself to something familiar while going through the transitional stages that occur in any migration.

Distance analysis can be used as a supplement to regular office treatment, in the way of a technical parameter (Eissler, 1953). In cases of necessity or urgency, it is a resource for actual or potential use for highly dependent patients. The mere knowledge that they have the opportunity of reaching their analyst by email or telephone is comforting to them.

These "distance analyses" can lead to serious, deep therapeutic relationships, and strong emotional bonds due to the existential significance that the analytic dialogue can produce.

4 What and who can be considered "known" or "unknown" patients?

For many analysts, a face-to-face meeting with the patient prior to the beginning of the analysis is of great importance and therefore becomes a concern in reference to distance treatments. For these analysts, the mere fact of having a meeting with a prospective patient in the office is essential in deciding whether or not to implement a distance method.

This situation leads to the formulation of a number of key questions:

- What do we mean when we refer to known or unknown patients?
- Is one meeting in the analyst's office enough in order to consider the patient to be *known*?
- How significant is the fact that a psychoanalyst feels that he/she "knows" a prospective patient?
- Can we consider a prospective patient to be "known" after having read his/her clinical history or via the referral of another analyst?
- Is it possible for an analyst to consider a patient as "known" if he/she analysed that patient many years ago?
- Are there greater risks (clinical, legal) in psychotherapeutic practice if there is little physical presence in the analyst-patient relationship?
- Is it possible to psychoanalyse someone when he/she has only been interviewed via communication technology, without going the office?

One of the stumbling blocks in finding a general agreement about these questions is that the answer depends on what a "known patient" means to each analyst. This is related to the parameters that each analyst uses in order to identify a patient as "known".

The fact of knowing another person can be conceived from different conceptual perspectives. New technologies, with their different codes and logic, provide new paradigms which, at times, can upset the absolute character of previously established logical preconceptions. For people born before the 1980s—*digital immigrants*—the idea of knowing another person is intimately connected with the physical presence of that person in a small area and with a visual perception of that person's body without the intermediation of communication technology. Is what until not long ago was considered impossible, still valid today? In contrast to the generation of analysts coming from the pre-digital era, for those who have become teenagers and young adults in the first decade of this century—*digital natives*—the concept of "knowing" another person is different. They can easily conceive that two people can *meet* and get to know each other although only having contact via written chat. Although this position opens up a whole new social and philosophical chapter in the current human condition, it is a fact of life and as such it is emerging as everyday reality. It is a contemporary way of "being in the world". Rejecting it from the outset could mean a withdrawal of the analyst and would take away the prospective patient's opportunity of operating psychoanalytically with him/her.

The internet cultivates various kinds of links, such as "chat rooms" and shopping sites offered by different portals located on the web. One can play chess, cards, billiards, roulette, or take distance courses which are delivered through so-called "virtual classrooms". This communication mode does not require the presence or even prior knowledge of the other. Nor is it necessary to touch the merchandise in order to buy it, given that the displayed photograph, price, and certain specifications of the product are sufficient. Viewing products indirectly on the screen has entered a new logic of *knowing*, in the same way that the words transmitted by telephone, or recorded on an answering machine, or seen in written form on the screen are being validated as equivalent to what has always been necessary to be said face-to-face, or when conducted from a distance, through a document that should be written and signed by hand, often in the presence of a notary.

In distance treatment, there are several conditions that are necessary in order to consider a patient as "known". All requests for interviews made by such means put the analyst in a position of increasing his/her attitude of inquiry. One important element is the countertransference feeling raised in this first contact. As it is not the same to interview a patient in the office as to do so by phone, this difference must be carefully addressed before drawing hasty conclusions about the trust or distrust that emerges from the interviewee. *A priori*, an interview in the office should be considered more reliable than one conducted by any technological means of communication, and perhaps less reliable if the prospective patient locates the analyst through an internet portal. This position can be established at the beginning and endure as a birthmark while maintaining the bond, which does not relieve the analyst from adopting a revision or corroboration of that position, which is almost axiomatic. The difficulty in trust should not be set entirely in the system of consultation. The analyst must be aware that, due to his/her habits and previous training, he/she is not wholly confident in being able to know a patient whose interview has been conducted through communication technology. After all, this does not seem very arbitrary. A paradigm of acquaintance which requires a face-to-face situation is applied in this categorization. However, new logic could be applied to process what elements are necessary in order to consider a patient as "known". This logic is increasingly within reach of a large section of analysts from the pre-digital era. The fact that there are patients who demand distance analysis is due to the acceptance by some analysts who believe that it is possible to carry out these new ways of implementing clinical psychoanalysis.

Anyone who goes an interview in a psychoanalyst's office is, in principle, also a stranger. However, the analyst has certain diagnostic instruments derived from his/her training in face-to-face interviews that allow him/her to assess the outstanding characteristics of the patient's identity. Implementing a psychopathologic and situational diagnosis is appropriate and necessary at the beginning of treatment. For distance analysis, this evaluative diagnosis is just as fundamental. Furthermore, it is necessary to implement a specific method of evaluation according to the adopted setting for the interview.

Even when diagnostic interviews take place in the analyst's office, it takes time for him/her to "get to know" a patient. Throughout the analytic process, the analyst will gradually assess whether his/her initial beliefs about a patient are to be confirmed or rectified. Close physical contact provides diagnostic tools that only arise from this particular type of encounter. In contrast, in order to begin any type of distance treatment, it is necessary to implement a strategy for obtaining the necessary elements of identification due to the fact that the different structure in the implemented technique may require another way of processing the act of "knowing the patient".

In fact, some analysts conceive that an important section of the analysis, even from its very inception, can be established without ever conducting diagnostic interviews in the office. Regarding this position, a cloud of shock and suspicion can be raised by a fairly wide swathe of analysts who consider this to be intolerably brazen. Should this case arise, it is advisable to implement a battery of tests to fine-tune the diagnosis, detecting a possible omission or deception by the patient. This practice is also observed in classic analysis and some analysts occasionally rely on a psycho-diagnosis. For those who carry out a consultation through an internet portal, it is necessary and desirable to do so with the corresponding computing resources. It is possible that increasing demand will bring about the creation of new computer software that will further help with the diagnosis.

For analysts who are "digital immigrants", a recommended method would be to interview the patient following the outline of the classic techniques of a psychiatric interview, which include an open part and another directed towards investigation as to the reason for the inquiry, the patient's symptoms, and a superficial viewing of his/her life history. The analyst can take this opportunity to explore why the patient is interested in a distance method, as well as his/her reason for choosing the analyst. In these interviews, the need to ask questions does not come only from the analyst but also from the patient, putting the former in a position of discerning which questions are necessary and appropriate to answer and which are not.

Everything related to the professional reality of the analyst must be answered, unless there are grounds for not doing so. It should be noted that the prospective patient will also ask him/herself whether or not to offer his trust to an analyst that he/she contacted over the internet. The analyst who publicly presents him/herself in this way should demonstrate his/her professional degrees, curriculum history, membership of a psychoanalytic institution accrediting him/her as a psychoanalyst, as well as his/her professional licence to practise. If a minimum or basic trust cannot be obtained, it will play a role in the acceptance or non-acceptance of being treated by the analyst, as well as the acceptance or non-acceptance of the proposed technological means. The qualities developed in the subjective exchange will influence the trust or distrust of both participants. In the case of beginning treatment, from the very start we must scrutinie in the material the amount of distrust that may exist. The matter of timing requires special attention at the moment of formulating an interpretation, especially at this early stage, given the amount of negative preformed transference (via the internet) that can be linked to the patient.

The outset of any analysis carries the possibility of being a "trial treatment" (Freud, 1913c), either because it is stated as such, or because it occurs without having been proposed. Direct contact of both members of the analytic dyad in the same physical environment provides diagnostic elements that only arise from the analytic situation. When it comes to another setting, the diagnostic path is different. With the framework of a distance treatment, the interpersonal relationship in some aspects or elements can be quite different. Taking into account these differences will allow the approach to receive the adequate adaptation to the adopted *analytic situation*.

5 Technical and epistemological reflections

Now and then, professional practice puts the analyst in unusual situations in which established guidelines do not suffice to accommodate the theoretical or clinical problems posed. These situations obligate the analyst to take decisions regarding his/her attitude and professional conduct when having to decide whether to begin or continue a treatment despite a change in a "constant"—the analytic setting—either because of geographical distance or due to other reasons that by virtue of their nature are acceptable. If the concepts arising from established theory and technique are not sufficient to implement a different type of analysis, should an attempt to remedy this be discarded? Those analysts who do not think so will have to assume the responsibility of putting their minds to the research of new theoretical concepts and the development of operational tools that make them possible. Although debatable at a beginning stage, this search should be harmonious with the basic tenets of psychoanalysis. When the analyst believes he/she can continue the analytic process from another instrumental perspective that affects the traditional setting, it is his/her prerogative to carry out the decision-making process in the way he/she sees fit. If he/she decides to allow the analysis to continue, its experimental nature should not be overlooked. The development of the analysis will be the judge of whether a new analytic process is being established in this modified clinical experience.

Although helping a patient is not always tantamount to analysing him, it is also true that an analysis that does not help is based on erroneous objectives. How valid is analysis if it does not help? In clinical work with patients, there is constantly a dilemma between the need to help a patient and the need to analyse without the urgency of thinking how much any particular part of the analytic process is helping the patient. It is well known that promoting better self-understanding in a patient implicitly provides a background of support. However, there is another level of analysis in which the factor of helping is more obvious and the analyst is inclined to attend more directly, although without forfeiting his/her neutral stance. That is why unilaterally addressing treatment in terms of a researcher who *analyses* or a psychotherapist who *helps* is sterile because it dissociates two positions whose aim should be to coalesce.

a Systemic changes

Given a set of integrated elements, if an addition or change takes place in one of its constituent units, this will produce an effect or influence on the rest of the set, in the manner of a chain of events that are jointly interconnected. When a phenomenon takes place, and it acquires the quality of being more than an isolated event, the social fabric absorbs a transforming effect that marks a "before and after" of the process. The technological revolution in the field of communications has exponentially increased the possibilities of exchange. The opportunities for connecting with others and spreading information of general interest among people located in different parts of the world have multiplied dramatically. With the internet it is possible to bring the world home and, conversely, take your home to the world.

From this perspective, it is possible to conceive the idea that patients living in different cities or remote and isolated places may require the professional services of an analyst who is geographically distant. Likewise, the analyst can offer his/her expertise in several different countries which may require his/her professional services. In order to offer these services with genuine validity, it is necessary to process the theory and the implementation conceptually in order to achieve the best results. Given the evolutionary stage that these methods are going through, in addition to being addressed in a spirit of clinical help, it is necessary for the analyst to research the process outside the session. Additionally, it should be processed at the group level, both domestically and internationally.

b Clinical psychoanalysis outside the analyst's office

It is well known that current communication technology provides excellent opportunities for conversational exchange. The integration of technological resources to classic psychoanalysis warrants a departure from the formal structure with which it has always been practised. People are already seeking psychotherapeutic help through internet portals. Thus, the following question arises: why leave out of the field of psychoanalysis those patients, as well as psychoanalysts, who see the clinical possibility of beginning analysis in this way? Beyond any personal opinion, this issue must be addressed institutionally. Promoting this conceptual exchange within institutions and in psychoanalytic congresses would contribute to the building of new conceptual structures which foster the development of psychoanalysis. In this regard, the issue was addressed in Chicago at the 46th Congress of the International Psychoanalytic Association (2009) by a panel of nine analysts.

For some patients, the clinical contribution acquired via distance implementation may constitute the only analytic experience in his/her life or be an abbreviated part of all tests they need. Does this not also occur with in-office analysis? Many of these processes end without having completed the necessary analysis of the patient or the possibility of resuming that process at a later date. It is a generally observed fact that, throughout his/her life, a person may go through several psychoanalytic experiences and the previous experiences should not be disqualified *per se*. Distance analysis can be established as an appropriate solution to the need for analysis in a circumstantial moment of a person's life.

Some analysts have claimed that a transaction of this type facilitates the performance of a manic fantasy in which both patient and analyst, when facing a situation of migration, continue with the analysis out of the desire to preserve the bond, denying the distance originating from the migration and therefore avoiding the mourning process. The latter statement is based on a model of psychoanalysis which is fixed, static, and contrary to the circumstances of the era and culture in which it is being conducted. It is not fair or correct to criticize the implementation of a distance method when one has access to the facilities offered by technological resources, the patient's desire to continue, and a psychoanalyst who is willing to do so. The analyst expects that the ontological quality of psychoanalysis will not change even if the implementation of this practice changes. If this were to be the case, the means of implementation should not be attempted.

The design of classically implemented in-office psychoanalysis adopted the model that the surrounding culture of the time offered it. An analyst who has no desire or ability to be trained for the implementation of distance analysis must differentiate his/her personal position from the claim that this type of implementation is impossible or improper. Conceptual adherence to the belief that this form of implementation is merely a defensive manoeuvre in order to avoid mourning for the loss of the bond with the analyst is based on the belief that psychoanalysis can only be performed in an office. Continuing analysis with the same analyst does not preclude analysing the mourning of the loss involved in no longer attending sessions at the office, nor the loss of the physical proximity or direct perception of the analyst. For this, it not necessary to interrupt the bond, and especially due to the fact that it continues, the analytical dyad can analyse the mourning brought about, while not forgetting what was gained in the whole process of migration. What was lost was the old way of implementation. What was preserved was the continuity of the bond with the same analyst and in the same language (Carlino, 1986).

Both analysts who have experience in distance analysis and those who do not but think that it is possible, will only mourn the part of the bond that involved in-office sessions without the need for communication technology. The active bond with the analyst is not lost, but rather continues in other ways and will be used precisely to analyse the mourning for the loss that migration entails. On the one hand, the decision to continue the analysis with another framework depends on the patient's request and the analyst's indication about its appropriateness. Other times it depends on the analyst's direct suggestion, if he/she deems appropriate. For ethical reasons, he/she will inform the patient that there is still no professional consensus that guarantees the analytic method, due to the fact that it is still experimental. If necessary, he/she will state that the progress of the analysis will be periodically assessed within the context of the new means of implementation.

Those analysts who continue to state in absolute terms that when a patient emigrates, he/she must change analysts demonstrate a theory based on an axiomatic approach, which although it may well have been in effect in the past, becomes anachronistic given the advent of the current means of distance communication. Indeed, before these technological advances, the idea that two people living in distant places could maintain a close bond of intimate and profound exchange several times a week by telephone was quite unheard of, due to the excessive difficulty of ensuring a call at a specific time, as well as the considerable cost involved. Only those who possessed great economic freedom could have absorbed the cost of the call, as well as been unconcerned about the telephone company's punctuality in establishing communication with the analyst. On the other hand, the analyst could only have accepted this means of treatment if he were able to attend the patient at inexact times, given the lack of punctuality in the telephone company's ability to establish the connection. However, it must be emphasized here that this difficulty would have been logistical and not one of a psychoanalytic nature.

Digital natives and many digital immigrants who acquired new habits of communication are accustomed to communicating via written chat, text message, email, voice mail, or videophone. These people experience little or no difficulty in beginning treatment by such means of communication. For others, however, at some point it is necessary to carry out some kind of personal encounter without technological intervention. However, it is also important to take into account the needs that appear as the process develops. It is very valid that either the analyst or the patient, or both simultaneously, would see the need for a regularly programmed meeting in the office, and therefore include this in the framework. The most "natural" geographic location for the meeting would presumably be in the city and office of the analyst. However, it is also conceivable that the analyst, for whatever reason, would decide to commute to the patient's city in order to meet him/her there. Although it may seem like a bold idea, it is based on the framework itself. Let us remember that in these treatments, each member of the duo provides half of the material elements of the setting. Each one is responsible for purchasing and maintaining his/her own communication technology in order to carry out analysis in the chosen medium.

Operating analytically with patients who live in distant places (perhaps on another continent), with different values, traditions, and customs, far exceeds the mere idea of learning a different technique in order to analyse at a distance. It means that the analyst, both when listening and intervening, must take into account cultural differences, habits, and customs established in the patient's mind, as a result of his/her culture. It opens an outside world that takes us far beyond the psychoanalyst's office and includes the patient inserted in and as a product of the world that surrounds him/her. As a new method, it offers the analyst and psychoanalysis first-time experiences that may contrast with his/her own. Quoting Bion (1965), we could say that these experiences contain "thoughts in search of a thinker". Conversely, this experience also opens the door to other disciplines: sociology, anthropology, communications, law, and computer technology, which also form part of and contribute to the contemplation of this new experience.

By implementing these treatments, a psychoanalyst realizes that he/she has not only opened his/her office to the outside world, but has done so in "offshore" fashion. In fact, he/she has established him/herself as part of the greater world. The analyst is now facing different types of borders. Although the borders established by political geography do not disappear, the world's countries become part of a computer unit— the internet and other communication networks. This is in line with the concept of the so-called global village. Ethnological differences appear in the long run, but they contribute much more to the process than they obstruct it. One difference that must be taken into account in order to avoid semantic confusion is the contrast that might exist between one's own language, as compared to and contrasted with the way it is used in other regions. If the analyst adopts the patient's language, there may be differences between the everyday speech of the patient and that which the analyst learned in an academy. The analyst may also have learned a version of this language which is more typical of a nation or region which is different from that of the patient. This communicational intertwining may be an obstacle that can operate as a communication difficulty or, conversely, it may become a source of mutual consideration and communication, thereby awakening eagerness for communication, depending on the predominant sign in the transferential ambience. In this type of communication, the analyst may encounter patients who live in countries with very different and contrasting idiosyncrasies in their existential stance which, although a hurdle at the beginning, can contribute to building a richer perspective for the analyst. For this to occur, it is necessary for the analyst, when listening, to move away from his/her *base logic* and enter that of the patient, thereby having greater "contact" and "encounter" by understanding the conceptual paradigm from which the material has come. Accomplishing this is tantamount to truly understanding the patient, which is the first fundamental step in being able to interpret him/her properly.

One must keep in mind that the functional quality of communication technology is not internationally uniform and this can sometimes become a source of difficulty or conversational complication when the technology does not allow one to understand clearly what the other wants to say.

Working with an open mind can allow one to develop new perspectives which are adapted to new situations. In adopting this epistemological mindset, it is necessary to rely on the nourishing vitality that can only emerge from non-cumulative experience produced by the spark generated through the friction arising from the clash of the mistakes, successes, and doubts which generate an appetite for new knowledge. With this starting point and the unique perception that each clinical experience includes, an analyst can place him/herself in an epistemological position that constantly brings him/her up to date.

c   Semantics and type of communication

The tracks left by hundreds of thousands of performed psychoanalytic treatments should not be taken as being equivalent to a *single and permanently unchangeable path*. The fact that the patient does not have the analyst at his side continues to offer the possibility of taking the analyst as a transference object. In fact, this may even occur to a heightened degree, due to the absence of a clear connection to reality which would be implicit in physical proximity. One might think that this contingency also maintains a certain parallel with the feelings of the patient lying on the couch in the analyst's office. When there are so many sensory organs whose intervention has been intercepted, it is necessary to resort to what is colloquially known as a "sixth sense" or "clinical eye", which is connected to the analyst's perceptive astuteness provided by training and experience. This "clinical eye" allows him/her to perceive, or at least infer, both the implicit and the latent. The mere fact of not facing the analyst may facilitate the "smuggling" of resistance, although this should only occur in those patients who have an increased willingness to do so and that an experienced analyst should be able to detect.

An old saying goes "All roads lead to Rome". It is based on the idea that there are many roads that arrive at that city. These roads were built to arrive in a city that was always in the same place. In contrast, the expected goals of psychoanalysis, considering the singular qualities of any specific patient and analyst, are not determined *a priori* to arrive to a particular place. In fact, that place does not yet exist and it will not be the same for everyone, although there are basic and general proposals described by well-known authors such as: Ferenczi (1927), Freud (1937c), Klein (1950), Bleger (1973), Garma (1974), and Polito (1979). The most immediate goal that an analyst has to reach in each contact with the patient is to analyse him/her according to what he/she considers to be the "point of urgency" or the appropriate timing in trying to make his/her interpretation serve as a significant contribution to the process. Experienced analysts know that the *how much, where,* and *when* can not be known *a priori.* The same is shown by Freud (1913c), when he metaphorically said that, just like in the game of chess, the only plays that are known in the analytic process are those that correspond to the openings and endings. The middle moves of the game would be more comparable to Antonio Machado's lines:

> *Traveller, there is no pathway,*
> *The pathway is made by travelling along it.*

6   Characteristics of the voice in distance analytic dialogue

The emission of the voice carries with it certain characteristics that should be noted. The act of speaking has a motivating intention. Its realization is performed by the operating of a vocal apparatus comprised of:

1. The oral cavity in which are included the palate, tongue, and lips.
2. The nasopharyngeal cavity that functions as a resonator.
3. The larynx, which contains the vocal cords.
4. A rich and complex innervation, superior laryngeal nerve, and inferior laryngeal or recurrent nerve. Its injury would produce dysphonia or total aphonia.

The combination of the different ways in which the vocal cords vibrate produces sounds that are emitted by the passage of air from the lungs. Their successful articulation is basically influenced by the anatomy of the throat and its surrounding organs, which function as a sound board, and which together form the vocal apparatus. In turn, the implementation of phonation comes from stimuli arising in the cerebral cortex that are sent to the vocal apparatus by the peripheral nervous system through the mentioned nerves. This detailed description is given with the purpose of displaying all the constituent parts that play a role in the production of speech. This, as a function of all the complexity described, emits signals that give information about the body and mind of the emitter. The emotional aspects influence the actions of neurological stimuli passing on features that can be detected in the physical emission of the voice. These can enliven the awareness and interest in what is transmitted, provoke increased attention and even invigorate the listener. In fact, this possibility is utilized by fitness trainers to mark a rhythm for gymnasts or by military commanders to give orders to troops. When applied inversely, it can cause drowsiness, boredom, disinterest, distraction, etc. (Cesio, 1960, 1962). Emphatic intonation can have compelling effects beyond the rationality of its content. The analyst will be very attentive to the amplitude of modulation, rhythm, pitch, and musical tone being emitted. Some patients tend to use this property as an acting-out process in order to convince others about a way of thinking. The characteristic given to intonation may involve support or rejection.

The tone and pitch of the voice, in principle, are part of the speaker's identity. Their perception would be almost equivalent to that of his face. When babies are emotionally distressed, the voice of their parents often stops or mitigates their cries, sometimes even if that voice is transmitted by telephone. In the session, the fact that the patient can hear the voice that he/she identifies with the analyst and the fact that the analyst can hear his/hers provokes a longing for contact, or sometimes a sensation of rejection, according to the transferential sign of the beginning of the session.

As we see, the paraverbal aspects of speech influence the listener and in turn offer rich semiological information that should be taken into account. Guiard (1977) describes some of the peculiarities that intonation and its cadence and musicality take in the final stages of an analytic process.

On the same subject, but this time referred to throughout the analytic process, Zac de Filc (2005) emphasizes the importance of language sound components. He affirms that the phonetic aspect of speech makes a valuable contribution to the semantics of the message emitted because it contains nuances and signifiers provided by intonation and gestures. He further stresses the container role of the *analyst's bodily presence*, especially in patients whose development has undergone significant emotional abandonment. On this last point it is important to assess whether, in distance treatment, there exist the necessary resources to substitute for the need for physical proximity with some equivalence of a different nature. This could be offered by the combination of *"presence-contact-encounter"* contained in the appropriate interpretive interventions that possess an adequate amalgam of "form" and "background" in order to provide the patients with a sense of accompaniment.

In a distance psychoanalytic session, the action of placing the possibility of perception solely on sensory organs would be a misconception based on ignoring the permanent mental work existing in that operation. The sensory organs undoubtedly play an important role by bringing information to the mind. However, it is the mind that permanently processes all it perceives, as well as what it does not perceive (precisely due to its absence). However, it is always clear that in situations of physical proximity, the dialogue takes on different characteristics than when this physical proximity does not exist.

7   Additional diagnostic resources

In order to evaluate the clinical possibilities of distance analysis, it is necessary to create some new diagnostic tools in case it is not possible for the patient to go to the analyst's office. These shall only apply to those prospective patients that the analyst believes would have difficulty in visiting his/her office. A series of distance interviews can be carried out with the addition of an ad hoc battery of real-time tests which may include drawings, a questionnaire with anamnesis-type questions and others that encourage open answers, to be sent by chat or email. It would be an option for many but not for all. It would entail asking the patient to write what encourages him/her to seek distance treatment and the reasons that lead him/her to do so at the present time, as well as his/her symptoms and existential problems. A third element, perhaps in a second communication, would be to ask him/her to recount his/her life story in broad strokes and to put special emphasis on the events that have left footprints in his/her life history. Both letters have to have a length that complies with the analyst's criteria in terms of what he/she believes appropriate in each case. All this would allow for a first diagnostic approach to the patient and ultimately provide data similar to those that a physical encounter offers. Once the therapeutic relationship is on track, the psychotherapeutic or psychoanalytic process will decide what can be achieved.

When attending a patient who has established contact through a website, that bond is affected by preconceived ideas about the quality that can be expected from that source, depending on the degree of trust or distrust that emerges from the portal (Levis, 2005). This will operate as functional psychic content in the form of preformed transference.

8   Indications: contraindications

Regarding the indicating of distance treatments, there must always be an explanation for this due to the fact that it is an innovative form of treatment as compared to the established *modus operandi*. Given the short history of its implementation, this method can only be recognized as a second option, although presumably this will not always be the case. Its implementation still needs to be justified. The initiative to encourage this type of analysis may come from the patient or the analyst.

When the proposal comes from the patient, the analyst does not necessarily feel obliged to take it as such, but rather as simply another fantasy. If the patient insists, at some point it should be asked whether that fantasy has now become a proposal. If so, the analyst elaborates with the patient and scrutinizes whether to assume the professional responsibility of initiating a distance treatment with the patient. The initiative may also come from the analyst, who recommends or perhaps indicates a distance treatment. A third alternative is that the "indication" may come from an "imposition" coming from a material reality that only allows for its acceptance or rejection.

As can be seen in the professional field of psychoanalysis, this different way of conducting treatment is here to stay, not only as an alternative when facing the inability to arrive at the analyst's office, but as a step in the evolutionary process of clinical psychoanalysis. At the present time, analysts generally do not imagine that, for whatever reason, in the case of not being able to work regularly in the office, the idea of conducting analysis from a distance in another location would be possible. Of course, this could be done by making room in the framework for the possibility of undertaking distance analysis when he/she must be away from the office during a typically non-vacation period.

There is no intention here to provide a list of clinical cases in which patients are specifically recommended to be treated with a distance method. Rather, it seeks to clarify which patients and analysts could fit well into its framework.

Berenstein and Grinfeld (2009) argue that all changes occurring in the field of technology affect society and produce a "socio-cultural change of mind". Therefore, there emerges a new and different socio-cultural perspective based on the logic arising from the spread and possible use of such technological means. They argue that "in certain social and cultural backgrounds" this social phenomenon is intensified and condensed, and they include analysts as a strong component of this group. Among those who manage and move socially with some skills based on digital communication techniques, these authors will find those whom they refer to as "the appropriate candidates for this type of analysis", due to their ability to easily adapt to the method.

This would allow the union of two people with criteria based on the changes which have occurred in present-day thinking and subjectivity. In an analytical dyad of these characteristics, the ideas of *distance, presence, contact,* and *encounter* are detached from the need for a concrete physical meeting, but are rather seen as abstract or symbolic.

The ideas just presented have relevance at an intermediate time of socio-cultural transformation like that currently underway. Not long from now, a generalization of what is now described as "social strata" will take place. These are qualities that, although currently considered as special, will eventually become commonplace. This is a phenomenon that psychoanalytic institutions should not overlook. Psychoanalysis, although linked to and influenced by its governing institutions, develops independently by learning from the experiences of its day-to-day implementation. For the good of psychoanalysis, it is hoped that the wealth of experience emanating from this "empirical" base provides us with a teaching that can nourish psychoanalysts and simultaneously contribute to methodological research led by the governing institutions of psychoanalysis.

In regard to the psychopathological aspect, distance treatments are not designed to be implemented indiscriminately, bypassing the diagnostic "eye". When correctly indicated, they should yield psychoanalytically fertile effects.

We saw earlier that there are people who suffer from social phobia, agoraphobia, or symptoms of everyday despair who do not consult an analyst because, in so trying, they face the very symptom that prevents it. Others are not able to arrive at an analyst's office due to serious physical handicaps. Still others are unable to visit the analyst for geographical reasons that imply spending most of their lives in their place of residence. What might happen if they were given the opportunity to consult with an analyst without having to first leave their own "comfortable" habitat and if this opportunity would, at the very least, also be an initial step in the evolutionary process of a treatment? Another possibility would be to indicate the method as a follow-up (Guiard, 1979) after the completion of treatment in the case where the patient were to find it difficult to attend sessions at the analyst's office because of having changed his/her place of residence.

As for the contraindications of these methods of implementing distance analysis, one must first appeal to the general experience of the analyst, given that distance analysis provides for little. Prudence, both in indicating and monitoring, is an appropriate analytical approach to something new. While some contraindications are very clear, as we shall see, others rely on the discretion of the analyst.

It is important that every analyst understand how to differentiate between a personal decision and a comprehensive approach.

Distance analysis is contraindicated in the following cases:

1. In patients who are going through a period (or state) of major depression which is resistant to drug treatments.
2. In borderline patients who cannot be held responsible for the direction of their conduct.
3. In psychotic patients who are in a state of hallucination and delusion.
4. For those who are diagnosed as psychopaths with a history of continuous disruptive social behaviour.
5. In chronic alcoholic patients who do not have a clear resolve to fight the disease.

Although some patients are diagnosed as psychotic, distance analysis may still be suitable for them if they maintain a stable social position and are employable, as well as not displaying frequently impulsive or suicidal behaviour. Several chapters of this book have stressed that these treatments expect more collaboration from the patient than what would be expected of those who take their sessions in the analyst's office. This is due to the material aspect of the framework—the possession and maintenance of sensitive communication equipment. In more regressive patients, another useful element is the guarantee of continued family support. Last but not least, in these cases of regressive patients, one must first justify the reason for distance treatment. After this first step is taken, the other items on the list can be considered.

9   Termination of distance psychoanalysis

The question arises as to how and when to conclude these analyses. We are undergoing an evolutionary moment in the design of these analyses in which they are almost entirely based on the inability of the patient to meet the analyst in his/her office. If such difficulty were to subside, the distance implementation would be concluded and the analysis would return to its classic form. It can also occur that the reason for analysis has ended and therefore the treatment concludes. Freud in "Analysis Terminable and Interminable" (1937c) refers explicitly to this issue. What must be added in distance treatments is the consideration of whether they can cover the entire spectrum of analytic treatment that a person requires. There is not sufficient solid experience so as to endorse a specific, accurate response. The completion of analysis with a particular analyst also depends on the purpose that was established at the beginning of the analysis and others which emerged during the process. We know the need for analysis is endless, but not so the motivation or capability to carry it out. It is for this reason that the indication and continuity of the distance method cannot guarantee to match all the analytic needs that a person may have. Nor can it be conceived *a priori* as the sole and definitive indication. Now we will refer to the completion of its clinical implementation with a particular analyst.

a. Termination by gradual and spontaneous mutual agreement due to having fulfilled the stated objectives or due to a termination of the need for the analysis to be conducted at a distance.
b. Termination due to an initiative taken by the patient and the agreement of the analyst.
c. Decision taken by the patient but without the agreement of the analyst. In this case, it is considered that the analysis has not finished, but rather has been interrupted and left incomplete.
d. Unexpected and sudden termination on the part of the patient by failing to connect without notifying the analyst.

The first two [a. b.] can be conceptualized as a true completion. In contrast, the third [c.] is clearly an interruption of the analysis. Regarding the final possibility [d.], when psychoanalysis is conducted at a distance with a patient already established as such and without having given any indication that this could happen, the situation can be felt with a certain degree of concern or anxiety by the analyst. Let us recall that the idea of "presence" in these treatments is inextricably linked to the idea of "contact" and "encounter" in the broad, symbolic sense of these terms. Therefore, in losing the sensation of "presence" the bond becomes empty or even absent.

Regarding the technique for concluding analysis (Carlino, 1981), we have observed in the analytic processes that the elaboration of the farewell and approaching mourning occupies less space than was traditionally dedicated to it. Nevertheless, this elaboration continues to be worthwhile.

In distance analysis, the contingency of termination is operating latently but with a higher density and frequency than in an in-office analysis. The support of these commitments depends on many factors, some of which were added subsequent to those established at the beginning of the analysis. These are analyses that function with little inertia. Their commitment must be sustained with proper contact. The patient must feel a sense of renewed encounter obtained through the content and form of dialogue with his/her analyst. Although this is in part a requirement, if properly managed, it can become a merit. In this analytic situation the technical neutrality of the analyst must not be lost. However, it must be handled in such a way that it does not affect the sense of contact and encounter. It is necessary that the analyst not lose *presence* in the mind of the patient.

A patient may be undergoing very positive analysis but for several situations decide, from his/her adult side, to end an analysis even if it is incomplete—with or without the clinical agreement of the analyst. These situations occur quite frequently and, in a percentage of them, the decision may be taken with or without awareness of the degree of improvement achieved or of the remaining elements that require further analysis. From this perspective, the analyst, beyond showing his/her disagreement, should advise the patient that the return to analysis is always latent, either with him/her or with another analyst. This focuses on the work of mourning, not only in the loss of contact with the analyst but also with analysis as an auxiliary resource of the mind. Some analysts must be wary of becoming angry with a patient who "deserts" him/her, despite the frustration caused by the unachieved expectations placed in that analysis. In these cases, when the patient's decision becomes irreversible, the analyst should explain to him/her that there is always a latent opportunity to return. In so doing, the analyst can avoid analysing the termination of the sessions in terms of a mourning caused by the alleged definitive termination of the analysis.

CHAPTER SIX

Clinical anecdotes

This chapter includes some stories taken from clinical experiences.

The first two are intended to illustrate how two separate analysts, whom I will identify as Analyst "A" and Analyst "B", for the circumstances that I will describe, establish a telephone treatment for the first time. One of them takes place in a stable setting and the other as complementary to an office setting.

1   Analyst A

Three years after having interrupted his analysis, a 33-year-old male engineer, who was married with three sons, contacted his former analyst via email. He had emigrated to Europe two years previously. Taking advantage of his annual visit to Buenos Aires for the holiday season, he requested an interview to be held shortly after his arrival. In the course of this interview, he explained that he was distressed by the difficult work situation that he was going through. He further recognized that he was partly to blame for this and that he was terrified about losing all that he had built as a result of his migration. Anticipatory anxiety was the most noticeable symptom. He wanted to protect himself from all possible contingencies, predicting very difficult but imaginary situations that could take place in the short or medium term. Although he knew he was exaggerating, he could not stop guessing and behaving as if what he was thinking were a real or imminent event. As this was a patient who already had a bond with the analyst, and because his stay would be limited to thirty days, both agreed in the first interview that it would be advisable to schedule five sessions per week with the idea of completing a total of twenty. A week after beginning, the patient calmed his anxiety and began to link the reasons for it to situations that made him remember his own childhood home. Motivated by the sensation that the remaining sessions were not enough, he decided to lengthen his stay by ten days. Furthermore, a couple of sessions before his return, he suggested: "Can't we continue doing this by telephone? What we did helped me to face the problems that I brought to the interview but by talking and talking, other things have come out, and they're still hanging in the air."

The analyst agreed with the patient that the new things that had arisen had not been addressed, and therefore were "hanging in the air", to use the words of the patient. However, he did not agree with the proposed solution of "continuing by telephone". The analyst had no previous experience in this type of analysis, although he had no particular stance on the subject at that time. He felt that the patient had offered a naïve solution, given the fact that it was out of any preconception of clinical praxis that he had conceived to date. The spontaneous response of the analyst could have been to say that, although he also wanted to continue the analysis, trying to do so by telephone was not possible. Moreover, as a result of this unexpected proposal, he thought that the telephone could only offer a parody or mock analysis. However, he felt that this clear and convincing interpretation that he had in his mind was not enough. This request, which was motivated by a desire to continue the analysis, seemed to deserve attention and therefore the analyst began looking for an answer, albeit only to satisfy himself. He agreed with the patient that he would communicate with him by telephone only if the patient still felt the need to continue having returned to his country of residence. There would be no commitment to do so and it would depend on the patient's need. These instructions were given at the final session because the analyst was not sure whether the proposal had been made in order to alleviate the pain of separation or whether it was a genuine desire to continue by telephone. That is to say, he was not sure about the patient's feelings. Nevertheless, due to the firmness and insistence with which the request had been made, the analyst considered that perhaps it could be genuine and legitimate.

A week after returning to his place of residence, the patient sent the analyst an email to ask what day and what time he could call him. The analyst acquiesced to the patient's formal request and proposed a time slot in which he was free. The patient called very punctually, which was an important detail for the analyst, although he continued to think that the patient might only have the fantasy of entering a session. The analyst maintained an attitude of receptiveness and listened to his comments. It was not in his mind to offer any interpretative proposal. He listened with a basic attitude of expectation to "see what the patient would come up with and what he would propose". He did not want to prejudge the fate and development that this telephone "conversation" could have. Although he did not consider that this was an analysis session, it was also clear that it was not simply a friendly chat. He remained alert to observe the quantity and quality of the patient's demands while simultaneously scrutinizing himself to see how he would react to them. Upon finishing the call, the patient asked if he could call again the following week. They agreed to a date and time. The analyst was left wondering about what had happened in that "conversation". Was it a session of analysis? Was it simply an extended farewell? The analyst preferred to continue contemplating the question and wait for the next "conversation".

The patient called promptly at the appointed time. Among other topics discussed, he insisted explicitly on continuing his analysis in this way. The analyst not only perceived the patient's firm resolve to continue but also simultaneously observed in himself a willingness to continue in this way, albeit on a trial basis. The lack of specific knowledge about this practice led the analyst to exercise the attitude that he typically adopted when facing something new. His first thought was that he had to design an ad hoc framework, which could be precarious due to his lack of prior experience but, as long as it did not show any shortcomings or failures, would have to be the track along which this analysis would travel. "Without a framework, there is no analysis, but rather only conversation," he thought firmly. From this premise, it began. It was proposed to attach the usual therapeutic goal of analysis intended to research the progress of the process by testing the quality and direction that it was taking with that framework. He and the patient agreed to an analytic contract adapted to this singular and specific setting. The analyst decided not to charge for the first two "conversations" to differentiate them from the following, which were structured with the bilateral agreement of a new analytic contract that included the telephone setting and its derivatives: policy regarding holidays, schedule, dissimilar vacation periods, amount and specific form of payment, etc.

After a couple of months, the analyst could understand that this request for analysis conducted by telephone was supported by patterns of the patient's own life experience. His parents divorced when he was a child. The experience of communication by telephone with a person who loved him and cared for him was established in his own child-hood relationship with his father. This was impressed upon his mind's logic and functioned as transference in his willingness to achieve goals beneficial to his mental health. There were also added transference stimuli, as this patient, in his work, was accustomed to communicat-ing by email with companies based in different continents. In contrast, the analyst did not have this professional habit. Moreover, he restricted telephone contact with his patients to the leaving of simple messages. Whenever a patient began to speak too much on a problematic issue by phone, the analyst issued an automatic response: "We should discuss this during the session." This was correct, given the framework of clas-sic analysis. The possibility of distance psychoanalysis was unknown to him and did not appear in either formal or informal dialogue with his colleagues.

In a session at this stage of the analysis, it became clear that when the patient said that many things were "in the air", he referred to the area of communication—generically called cyberspace—which does not refer to the analyst's office or to any geographic location.

A year after beginning this experience, the patient returned to Buenos Aires on his annual visit to relatives and friends and he asked to continue his sessions for the duration of his stay. The analyst agreed, taking for granted that the sessions would be in his office. However, in the fourth session, the patient told his analyst: "Why should I come to your office when I can call you on the phone, as I normally do? If you agree, I prefer to continue taking my sessions by telephone, although I'm here in Buenos Aires." The analyst did not agree. He thought that it was a denial of the patient and that he wanted to ignore the real-ity that he could come to the office and have direct contact with the analyst without the need for technology. The analyst also felt a sense of discomfort, as if the patient's request were expressing what little importance he attributed to the office sessions.

The analyst's reaction deserves some attention. It is possible that the analyst processed that request with the paradigm that usually applies to the understanding of his work in the office setting. Because of this, at that time he failed to understand from what *base logic* that request was made. This patient already had the telephone setting inherently built in and the abrupt change in returning to the office meant a strange and sudden disruption of his usual analytic setting. The analyst, however, was far more accustomed to an office setting and considered this telephone analysis to be an exception. In contrast, the patient now considered that it had become the rule.

This telephone treatment lasted for a little more than three years, with a frequency of three weekly sessions of fifty minutes during the first year-and-a-half and two sessions per week until its completion. There was a great deal of stability in maintaining the schedule and attendance at the sessions. The patient, on his own initiative, decided that he wanted to conclude that analytic experience. He felt he had fulfilled his expectations. The analyst agreed.

2   Analyst B

A 45-year-old patient asked for an interview with the analyst because he was going through a transitional time in his life. He had put an end to a significant commercial partnership in which he had been successful. He had started up a new project approximately three years ago, but did not feel much affection for it. He was single and had no children. Although he was successful professionally, he felt that he was advancing in his career out of obligation to guidelines of conduct that he had acquired in the past, which made it more difficult for him to adopt more current models. He was not sure whether to continue living at home or move to another country where he also had a business office. His daily routine was very busy, and he often took business trips with short stays, interspersed every so often with a longer one. He described his love life with the phrase: "It's what's left over from something that used to be." He and his girlfriend had decided to separate, but he said that he could not completely detach himself from her. The relationship had been going on for ten years. There were moments in which he could not distinguish whether he is as he appears to be or whether he has been playing a character that, according to him, "seems to be able to sell everything to everyone, including to myself". He explained that although he had gained both social and professional prestige, he could not enjoy his achievements and sometimes could not even experience them as if they were his. Those who know him appreciate his success in the professional field as something of value. In contrast, this was not his case.

He claimed to have a pessimistic view of "life", which, of course, also applied to his own. He was not convinced by other people's definitions of happiness, although he made it clear that he did not consider his life to be one of non-conformities or suffering. He had an excellent economic position, but he did not know whether to consider himself to be fortunate. He described himself as being in a position halfway between what he liked and took interest in and what he did not. The degree of ambiguity and ambivalence was very high.

At this point, the analyst placed himself before someone who was opening a door to show his problems, but he could not be sure of the firm intention to include him as an analyst in order to solve the "halfway" monologue of being caught between feeling achievements as his own or as something that social values had imposed upon him. The analyst considered that his philosophical and existential statements operated on him as an equation of equal values of opposite signs. This led him to a neutral result (neither one, nor the other), which in turn acted as a factor of ambiguity. All of this speech was presented with exquisite packaging, highlighted by the quotes of philosophers and famous writers. This led him to end up being trapped in his own net. It functioned as a compelling package that kept him in that intermediate and undefined situation. This situation was well illustrated by his description of his relationship with his "ex"-girlfriend: "I'm with her, and I'm not with her." "I can't turn the page and focus on the future." His entire system of thought left him clinging on to the *status quo* by "not turning the page". This was also a reason for him to request analysis.

The analyst contemplated the situation of the prospective patient's frequent travels and the resulting instability of residence, due to the fact that it did not coincide with his habitual criteria for beginning stable analysis. On the other hand, he considered that although this lifestyle was not similar to that of common people, the patient's potential for analysis should not be discarded outright. The instability of residence caused the analyst to reach the conclusion that the framework that he used for analysis was inadequate. It should be noted that this reflection was built from a *base logic* that perceives the world by measuring the distance between different geographic locations in traditional modules—that is to say, with the idea of presence in the classic sense of both people being present in the same place. However, this framework was the only one available to the analyst. He knew no other. From that moment, they agreed to treatment twice a week, one day after the other, in order to leave the remaining five days of the week available for short trips. However, they also agreed that if the patient could not leave this situation of always being in a "halfway" position, the analysis should be increased to three sessions per week. In this framework, they were not able to resolve the potential effects on the analytic process if, from time to time, the patient were obliged to miss three weeks of sessions due to longer business trips. On the other hand, the analyst considered that the patient took his commitments seriously, given that he was productive in his professional life, and was therefore optimistic about the patient's ability to be responsible for attending his sessions, except of course when he could not attend due to distance.

The analyst began pointing out to the patient that he constantly manifested elements that had a certain value or quality but that became nullified by another explanation of the same situation that was of the opposite sign. Therefore any progress in his "intelligent" thinking became inert and did not permit him to "turn the page". This patient was consistent in his irregularity, given that every forty-five days he had to travel to another continent for two or three weeks. The analyst felt that he was faced with a patient who wanted to but could not comply with the (classic) method of treatment that was required.

After some time had gone by, the patient attended his first session of the week and said that he had been in a province that he regularly visits and that at one moment he had begun to feel quite anguished. He further commented that he wanted to call the analyst but refrained from doing so because he did not consider it to be proper. He described his symptoms and commented on their connection with existential ruminations that caused him much distress. He specifically complained about this because it did not disappear or even become mitigated through the practice of analysis. The analyst interpreted that this anguish may have been heightened due to the fact that the patient was about to begin another long absence on a trip to another continent. The situation continued in this way for a few more months. The analyst felt that, despite the interest in analysis demonstrated by the patient and the effort made in trying to maintain it, the circumstances of his own lifestyle placed him in a category that could be popularly denominated as "touch and go". "After all, this is the patient's life and he organized it in this way," thought the analyst.

At this stage of the analysis, the treatment already contained an initial impetus. It occupied an important place in the life of the patient and also in the analyst's current professional work. The analyst realized that the patient assumes job commitments that will make him leave his country. Due to this, in a session, the patient asked whether he could call the analyst by telephone at the regular time of his sessions during a long business trip that was about to begin. The analyst was initially surprised by the proposal. However, he did not consider it to be strange, but rather simply different from what he had become accustomed to in his work. The patient had been demonstrating enthusiasm, and the request was an example of this. He wanted to maintain continuity in the analytic dialogue, albeit through different means. The analyst told the patient that he had no experience in this type of treatment but that he would be willing to try it and evaluate the results.

This position shows an analyst who, despite his lack of specific experience, was open to trying a new kind of analysis in the spirit of a researcher with an ethical attitude. He decided to create a specific framework for this patient, setting aside one that was becoming increasingly inadequate for a patient with these characteristics. The analysis was structured around a mixed framework that combined analytic telephone dialogue whenever the patient was away and in-office sessions when he returned to the analyst's city of residence. The analyst noted that when he talked on the phone, this patient had a keen ability for verbal expression, which was superior to that of the in-office sessions. He demonstrated the capacity to include verbal nuances in order to compensate for the analyst's lack of visual perception of his gestures. The patient included this *modus operandi* immediately and automatically.

3   Vignette 1

Influence of social and professional paradigms

A colleague told me that twenty years ago he had gone through a very difficult situation in his professional life. A patient who had been in analysis for nearly three years phoned him to say that he could not go to his session because his wife had suffered an accident and that he had learned of this just a few minutes before he would normally be leaving for the analyst's office. The patient did not know the degree of severity of the accident. The next day the patient phoned again notifying that his wife had suffered abdominal trauma with a visceral injury that required her to undergo emergency surgery. It was a serious accident and carried the prospect of a long recovery, if in fact her life could be saved. The following night the patient called again to tell the analyst how he was coping with all that had occurred. The analyst listened carefully but spoke very little. He just listened, with the intention of allowing room for the cathartic need of the patient, while maintaining a position of reticence. As the patient continued talking for another fifteen minutes or so, the analyst interrupted to say that he could not analyse him over the phone. He suggested that the patient come the next day at his habitual time, considering that the hospital was not far from his office. The patient replied that he could not and would not get away from the hospital because he feared for the situation of his wife. He added that he could not even go to his own home for fear that his wife would take a turn for the worse. The analyst insisted that the patient come to his office, given that he could not analyse him by telephone. The analyst could not convince the patient. At that time (1989) there was no latent idea in his mind, nor in the minds of those in the analytic community to which he belonged, that one could have "telephone sessions". The most that an analyst could offer was to listen to a patient without offering any interpretation. Moreover, when taking a phone call from any patient, his *a priori* feeling was that he was speaking outside the setting of a session and therefore was not able to guarantee an analytic attitude regarding the material and hence should not rely on his interpretative ability. He rightly believed that it was only valid to interpret a patient during an analysis session. For this analyst, talking on the phone had a domestic connotation (maintaining a conversation) or a professional one (giving or receiving information).

After hanging up, the analyst felt a terrible void. He felt that his fine-tuned technique was absolutely useless to a patient who was going through perhaps one of the most distressing moments of his life. He asked himself how much this refined technique was really worth if it left the patient isolated from his analysis. He thought well and even though he believed that it contradicted his role as analyst, the next day he went to the hospital to try to locate the patient. He was successful in finding the patient and offered the patient a session in a secluded corner of a café across the street from the hospital. He knew that he was not conducting analysis, although he simultaneously felt that he was helping the patient cope with his anguish. He felt rewarded by carrying out his vocation of aiding the patient.

Years after this experience, the analyst, upon reviewing this clinical situation, understood that in his decision to visit the patient at the hospital, he had left aside the misleading idea of using psychoanalytic technique as a Procrustean bed. He understood, although perhaps not in full detail, that the framework that had been established for this patient was rendered useless due to the special (albeit temporary) situation that he was going through. Therefore, while this situation lasted, there were only two possibilities: one would be to interrupt the analysis due to the impossibility of carrying it out, as he had determined when he interrupted the phone call. The other would be to change the setting for one that would suit the new existential situation that the patient was experiencing.

An innovative decision of such importance is not easy, but by no means should be avoided, assuming that the analyst feels able to face it. In a change like this, the transference field becomes more complex, due to the sporadic addition of other players to the setting—i.e., doctors, nurses, family members. It is also probable that these new players have no idea about the influence they are having on the analyst-patient link.

The case reported deals with a psychoanalytic treatment in a clinical care situation, which may contain infinite variables that analytic theory cannot cover entirely. This patient, in this situation, was not always able to receive transference interpretations or hear the revealing of all the latent feelings contained in the material emitted by him. Although this is an extreme case, we could say that any analytical treatment bears the possibility that there be sessions in which the patient is not able to receive deep interpretations, but rather only psychotherapeutic support, due to the mental state that he/she is going through.

Asbed Aryan (2004), when referring to several situations that clinical experience can bring about, said: "It is recommendable to separate the practice of psychoanalysis from psychoanalytic method. Psychoanalysis is a human science that studies the functioning and the disorders of the psyche of *a person*. Psychoanalytic method is one that takes place between *two people*." As we see, this author highlights the leap from a theoretical concept to its clinical application. Here we have two people in a position of medical reality in which it is possible they will have to pass through labyrinthine paths which must be conceptually contained as possible contingencies, although they cannot be included in detail in the abstract content of a technical concept.

Returning to the clinical vignette, the accident of the patient's wife changed his reality. In situations of this nature that contain sudden and unexpected changes that are experienced as tragedies with the possibility of traumatic after-effects for the patient, the previously established framework is inadequate to cover the new needs and current possibilities of that patient and, therefore, of the analytic dyad. In this case, the patient wanted to continue the analysis with his analyst and a change in framework was carried out in order to establish a new analytic contract for the duration of this circumstantial crisis. This is an example of a model of analysis which has modified the traditional setting, in this case outside the office, without physical distance and "close" to the person of the patient—a very specific example of the need for a change in setting. Technically, it could be categorized as a technical parameter (Eissler, 1953).

Not only does this make the meeting possible, but it also provides an analytic attitude of sincere support and solidarity. In these situations, the analyst is specifically introduced into the material reality of the circumstances of the patient, which spontaneously promotes a contact with the family, which was neither stipulated nor regulated. This type of setting absorbs too much concrete reality immediately to elaborate the latent and symbolic material. One must wonder whether such a contaminated environment can ensure the conditions for free association and free-floating attention. It would seem rather difficult. The patient's anxiety forces him/her to focus his/her attention on the traumatic event, which greatly affects this possibility. As we see in this case, what changes is not only the setting or the analytic situation, but rather both of these analytic postures, which are basic and necessary for establishing an analytic dialogue. A possible solution would be to implement an internal framework in which the analyst, after the session, would be given the opportunity to continue processing what has taken place in it—similar to what occurs with a message that arrives by email. In such situations, the analytic elaboration takes place temporarily in the analyst's mind. The analyst will only inform the patient as to what he/she sees fit and appropriate.

All this shows that when a psychoanalyst treats a patient, in principle he/she should be put to the service of that analysis. However, when this process goes through a special set of circumstances, the need for analysis temporarily shifts to the patient's need to be helped. What does this analyst do if the minimum conditions for the analysis are not met? In such cases, the analyst must recognize the new situation, as well as research and evaluate what the patient needs and is capable of accepting. It is not advisable to stop the treatment although the analyst may have to postpone the offering of some interpretations to the patient. This does not mean that the analyst should stop thinking psychoanalytically about the patient's material, but rather must assess the current situation and the patient's receptive and elaborative timing. The agreed solution at that time and in that environment was valid and appropriate not only given the circumstances but also the resources available. The analyst in this case, although he hesitated at first, immediately rectified his decision. He demonstrated clinical elasticity. This solution, although at that time it was unknown to the analyst, is now widespread and by no means considered "out of place". Furthermore, it yielded positive results. Well known is the boldness and effort that the analyst must exert in order to carry this out and sustain it over time.

For the purpose for which this illustrative case was included in the content of this book, it is not worth going into details as to the content of these sessions. It would suffice to say that the analyst had to maximize his clinical skills in order to overcome all obstacles that the new setting created.

4   Vignette 2

Experience of (a type of) "reality", or delusional experience?

A 21-year-old man had a girlfriend who had emigrated for a few months for a study programme. In an analysis session, he described a unique way of staying in "contact" with her. Every weekend, the two connected to the internet and conversed via "video chat". According to the young man, he and his girlfriend interacted for about five to six hours, and they "shared" a pre-planned lunch in which they both had the same dish. During that time, he said, they talked and did "other things". This latter comment was expressed with a mixture of modesty and irony, adding later in the same vein: "If I cannot do something, I can do something else."

This is exactly what it's all about—using what you can as a substitute for that which is not obtainable. With the everyday application of communication technology, such as a web camera, one manages to feel proximity and even a sense of reality towards something that is not "real" in the traditional sense of the word. This is "another" reality that was experienced by these two people who substituted one thing for another. This is included in the concept of the expression, "half a loaf is better than none". This story refers to the substituting of a classic material reality for an experience of a different type of reality, of which both protagonists were fully aware. The experiences felt by these young people show a *different* reality. The narrated episode *per se* was a reality that produced intense experiences during those hours in front of the screen, in which they emitted and received interactively a package of images, actions, and words full of ideas and feelings, accompanied by gestures.

The perception of what is displayed on the screen produces an experience of reality, notwithstanding the fact that the display is a representation of what happened on the other end of the line. This perceptual experience consists of the amalgamation of what the screen emits and what is processed by the perceiver as a new reality. The perceived image has its origin in a distant place, and it appears as images, colours, movements, and sounds. Moreno (2009) says of these images: "They are known by the contradictory name of 'virtual reality'. I believe that they should actually be called 'computer reality' because they are associated with configurations that have permanently altered the space we inhabit." I would agree with this statement if the author refers to the reality that only took place on the screen. But, when this "computer reality" acts as a mechanism that provides the interaction between two or more persons, and this contributes to promote thoughts, actions, and emotions, we are facing the creation of another reality that does not need adjectives. This, even though it includes "computer reality", in fact exceeds it substantially.

This is an interactive experience in which the mutual influence is in real time. Here, technology participates on one end. On the other, we find the direction and meaning that the mind of this young protagonist gives to all the elements received and the answers that emerge as a result. A similar situation is perceived on the movie or TV screen.

When a TV news reporter puts questions to an interviewee on topics of his/her area of expertise, and the interviewee answers his questions from a screen, we do not doubt the reality of the interview. This would be a replica of the same reality of the experience of the young man with his girlfriend.

When expressing "If I cannot do something, I can do something else", he is showing that he knows that this is another reality. This brings to mind the attitude of children when they play "make-believe". When they take the role of different characters, every child "becomes" this character and gives the same treatment to the characters assumed by the other participants of the game. Nevertheless, no one considers that a child or a theatre actor is delusional when he/she correctly interprets his/her role. This comment is made in response to the question that precedes this section.

5   Vignette 3

Non-conscious motivations involved in requesting distance analysis

A colleague in a situation of clinical supervision described the case of a patient whom he attends by telephone. This patient began her analysis a few months after the death of her father. She currently lives with her family in another country, which is her husband's native land. The country of her upbringing coincides with that of the analyst and is also the country in which her father resided until his death. She has two sons, aged thirteen and fifteen. Her relationship with her father was very conflictive. However, she maintained contact with him through relatively frequent telephone calls. Her father's death was sudden and surprising.

Among the reasons for which the patient had chosen to be analysed by telephone and with this particular analyst were the professional references that he had, and the fact that she wanted to conduct her analysis in her native language. She further stated that she had little trust in the analysts of her place of residence. She defined them as "psychiatrists, not psychoanalysts" and added: "To make matters worse, there are few people where I live and we know each other all too well." Both the choice of analyst and the distance format seemed to be well justified. Furthermore, they were reinforced by two elements which were not consciously connected by the patient at the time of the interviews.

One was the fact that the analyst lived in the same city in which the patient had been brought up and educated, having emigrated seventeen years earlier at the age of twenty-eight, and settled down in her current place of residence, which is her husband's native country.

A few months into the analysis, there was a revelation as to a further unconscious motivation in requesting telephone analysis. It had to do with the fact that she communicated by telephone with her analyst three times a week, and in the same language that she spoke with her father. This had a transference effect, linking the figure of her father with that of her analyst and made her feel that there were still possibilities to resolve the conflictive relationship that she had had with her father, which was cut short by his untimely death.

This illustrative case shows how important it is that the analyst maintain a question mark in his/her latent attitude in order to allow him/herself to be surprised by an unconscious motivation which may have brought about a patient's request for distance analysis. Had this patient not become aware of this, her telephone analysis would have contained a split aspect which would have operated as an unconscious motor in the analytic encounter. This would have caused her mourning process to remain frozen.

6   Vignette 4

Feelings and fantasies of the analyst, which are not subject to countertransference

This is the case of the telephone analysis of a patient living in a small town and in a different continent from that of the analyst. In one session she connected from the home of a relative whom she was visiting. It was a summer day and she spoke from an apartment on the eighth floor with the window open. Suddenly, the wailing of the sirens of several ambulances was heard. The analyst thought they had stopped at the entrance of the building from which the patient was speaking. At that moment, her speech became more withdrawn and lethargic, giving the sensation that she felt curiously attracted by what was happening on the street. The window of the high floor from which she was speaking pointed exactly in that direction. Suddenly, she told the analyst, "Wait a moment, please ...." Shortly afterwards, she returned to the phone and told the analyst that there had been a car accident with injuries in front of her building.

The analyst then thought that if that situation had taken place in front of the building where his office was located, he would not have interrupted the session to find out what was happening on the street. Then it became evident to him that the patient is responsible for 50% of the material aspects of the framework and that he/she will manage it according to the criteria he/she has in mind at all times. The other thing that impacted him emotionally, at a personal level, was that he never ceased to be surprised—or in fact, amazed—by the possibilities offered by modern means of instantaneous communication. He felt that this technology could allow a real event to have sensory impact on two people living in distant places, as if the act itself had acquired the aspect of ubiquity. However, this was not entirely the case. It was due to the signals that were added to the fact itself: the wailing of the sirens and the alteration of the circumstances in which the patient was included caused these events to be simultaneously experienced in two distant places. The analyst was shocked by having experienced the very moment of the accident that had occurred 10,000 km away and by being able to hear the sound of those sirens simultaneously with the patient. Then he asked himself: "Why am I so amazed? The same thing happens with my voice and that of this patient during every session. Obviously, we speak to each-other from the same distance as now." He continued thinking and concluded that only something new to people calls their attention, or at least which people had not become aware of previously.

7   Vignette 5

Disinhibition achieved through telephone analysis

This case describes the situation of a female patient who was treated for nearly three years in her male analyst's office. She believed that the analysis was going very well and that her objective of seeking "qualified" guidance in order to address her everyday problems was being achieved. The analyst, despite the patient's satisfaction, believed that she was defensively camouflaging the transferential link, just as she did in her private life. He believed that the analysis was failing in that regard because it was not helping her break the barriers of her personality. A purely coincidental situation will illustrate this assertion. The patient, two weeks earlier, had agreed to change the schedule of one of her three weekly sessions. The second time she attended the session corresponding to this new time, she became confused and got to the area near the office an hour early. She realized this mistake when approaching the building of the analyst and therefore refrained from ringing the bell. She subsequently decided to walk a bit, so as not to stand there waiting. During this walk, she came across the analyst, who was walking in the opposite direction along the same pavement. Upon seeing her, the analyst raised his head with the intention of saying "Hello". Nevertheless, she walked past him as if nothing and no one were there. This posture did not seem forced, but rather quite natural for her. This episode brings to light the armour she wears when she "walks through life".

A few months later, for work reasons, the patient had to move to a location which was nearly eighty kilometres away from the analyst's office. All concurrent availability changed abruptly. They agreed to a new timetable which was theoretically possible, but very difficult to carry out. This brought about a number of absences and late arrivals to the sessions, which had not occurred previously, and it caused the progress of the analysis to suffer. Given this situation, the patient decided to "suspend"—in her words—her analysis for a time. In fact, six months later, she requested an interview and asked her analyst to consider the possibility of treating her by telephone. This was a patient who was accustomed to a rigorous professional use of the telephone. This seemed very natural to her, and she also clarified that she knew a person who was doing so. The analyst agreed, as he had some experience with this means of implementation. Once this new setting was established, the analyst noted that in the material, there appeared several references to the patient's sex life, as well as thoughts on her love life that she had not previously brought to session. The situation of not being physically near her male analyst automatically enabled her to shed the defensive armour that was previously mentioned. This change allowed her to engage herself more and establish an ambience of comfort in which to speak of intimate topics. However, it is legitimate to conclude that the distance acted as a new set of "armour", which made the previous one unnecessary. She was able to talk about her sexuality, not because she felt more trust in her analyst, but rather because she felt more trust in herself, due to the physical distance from her analyst.

While it is clear that the patient did not shed the armour inherent to her personality, this new option of telephone analysis allowed her to show what had previously been automatically dissociated. It remains to be seen what effect this will produce on all of her defensive apparatus. Time will tell whether she will continue to need it after the process of elaboration takes place on whatever remains locked up in her defensive shell. The new analytic situation, which included facing the analyst under different circumstances, specifically functioned by decreasing the inhibitory defensive problem. However, it should be clear that this is only weakened or disabled as long as that distance remains in place. Nevertheless, it contributes to the possibility of establishing better contact with her inner world and with the analyst, which contributes to making her aware of her inhibitions and making them available to the analytic process.

CHAPTER SEVEN

Clinical psychoanalysis carried out in written form

"Suppose a painter sees a path through a field sown with poppies and paints it: at one end of the chain of events is the field of poppies, at the other a canvas with pigment disposed on its surface. We can recognize that the latter represents the former, so I shall suppose that despite the differences between a field of poppies and a piece of canvas, despite the transformation that the artist has effected in what he saw to make it take the form of a picture, *something* has remained unaltered and on this *something* recognition depends. The elements that go to make up the unaltered aspect of the transformation I shall call invariants."

—*Transformations*. W. R. Bion. (1965)

1   The written word in distance analytic dialogue

The written form of therapeutic communication can achieve considerable importance in clinical experience. This premise justifies that the topic be included in a chapter in this book. This form of treatment includes the written word as a major player in analytic dialogue. It will play a rich, complex, and diverse role. It serves as a first destination to which the ideas born in the mind arrive. As it is used for reasons of conversational exchange, it sets itself up as a container and also as a suitable vehicle for contact for the conversational encounter.

The fact of writing born in the mind simultaneously promotes the objectification of its content, thereby allowing what is written on paper or a computer screen to become an object of knowledge, first for him/her who writes it and then for the addressee. What is written and sent by the patient is the manifest content of the material. It "speaks" for what it says explicitly and for what it may denote. Furthermore, there is the latent content which the analyst can infer in his/her analytic reading. Sometimes, its meaning is found in what it does not say.

Estrada Palma (2009) presented the statistical results of a survey she conducted. Of the thirty-two analysts who responded to her survey, in response to the question as to whether they would continue a psychoanalytic psychotherapy by written chat, six analysts responded affirmatively. In reference to whether they would do so by email, five analysts responded affirmatively.

However, there were different figures in response to the question as to whether they would agree to continue a psychoanalytic treatment by written chat or email. In response to the question regarding psychoanalytic treatment by written chat, three responded affirmatively, and regarding that conducted by email, only one responded affirmatively. Presumably, one of the principal motivations involved in the responses was connected to a pre-established sense of commitment to a patient.

In reference to the willingness to begin a psychoanalytic psychotherapy by written chat or email, the affirmative answers were seven and eight respectively. In contrast, in response to the question of whether psychoanalysis can begin by using written chat, only one answered affirmatively and no one answered affirmatively in reference to email. All the analysts who responded to this survey have vast clinical experience. One could presume that the age group of these analysts surveyed would place them in what Marc Prensky (2001) would call the generation of "digital immigrants". Today, written analysis can be related to the easy access to and simple management of computer communications. It is a practice that seems to be more easily managed by those who have been born and brought up according to the new requirements promoted by current social dynamics. In this social context, distance communication habits have been developed in the youngest generation, the "digital natives". Some of these young people, currently or within a short time, can become psychoanalysis patients. Some may even become analysts themselves. Either of these events will greatly increase the acceptance of analytic dialogue via written chat. As for email, it can be supposed that it will become established as a complementary form of analysis or will occupy only a part of the total process. In Argentina, this therapeutic method has gained some public attention. Andrea Ferrari (2005), a reporter from the newspaper *Página 12* of Buenos Aires, dedicated two pages of the main section of the newspaper to this topic. In this article, she reports on the interviews that she conducted among a number of psychotherapists and psychoanalysts with certain clinical experience in distance treatments.

Currently, the written form of therapeutic communication is being used as an alternative or complementary resource to classically known therapy although it is not always clear *what, how,* and *in whose hands* it is being conducted. The results of this method are also not well known. One might think that the time has come to try to psychoanalytically cover some treatments with this form of therapy and apply a methodology of research in order to fully understand the potential scope of this kind of treatment, as well as its complexities and impediments.

2   Ideas and emotions expressed in writing

It is important to note that the writer understands that the existence of the written word transcends the barrier of the instantaneous. In asynchronous analytic dialogue, written communication is undertaken with the knowledge that the writer will not be present at the time of the reading, and therefore will not be able to explain anything that the reader does not understand. This, of course, contrasts with what would happen in synchronous dialogue. All this will surely have an effect when producing a thought expressed in writing.

Walter Ong (1992), an anthropologist who studies and compares cultures that have not developed written languages with those which have, noted that writing has an effect that goes beyond the mere recording of thought, but in fact also influences and contributes to the self-development thereof.

It is not always easy for the mind to objectify what it produces. At the beginning, the ideas that are created in the thought process operate in the manner of an eye that sees but cannot perceive itself, unless of course a mirror is introduced. This is precisely one of the functions of writing: to mirror one's own thinking. Writing changes the functioning of the human mind, contributing to the task that involves organizing ideas. It is an activity that offers the possibility of greater semiotic precision in that it helps one to think and express oneself clearly. One must write objectively, thereby making it easier for others to inquire about what one thinks about the topic being addressed. Once a thought has been expressed in writing, it creates distance from the thinker, thus allowing him/her to re-examine it with a critical approach. The very act of writing is an activity that promotes thinking. It creates the sensation of a learning experience carried out by travelling through the intricacies and mazes that their action entails. The mere fact of beginning to write brings about a change in the basic attitude in which one elaborates what one feels and thinks, given that it is done with the implicit knowledge that it will be recorded. This will inevitably make the final product different from that which would have come about if it had merely been spoken. Further ahead we will see what effect this has at the moment of expressing oneself, applying the Fundamental Rule.

Writing is like an object with multiple facades and different effects to consider. It can provide an instantaneous and synchronous service, such as that of writing chat on a screen, writing on a white board during a class, or a note that one has written to oneself. In contrast, written material that is to be deferred or read asynchronously is done with the intention of circulating it, much like what occurs in deferred dialogue. Another intention can be to allow it to endure throughout time. As the author will not be present to clarify anything that might not have been understood, this requires more idiomatic resources of expression, a precise and adequate use of vocabulary, correct verb conjugation, and command of correct punctuation.

Due to the linguistic union among users of each language, written forms are presented as words, phrases, or sentences in a coded form representing a more complex idea or thought. Writing may be the record of a spontaneous thought and remain as such. Another possibility is that each written concept be considered to be provisional and at the service of reflective, recurrent, and progressive thinking. In this case, the original thought will fulfil the role of a temporary station or step in order to continue the elaborative process vis-à-vis free association until finally arriving to a concept that is acceptable as a final written version. The graphic aspect of the writing is in itself a concrete object. There is a proverb that says: "Ideas that are not written down evaporate just like drops of water do." The conceptual nature that is "trapped" in writing will only find development or virtualization (Lévy, 1995) if there is a reader who can decode it and perceive the abstract and symbolic content represented by the drawing of its letters. At the moment of reading, the virtualization process of the "encoded" memory contained in the writing begins. The Rosetta Stone is an illustrative example of this type of memory.

In psychoanalytic dialogue conducted by email, the received written material is considered to be the *manifest content*. Then the analyst will carry out a second reading, which allows his/her interpretative inference to "unlock" latent content. This decryption can only be considered as a hypothesis that is put to the test in the elaboration that can be achieved with the patient. As this is a deferred-time dialogue, it is necessary to take this into account when sending an alleged or convincing interpretative statement. It must be stated in a way that is absolutely devoid of ambiguity, but without losing the sense of interpretative hypothesis that needs to be complemented by the patient's elaboration.

Secondary and tertiary processes

The *secondary process*, as understood in psychoanalysis, finds both a container and a tool in the structure and content of the language. The resources of the language serve as auxiliary support at the time of feeling and thinking. They offer the thinking process their vocabulary, as well as their syntactic and grammatical structure. The act of perceiving the writing itself operates as a kind of "feedback" that will somehow influence the thinking process of what was first emanated in its most primitive origin, called "O" by Bion (1965), *primum movens* of the ideas that are later processed. The development of "thinking writing reading this writing rethinking rewriting" implies a permanent re-conceptualization of the first thought that emerged. The fact of re-editing new thoughts while writing adds another step to the secondary process just described and therefore provides greater complexity. This other step can be thought of as a *tertiary process*, which is specific to thought developed in the act of thinking while writing.

3   Writing as clinical material and interpretative input

The contents of the writing sent to the analyst are the patient's core contribution in this epistolary dialogue. One must add the consideration of whether it was submitted within the terms of the framework or outside it. The analyst will, in turn, respond with another piece of writing which will be his/her input. This epistolary "back and forth" makes for an exchange of unique analytic dialogue. As shall be seen, it contains and is structured by several dialogues. The patient, when writing what he/she supposes that he/she feels, is simultaneously recognizing whether what he/she has written agrees or disagrees with his/her original thinking. In this text, the patient longs to objectify in the writing the last step of his/her feeling and thinking. Between the "O" origin, and what the patient accepts as final and submits to the analyst, there is a rectifying and elaborative journey that will not arrive explicitly at its destination unless the elaboration is included in the material. In turn, the objective message sent contains the manifest and latent aspects of the material, thus creating a context of meaning searching for signified.

The writing of the analyst must address several fronts: understanding the manifest meaning of the material received and the latent material that it may contain, including mnemonic and spelling errors, as well as omissions and *lapsus letrae* that are considered significant as unconscious expression or as the voluntary censorship. Finally, when writing his/her interpretative elaboration, he/she must take into account the content and form that are most adequate regarding the timing established by the unique characteristics of each patient. Due to the asynchronous nature of this communication, it is worth repeating that the analyst must be careful not to send a text that lends itself to ambiguity and/or confusion or even to a "conclusion". The interpretations do not conclude an idea but rather should serve to open the possibility of other relevant new ideas.

The opportunity of objectifying what one is thinking or writing creates a kind of "chat" or dialogue with one's own ideas at the moment of producing them, which influences the original thought. Indeed, considering the patient's written participation in this asynchronous dialogue, it is observed that it is preceded by dialogue that occurred in the *Intra space* between the first original idea appearing on the screen and that which was objectified at the time of its reading. While the analyst knows that this happens, he/she does not have any direct details of this process, except for some indirect manifestation. The written record of a spontaneous evocation of the patient may be permanent or simply a fleeting support that leads to another and another, bringing about evocations that at times will be expected and other times may cause surprise. The latter may imply that a conceptual jump has occurred given the new viewpoint that may provoke a different perception. This is similar to what would happen if one were to support one's foot on the stones of a river-bed with the intention of using them as a walkway to cross to the other side. This operation sometimes takes unforeseen turns in that it finds different support stones from those previously calculated, which leads one to take a different path in order arrive at the other side of the river and therefore, when arriving, observe a different panorama than the expected one. Charles Peirce (1931–1958) described that every conceptual object has the possibility of becoming a sign that may represent another object, which in turn can be changed to another sign that represents another object, and so on. He used the term "unlimited semiosis" to refer to this semiotics process in multiple subsequent signified.

Spontaneous thought, once written, offers greater objectivity to be considered, which allows for adjustments, corrections, and/or cancellations. Some of these may be the product of resistance. The analyst will find it difficult to know this directly due to a lack of direct perception in that reflexive process. He/she will only be presented with the latest version of the text received. If one were to take this hypothetical resistance possibility to the extreme, one might even assume that one is analysing a text and not a person. This limitation that the method may present, without wishing to minimize its importance, can be considered and assigned to any method used, including that of the analyst's office. The important thing is to know the specific limits of each method in each specific patient. It is known that the repressive process contains some inefficiencies and that what was repressed tries to escape from its confinement through other manifest means, whether directly or through derivatives of the unconscious. An additional resource will depend on the analyst's own astuteness in detecting what was repressed by "diving" into the latent content of the material and using his/her own countertransference.

4   Technical communication resources

The advent of present-day communication possibilities is *per se* influencing the development of new techniques for distance assistance.

Some of these practices are advertised and offered through an internet portal for psychotherapists who attend from a distance, either individually or as part of a team. Queries are addressed in the form of answers to the central issues raised. Although this only claims to be "psychological orientation", it cannot ignore the circumstances surrounding the reason for the consultation, such as the situational context of the present, the past, and the surrounding social environment. There are other psychotherapeutic practices that yearn to achieve good contact and a good conversational encounter. When the therapists are psychoanalysts, each time the addressed issue includes something that becomes evident in the transference bond, they can identify it and evaluate the best way to implement it.

It has been observed that this innovative approach, as well as those of distance synchronous communication, is likely to receive rational objections. However, it should be mentioned that these methods are not entering timidly or asking permission to establish themselves among the general population. In fact, it tends to be accepted by some as a possible instrument on which to rely when addressing their psychological problems. It also tends to be a resource for some therapists in their clinical work in the field of psychotherapy and psychoanalysis. A form of focal non-psychoanalytic psychotherapy structured with a specific framework to be conducted on the internet is becoming widespread, with the structure of question-response. The one who requests such assistance explains what motivated him/her to seek treatment in this way. The professional then responds, focusing primarily on the topic of the consultation, framed in a number of previously arranged, pre-paid sessions.

In treatments that are conducted in written form, as seen, it is necessary to bring into play the greatest potential of writing, so as to allow what was produced in the mind to come out with the least distortion possible. In principle, we need to ensure that the expressive potential of each of the protagonists of this dialogue is maximized so as to enable his/her thoughts to reach the other in written form without losing the richness of their original meaning. When for reasons of resistance this fails to be achieved, it will not be due to inability, but rather as a manifestation of his/her own neurosis.

In written chat dialogue, specific communication tools are made available. When properly used, they allow for the implementation of new expressive signs, added to the possibility of shorthand abbreviations and simplifications that alter the spelling of words by removing some letters. In fact, over the last approximately fifteen years (in which the use of written chat has been widespread) the form of writing in this field has constantly been taking on new features that tend to shorten the number of characters and the way of representing words and ideas by using acronyms, abbreviations, figures, etc. Another item that has a similar feature is the use of emoticons. For a more precise development of this form of communication and the avatars that a user may apply— outside the therapeutic application of chat—reference can be made to the work of Diego Levis (2005) which, from a sociological perspective provides a brilliant in-depth exposition on the subject of love relationships on the internet and the various forms of graphic expression used to communicate through this medium.

These short- cuts, although good time-savers, are sometimes used improperly or misunderstood. This can decrease the depth of expression by simplifying the complexity and richness that both the words and the grammatical rules provide. These codes transmit messages in which their expressive potential can be affected by the various connotations attached. In this regard, the meanings of the expressive emoticon figurines, as understood by the reader, may differ from the intended denotation set by the writer.

5   Current tasks of the analyst

The beginning of every analysis is an attempt or "bet" that the analysis will be achieved in the very development of its implementation. Major contributors to this are the indication and design of the framework with a specific alignment, such that it harmoniously combines the methodological requirements of the treatment and the patient's realistic possibilities.

The current work of an analyst is reaching a degree of complexity that requires not only good management of the already known concepts of the science, but also attention to the new needs that the gradual transformation of society will demand. If one adopts email as a communicative method, one must also develop a specific skill for the requirements of the method: basic computer skills, skills for expressing oneself through writing, and training in the reading and elaboration of written material in asynchronous time. This last step will help the analyst to better position him/herself in order to detect the "cross-outs" and changes to the original material. Similar considerations, although in lower percentages, are applied to oral and spontaneous material, beyond what its intention was or whether the patient was aware of it. The analyst will not overlook the fact that the ego in its three forms of resistance: repression, transference, and secondary benefit of the illness, can function as an ego of the unknown, so he/she must always be ready to detect this possibility, either in the patient or even in him/herself, notwithstanding the method used.

6   The clinical material and its "transformations"

The quantum of fidelity in the communication process brings us to evaluate the "invariant aspect" found in a transformation (Bion, 1965), being that which legitimizes or nullifies whether the received message contains the core idea that the sender wanted to convey. When the patient and/or the analyst do not possess the minimum capacity necessary to represent in writing what they think and feel, the communication will encounter difficulty and a conversational misunderstanding will occur. A possibility, always latent in the asynchronous communication, is that a "pragmatic distortion" takes place (Liberman, 1970). This would occur when the patient uses the material for other purposes that go beyond the analytic work. There is also the possibility of "semantic distortion" in the received message. This is typical of patients in whom predominate depressive aspects of their personality. They will delve into every word or expression received to determine the quality and amount of affection that the analyst has regarding him/her. In patients with prevailing susceptibility and mistrust, both distortions could occur. They may make improper use of the material by scrutinizing the interpretative text over and over again with the intention of looking for "clues" or signs of an implicit second message. They may also simply give them a distorted meaning as a result of their mistrust. The hashing of the text must be taken into account by the analyst when writing his/her interpretative message, which will surely be read and scrutinized according to the personality traits of each patient or the transference stage that he/she is going through. The written interpretative intervention can be transformed by the patient into an object which is liable to conform to the distortion that he/she is willing or able to give it.

As for the manifest content, if it adequately represents the original idea-affect, the "O" origin, the outcome will provide similar effects to what this author describes about moving from the visual perception of a poppy field to a "canvas with pigment disposed on its surface". Bion carried out a thorough study on this subject in his book *Transformations*. There he describes the similarities and differences between an original object and its representation on the canvas of a painting, as was included as an epigraph to this chapter.

this is not a pipe

Painting by Beatriz Viola.

René Magritte, a distinguished Belgian painter of the last century, was a keen researcher interested in the relationship between reality and its representation. In several of his illustrations included in *"Les mots et les images"* ("Words and images") he warns of the fallacy that could occur when incorrectly linking an object to its representation and, conversely, the representation to what it represented. He questioned the true relationship between images and things when they are viewed from their representative similarity. The painting referred to here is part of a series called *"La trahison des images"* ("The treachery of images") that Magritte painted in the late 1920s. We see an illustration of a painting with a legend provided herein. This painting and its legend invite us to think reciprocally about the similarities and differences that relate the original object with its pictorial representation and the word "pipe". Indeed, in this painting the artist shows us a pigmented canvas set up with shapes and colours that allude to a pipe. Below is a written legend that says: "ceci n'est pas une pipe" ("this is not a pipe"). Magritte not only produced the painting, but also named it "*Pipe*".

Something similar occurs with the image and legend of the pipe included in this book, which is a graphic impression of the original legend by the plastic artist Beatriz Viola, who in turn produced her work with the intention of representing the painting and words of Magritte. These three, although they share the quality of recalling a pipe, are very different. The work of Magritte was inspired by ideological content and is of his own creation. In contrast, the work of Viola is an allusion to that of Magritte and that which is illustrated in these pages is a black and white graphic reproduction of the latter. However, despite all the transformations which have occurred from the original object, something remains in all the paintings—the "invariant" in Bion's terminology—which refers to the original object that they represent—the "pipe". The French word, "*pipe*" and also the English word, "pipe", through conventional language usage, both make reference to the object pipe. However, they are not pipes but rather linguistic symbols that represent them. What can clinical material be, if not simply a representation of the original ideological and emotional content?

The psychoanalytic perspective with which an analyst perceives the material is comprised of his/her free-floating attention and the analytic theories that operate in this perception. As should be noted, it is not a neutral perception. What is referred to as latent content corresponds to what the analyst infers when formulating his/her interpretation. At the moment in which this interpretation is formulated, it takes on some content and shape after having gone through a transformational process of the "O" origin, beginning with the analyst's thinking and ending with his/her writing. We can see that the analyst, in a first moment, operates with the last transformation of the original idea after it has gone through its subsequent presentations and representations stemming from the "O" origin of the thought. The patient's material is influenced by the effect produced by the interpretative hypothesis that came from the analyst. The ideas and feelings that will constitute a written response will surely undergo the transformation process described above, to which will be added the transformations that the process of repression itself produces. Furthermore, there will be the addition of a "tertiary process" operating at the time of transforming one's thinking into writing.

In the field of philosophy, Kant (1781) refers to "noumenon"—in our case the pipe itself—as that which lies outside the framework of a possible experience. One's greatest expectation would be to think of the concept of that thing because it would be impossible to become familiar with it through a sensory experience. From this premise, one can make a comparison. The patient's material that reaches the analyst can be thought of as the transformation of a "thing in itself", comparable to the "O" origin. These two elements share the possibility of only being approachable through their outward manifestations. The "O" origin, can only be revealed in a very indirect way, after a secondary process that is influenced by the nuances of the linguistic style that the used language offers, as well as by the writer's literary skill. Subsequently, a "tertiary process" is added, which produces the successive transformations of the conscious material itself, until it is finally "edited" and sent to the analyst as material. It is appropriate to note and keep in mind that the final material of this type of implementation always includes a much greater review than spontaneous and synchronous material would.

In the mentioned transformations, we must include whatever has been intercepted and crossed out by the patient's unconscious repression and occasionally by his/her intentional censorship. It is well known that clear written expression requires adequate training, and better still if one has some literary skill, so as to include the nuances that a good representation requires. The original thought goes through a transformation process, which is subject to the Italian expression "traduttore ... traditore" ("translator ... traitor").

In Chapter Two we can find a detailed step-by-step description of the virtualization process that transforms voice-delivered material from the "O" origin, until the moment of being pronounced by the patient and perceived by the mind of the analyst. Now we will take this descriptive model and add to it the newly expressed transformative process that occurs in communication via written chat and email. Regarding email communication, we must further add the transformative effect of the *tertiary process*.

In the classic model of analytic supervision, there are more links observed in the chain of transformation. It is known that the material presented, at the moment of being enunciated, has undergone one or more mutations, and probably even some deletions. However, if the transmission preserves the "invariants" of what happened in the session, it can be validated as if it were equivalent. Furthermore, part of the ideological and emotional content that arises in the supervisor (for countertransference) is addressed for elaboration, although it has not had direct contact with the patient but rather with the "invariant" aspects transmitted. Grinberg (1986) goes even further. He considers that everything discussed at a supervision meeting, no matter how separate or marginal to the patient that it appears to be, could possibly be considered a metaphorical allusion to something brought from the session for the purpose of supervision.

Something similar might be considered for the reports of clinical material included in the records presented in publications in various scientific fields. They are seen as a reliable representation of what occurred in a session, although it is known that transformations have occurred, including the necessary deformations made in order to conceal the patient's identity.

As for the legitimacy of experiences achieved during the reading of written material, what has been stated can also apply to everyday life experiences. When reading a compelling article, the interest that arises is due not only to its content, but also to its communicative effectiveness, which manages to permeate the reader and enthuse him/her. Another noteworthy factor is the timing involved in the delivery of the article, so that its content and circumstances fit well with the reader and thereby stimulate his/her interest.

Contact made with ideas stemming from a recording, written material, or a figure, if they were well presented, can be felt as real and never virtual in the conventional sense of the term. The ideas are abstract and without concrete materiality. They need a container from which to be offered. If this container has the quality of being long-lasting, then it does not misinterpret the idea contained in it or rob it of the quality of being real. Books are among the greatest examples of this. A recorded message—oral or written—such as the allegorical painting of Magritte, the graphic image of a logo, or an audio signal, are not ideas in themselves but rather only in their symbolic content. Each of these mediators operates as a connector between the original idea and the receiver. From the idea, to its representation, and finally to the perceiver, a process of transformative "virtualization" takes place. At the beginning of the process, it moves in a certain direction until reaching a symbolic representative object, from which it will begin a reverse trip from there to the subject who perceives it. This subject faces and considers this object as if it were a real yet primitive object in *status nascendi*. Is there any magic involved in being able to pronounce a word or a more complex expression and have another person understand it without manipulating the object or the concept which is being expressed? A simple diagram will illustrate this:

Original object→subject 1 codifier→object symbolic→subject 2 decoder→original object

When an anxiously awaited letter arrives and gives written news, it is received with the feeling that the person who sent it was only a metre away. The reading of its content produces the subjective sensation of feeling great proximity with the writer although he/she is distant in terms of both time and space. Even the ontological quality of the object (letter)—the paper it is written on—is totally different from that of the person who sent the letter. Nevertheless, the experience may be created in which the sender of the letter and the written message form a unit of common identity. Although in different places and times, the written message is present in both places. At both ends of the communication, the writing played the role of representing the ideas and feelings that were present in the mind of the one who wrote it.

7   Specific qualities depending on the method used

a   email

The use of email as a container and vehicle of psychoanalytic communication provides the analyst with a material that is already defined because its participation is not simultaneous, but rather of successive emission. It is profitable for an interpretative reading which will receive analytic intervention in deferred time. Any material emitted by email is generally saved after being read. Sometimes it can be used to observe the overall development of treatment. Although the possibility of perceiving intonation and other aspects of verbal communication are absent, it may eventually be supplanted by the wealth of vocabulary and the proper use of grammar and expression that written language provides. As the communication is not synchronous, the material loses the opportunity of being subjected to questions or the interpretative interventions of the analyst. However, it gains in spontaneity and expressive identity.

The transformations that contain materials of successive emission and reception have already been described.

In this type of communication, some patients may acquire the habit of exposing ideas extremely carefully and sensibly. This automatically leads to the nullification of all that the Fundamental Rule asks of the patient. For this type of analytic exchange, the possibility of freely expressing one's occurrences is close to nil. The analyst will take this into account and therefore have another "perceptive lens" when reading and interpreting the material.

The motivation and analytic spirit that the analytical dyad puts into this method will have an effect on the perspective that will be configured in the therapeutic relationship. Both are placed in a situation of working analytically in a format whose methodology puts that of classic analysis aside. However, the concept of "material" as what is expressed by the patient and that of "interpretative intervention" as what is written by the analyst still have significance.

The Fundamental Rule and "free-floating attention" continue to be significant although they take the structure and shape that the method requires in clear harmony with what it offers.

α   The fundamental rule

The premises arising from the Fundamental Rule for spoken language are not adaptable to this method. Therefore, the method must find its own coherent ways. Asking the patient to write down everything that comes to mind without stopping or correcting anything is a model copied from another type of communicative operation. The benefits of such writing should not be ruled out when it comes to an exercise used for specific purposes or when the patient sees fit, regarding his/ her own occurrences. For example, the patient can syntactically write those ideas or loose words that come to mind regarding this or that issue. This would apply to associations about a dream, a slip, or an occurrence that took on a certain significance that justifies practising a brainstorming exercise, which to some degree mitigates the obstruction of spontaneity. This type of writing exercise may be born spontaneously or be proposed by the analyst or the patient him/herself. In the communicative freedom of synchronous sessions, the associations flow spontaneously while the patient speaks. The patient makes associations without realizing that he/she is doing so.

β   Free-floating attention

The free-floating attention, in principle, operates similarly to that of synchronous conversational dialogue. The analyst remains in a state of perceptive neutrality with the intention of not becoming anchored in the manifest aspect of the written text, so as to be able to delve into the primary process that spawned it. This implies placing him/herself in the position of carrying out an unbiased reading of the material and of the patient. It will furthermore take the analyst closer to the basic idea of paying attention "without memory or desire", which was postulated by Bion (1967). Positioning oneself in this way before the reading of the material is very difficult, but should still be attempted, although it may not always be appropriate or necessary. In ideal terms it is impossible to achieve, and in real terms this positioning can be achieved in coincidence with the *analytic attitude* of the analyst at that particular moment. For example, it would be achievable if at the moment of reading the material the analyst were located in the proper place, time, and circumstances. This would create an "ad hoc" setting for this type of diachronic psychoanalysis, which does not take place in the simultaneity that a session offers.

γ   The analytic setting in diachronic communication analysis

Where, when, and how does the analytic process take place?
Due to the fact that there is no classic analysis session in treatments conducted by email, the material will be better addressed if the analyst fully understands the transformative sequence that the received material has undergone. Here is a sequence: the birth of an idea ("O") → successive transformations until its written manifestation in the significant format and lexicon provided by the language used → transmission of the material to the analyst → reading and elaborative interpretation of the material → written interpretation → transmission to the patient, and so on—i.e., with a structure involving a diachronic series of events. This lack of simultaneity does not form a period of time for reading, elaboration, and interpretative intervention. It is for this reason that the analyst must allow for a geographic space and an "ad hoc" time for the analysis of the material. In order to acquire the status of "material", the written text should be read in a situation that constitutes the proper analytic setting in order to allow the analyst to perceive the latent content of the written material. Only in an environment

created with these characteristics will it be possible for the analyst to use free-floating attention in order to perceive analytic material in the written text, as well as enter into an analytic attitude and analytic frame of thinking. In this deferred meeting, each member of the analytic dyad works independently, although with the influence of the previous message and presence of the other member in mind. What prevails, as would be expected, is the dominant transference sign at each moment of the elaboration.

It has already been noted that the substance of the analytic process occurs mainly in the minds of its protagonists—that is to say, in their *Intra space*. Each one contributes from his/her role, in an "ad hoc" setting that each one has been able to create and exploit. Due to the absence of simultaneous encounter in email treatments, no analysis session takes place. The *Inter space* takes on a unique characteristic. It circulates in the content of the material sent and received by email. In this material, a conceptual net has been woven in which the received material serves as the intrigue and the response serves as the plot (Cabanne & Petrucci, 1988). The degree of *presence, contact,* and *encounter* of the analytic dyad will depend on the expressive quality offered by the patient and the proper perception and decoding of the analyst.

b   Written chat through the internet

Messages sent by written chat contain more spontaneity and urgency of response than those sent by email. They are sent and received in real time. The instantaneous nature of this communication does not allow for elaborative re-edition or corrective censorship. The material, from its "O" origin, would only pass through the inevitable transformation or secondary process already described in reference to email, which involves the moving of thought *in status nascendi* until it is finally reflected in a written message. Additionally, the computer will offer the option of using emoticons and stenographic abbreviations. Written chat, just like telephone conversation, does not allow for visual perception of the other, unless of course a webcam is used. However, the possibility of analysis and synthesis for both the participants' minds remains intact: "Out of sight, but not out of mind," according to Sharon Zalusky (1998). The visual pathway is made for the perception of the material received and that which is being written. This type of written communication allows for simultaneous visualization of the words at the moment in which they are being written, giving one the opportunity to objectify the writing.

Written chat for the purpose of psychoanalysis involves transfers which have been preconceived regarding this type of communication and that come from other situations which are similar, but not analytic. It is known that many may feel doubt and mistrust due to the preconception that written chat dialogue allows for the possibility of lying about one's identity and/or pretending to be someone else by using his/her *nickname*. In common internet chat—outside psychoanalysis—many times people will chat with someone who is unknown and therefore, in an *a priori* sense, considered untrustworthy (Levis, 2005). However, due to the brevity and low significance of the exchange, the person who is chatting may not give this much importance. Such experiences can occur in a transference sense at the initial period of a treatment conducted through written chat.

α   The fundamental rule

All the basic points referring to telephone communication are valid. Regarding the considerations referring to treatment by email, and therein lies the difference, one can consider that the chance of a tertiary process in the writing is quite meagre. As we have already said, this communication requires more spontaneity and expressive haste.

β   Free-floating attention

It is basic knowledge in psychoanalysis that free-floating attention offers the best conditions for achieving adequate psychoanalytic perception. It allows for the perforation of the dividing line between conscious and unconscious. Free-floating attention provides a perceptive freedom that will help the analyst to "extract" inferences regarding the *latent* content of the manifest material emitted by the patient. His/her mind perceives as material not only what is present in the written words, but also:

a. in the form of typing: emoticons, abbreviations, *lapsus letrae*, etc.,
b. in the omissions it may contain,
c. in the speed in which the material is received, if anything is suggested by that,

d. in the associative pertinence or in an evasive attitude,

e. in the context that accompanies the analytic situation, including the macro-context regarding socio-political-economic-family-work aspects, as well as others that may be more personal.

In summary, the situation of the patient and the circumstances surrounding the written material are taken as a communicative unit.

8   Privacy conditions

In reference to the private and intimate content of the messages that are sent in the treatments that take place via email, it is necessary to ensure their authenticity and that they can only be read by the intended party. Therefore, some precautions must be taken. One must verify that the address is correct and prevent the message being read by anyone else. On this basis, it is necessary that at the end of the page, there be a clarification as to the analytic objective of the content and that the use and/or circulation of the material for other purposes would constitute the committing of a violation of privacy of correspondence and of professional secrecy. It is necessary to add to this provision that its content only has value within the context in which it was produced and that it cannot be used as a document for purposes other than those for which it was issued.

In order to ensure the inviolability of the content and of the reading of the written material, nowadays one can send it as an attachment in Adobe PDF and establish the need for a password to open it. It is advisable to have a digital signature or, if it is manual, to scan it. These preventive measures are related to the potential use as testimony that could be put to the material, either by the patient or others around him/her and/or as evidence for legal purposes.

The following is a text that may serve as a basic model of warning as to the violation of privacy and also of legal prevention.

PRIVACY NOTICE

All the conceptual and informational content of this document is strictly confidential. This text is covered by the obligation of professional secrecy. It is sent for the exclusive use of the addressee, and only for specific use. It cannot be allocated for administrative and/or legal purposes. If you are not the intended addressee, I apologize for any inconvenience. You are hereby notified that the

9   Self-analysis

Performing an act of introspection using free-floating attention or capturing any spontaneous occurrence itself, a slip, or a dream for analytic purposes places a person in a situation of self-analysis. The results of this reflective activity that was carried out by Freud have always been recognized as an important contribution to the building of the foundations of psychoanalytic theory. It is very difficult to imagine this activity without the aid of reflective writing. Material arising from Freud's dreams provoked his interest in inquiring about his unconscious, taking himself as the object of his research. The book *The Interpretation of Dreams* and its first discoveries about infantile sexuality were written in conjunction with the systematic self-analysis that, according to Ernest Jones (1953), began in the summer of 1897, although this same author also records that the first time that Freud analysed one of his dreams completely was in July 1895. This synchronicity between his self-analysis and the simultaneous writing of issues that constitute the fundamental pillars of psychoanalysis provides an additional contribution to linking self-analysis to writing. The method of writing clearly serves as a support for recording what one becomes conscious of and allows it to be used for future discoveries. His memories, spontaneous occurrences, and dreams were taken as manifest material for Freud's self-analysis. Something from his mind shaped the material as a dialogue between him and the written record of his own thoughts, which were simultaneously put onto paper. Some of these written "dialogues" were carried out between himself and Fliess, with the purpose of further developing both the previous issues, as well as new hypotheses. These were the product of his relentless analytic elaboration.

When writing for self-analytic purposes, a structure is established in which one's own evocative occurrences are recorded in a specific space of time. The psychoanalytic part of the personality reads and elaborates what was written. It does so in search of meaning. This kind of "session" can be programmed as an ad hoc place of time, space, and circumstances. It can also coincide with other spontaneous moments that occur throughout the day, regarding occurrences that motivate addressing them analytically. As can be seen, when writing down the development of one's own self-analysis, the writing becomes a functional and auxiliary extension of one's own mind, as well as an "other", which is necessary for the dialogue. Spontaneous occurrences or those which have already been thought are transformed into writing and then return to the mind. This occurs again and again with the intention of reprocessing what is already known or which arises at that same moment.

Something similar to this last situation occurs with self-analysis of countertransference, in which the analyst often writes down his occurrences when an isolated mental operation is insufficient. It is almost impossible to imagine a comprehensive self-analysis which was free of writing. Here, the self-analysing subject finds the first possibility to objectify on his/her thoughts about his/her conflicts, dreams, and occurrences in his/her free and spontaneous association digression. Sometimes this operation is preceded by the utterance of these ideas in a loud voice in an attempt to achieve further objectification of their content. This also allows the ideas to be put in a situation of dialogue, given that hearing them as if they were coming from outside allows the imaginary creation of the analyst-patient dyad.

Regarding writing about oneself, I recall my own adolescent diary, which I now consider to have served the purpose of a primitive self-analysis. It was made up of a group of units connected by successive writings, many of which were preceded by readings and re-readings of previous units that were designed to allow for moments of reflective self-knowledge. The procedure consisted of first writing free and spontaneous occurrences, and then reading them to see where those reflections led me. Each opportunity for writing and reading was far from the previous one. Several days later I read what I had written about myself. This second round was very productive for the reflections—"interpretations" that my previous writings allowed me to make. When I could not identify with the content of the reading, I had an opportunity to process it again.

Spontaneously writing the thoughts that come to mind is also practised by some people as a method of unloading and of objectification of an experience. At a later time, stripped of the emotional climate in which it was written, it may serve as a testimony to the subjectivity of the ideas previously put into writing. This is similar to the personal story to which reference has just been made.

10   Acceptance and/or indication

Regarding analysis conducted via email, one does not only consider the distance at which the patient resides. Rather than regarding this as a strict indication, we may consider its feasibility for situations in which a person proposes being analysed through writing. In this case, one must ask oneself what purpose this method serves for the person who has solicited it and what results it may have. When requested by someone who feels that he/she expresses his/her inner feelings best in written form and has previous analytic training, the request for asynchronous analysis carried out in written form may be acceptable for a limited segment of a person's analysis. It is difficult to conceive of a complete analytic process conducted exclusively in this way, and it would therefore only be justified in very specific cases that so warrant.

Another very valid possibility would be to include analysis through writing as part of a treatment, alternating it with another synchronous method, whether this be conducted in the analyst's office or by telephone. What would change with this mixed method? Synchronous processing of the material adds the option of a simultaneous approach to the reflective occurrences, thereby giving the opportunity for the interpretations to be co-processed in simultaneous time by both members of the analytical dyad.

Writing *about* oneself is also a way of writing *to* oneself, although the communication is addressed to an analyst as one's interlocutor. It grants the opportunity to adopt a reflective attitude, which is a basic condition for accommodating a psychotherapy or psychoanalysis. It may help a wide variety of patients by putting a waiting period between impulse and action. The *sine qua non* requirement is that one has the necessary writing skill in order to put in writing what one feels and thinks.

Now that these comments have been made, we will register some specific applications of the method, although not with the purpose of excluding others that may also be pertinent. A perspective of good results can be found in the situations listed below:

1. As has already been described, as a method of self-analysis.
2. As one of the possible ways of conducting a follow-up on patients after ending his/her analysis. This agreement or recommendation foresees a promising result in that it can be assumed that the patient

already has a certain self-analytical capacity. Different types of instructions are likely to be made:

a. establishing a certain periodical frequency between the sending of emails;

b. allowing the patient to take every opportunity to write, without indicating how or when, but rather leaving it up to the discretion of the patient;

c. allowing for free choice as to the most suitable use of the written text. That is to say, it could be saved, sent to the analyst, or taken to a follow-up interview in order to be commented on, bearing in mind the sequential structure of its content.

3. In cases of patients who have little chance of establishing regular meetings with an analyst and in which excessive downtime detaches the patient from any attitude of analytic reflection. The act of writing, although an asynchronous connection with the analyst, finds synchronicity in the patient's need for analytic scrutiny. The one who writes in these conditions, although he/she may be positioned in an attitude of self-analysis by being in a therapeutic relationship with an analyst, albeit at a distance, will allow his/her mind to serve as host to the analyst's transference.

4. If an illness or other justified reason prevents the patient from going to the analyst's office, both telephone implementation (Zalusky, 1998) and writing methods—synchronous chat or asynchronous email—may be valid temporary substitutes. These coincidental and temporary situations that allow treatment to continue at a distance can be thought of conceptually as a "technical parameter" (Eissler, 1953).

5. As an additional element that gives structure to the analysis. A part of the analysis can take place in the office and another can be carried out through asynchronous writing. This moment of writing about oneself can serve as a way to "hold on" until the next session, or as a proposal that fosters self-observation and reflective thinking as opposed to an impulsive possibility.

6. Suitable for the hearing-impaired. This method can even be carried out in the analyst's office by conducting written chat between computers when the analyst does not know or has not mastered sign language.

CHAPTER EIGHT

Public and private law considerations of distance psychoanalysis[1]

Ricardo Carlino and Julian Hermida

1 Can psychoanalysis be conducted without knowing the full identity of the patient?

From a legal point of view, it is not advisable to treat a patient without knowing his/her full identity. Each time an analyst and a patient agree to carry out treatment, they both place themselves in a situation of facing potential legal liability. The analyst must disclose his/her full name, university degrees, professional licence, and address—both geographic and electronic. In turn, the patient must disclose his/her full name, age, gender, and address.

When the analyst and patient reside in different countries, the analyst should be aware of the laws in his/her own country, the applicable laws in the patient's country of residence, and the Private International Law rules on conflict of laws of both.

Should there be a lawsuit, whether it be in the analyst's country, the patient's country, or even a third country, the court that receives the lawsuit must first determine whether it has jurisdiction to accept it. Subsequently, the substantive rules, i.e., those rules applicable to the case, must be established. The court that accepts the claim must also determine the procedural rules, i.e., those which will govern the case. In most cases, procedural rules coincide with substantive rules.

a. *Procedural rules*: those that set the regulations governing proceedings before the courts. For example, the rules that determine who may appear as a witness or the specific requirements applicable in filing a claim.

b. *Substantive rules*: those that determine the rules applicable to a case. For example, the rules applicable to a malpractice lawsuit that determine that a physician who has caused harm to a patient must compensate for said damage.

If a patient who resides in a country which is different from that of the analyst files a malpractice lawsuit in the country of the latter, and if the court accepts this lawsuit, it is very likely that the procedural and substantive rules adopted will be those of that country. However, it may also be the case that the procedural rules differ from those of substantive law.

Continuing with the foregoing example, it could occur that the claim is filed before a court in the country in which the patient resides. In this case, the judicial process will be governed by the *procedural rules* of the law of that country. On the other hand, in order to resolve the substantive issue, the substantive rules of the country of the analyst may apply.

The applicability of the substantive rules in each case depends on the content of the rules of Private International Law of each country. According to the preceding example, one must identify what the rules of Private International Law prescribe in both states. If both agree on the applicable law, it will be this law that governs the conflict. If they differ, the applicable law must be determined by analysing the existing rules and principles of Private International Law regarding the resolution of such conflicts.

As a way of illustration, in Argentina for contractual disputes, the rules of Private International Law refer to the law chosen by the parties in the contract, the law of the execution of the contract, or the law of the performance of the contract. Argentine courts have established that the law of the performance of contracts related to mental health services is that in which the non-monetary performance is carried out, i.e., the jurisdiction of the analyst's residence.

In jurisdictions that follow English Common Law, one can generalize the following situation. In the very unlikely event that the patient and analyst agree on the law governing their contract, it shall be that law that will govern the relationship. In contrast, in the much more common situation in which no such arrangement is made, the law of the state that has the strongest connection with the contract shall have jurisdiction. In common law, it is considered that this jurisdiction is the place in which the contract is performed.

A third aspect to be taken into account, in addition to the jurisdiction and conflict rules of Private International Law, is that related to the recognition and enforcement of a foreign court decision. It may happen, for example, that a patient who resides in Scotland (where both the jurisdiction and the substantive rules are those of that country), decides to sue his/her analyst, who lives in another country, for malpractice. If the court rules in favour of the plaintiff, he/she must endeavour to make the courts of the analyst's country recognize and enforce the ruling, since it is very probable that the analyst has no assets or money in the plaintiff's jurisdiction, but rather only in his/her own country of residence. For these situations, there are specific legal rules governing recognition and enforcement of court decisions. In summary, such a ruling will be recognized unless:

a. The court of the analyst's country determines that the foreign state has no jurisdiction over the dispute according to the laws of the state where recognition is sought;
b. There has been fraud in the proceedings;
c. The ruling contradicts the public laws of the state. Some states, such as France, demand a fourth requirement. This additional requirement conditions the recognition of the foreign ruling to the existence of reciprocity agreements signed by the involved states.

Thus far, we have discussed the general procedural law and rules that can govern professional clinical activity when it is performed in different countries.

However, in cases in which the law specifies that professional services are subject to the law of the country where the services are held, the following question immediately arises.

2   In which country are the psychoanalytic activities carried out?

As we have seen, this question can be answered based on the fact that the choice of law agreed upon in the contract determining which jurisdiction will govern any potential conflict will be the binding law.

But this law is only valid if it does not contradict the rules of public order in one or both of the countries involved. Beyond the legal aspect, this topic is discussed in detail in Chapters Four, 1; Four, 5 α; and Seven, 6 γ.

3 Tax obligations

From a non-legal perspective, one would speculate that the contract takes place in the state where the analyst is physically present. Let us remember that, for psychoanalysis, distance analytic treatments are implemented with the premise that each member of the analytic dyad is responsible for half of the material aspects involved. We can say that distance analysis is carried out in a "space" that is devoid of nationality and beyond any criteria of geographic identification. However, from a legal perspective, this is not the case.

It is necessary to bear in mind that the logic of the analyst in considering these issues may agree or differ, either totally or partially, with the legal criteria. Legal logic is based on a method of reasoning that involves laws applied by courts in a way which the analyst generally ignores.

It is important to understand that the principles in the codes of ethics of the professional associations to which analysts belong may not always have legal validity. They function as private agreements that only require adherence for members in order to belong to the association. However, in many countries membership to professional associations may be a requirement to be admitted to work as a psychoanalyst. This can be taken into account by a court at the time of sentencing, provided that these rules do not conflict with local law.

The legal considerations concerning sessions conducted via communication technology could raise some concerns among professionals about potential legal problems. This is due to the fact that the existence of these sessions is likely to be corroborated. In light of these considerations, it is important to remember the "real" character of this dialogue.

One must keep in mind that the electronic or written telephone registry can constitute a document. In a lawsuit, a court may decide whether or not it has evidentiary value. There is a possible risk involved in the recorded material of the session. This can be used by a family member to learn about issues that the patient was not willing to include in his/her everyday dialogue. This can produce an unexpected conflict. This is in sharp contrast to the dialogue that takes place in an analyst's office given that the only recorded material would exist in the patient's own mind. The patient or even a family member could eventually decide to use recorded material to initiate a lawsuit.

An interpretation is a hypothesis that will or will not be validated by the subsequent elaboration that would result. The value of the interpretative statement given by the analyst may be either ephemeral or wide-ranging. For his/her psychoanalytic work, this distinction is not significant because what emerges in the dialogue stems from the deep complexity that is provided by the situations, circumstances, and history. The analyst's messages are included in a conversational mass, which are in a situation of *becoming*, rarely in one of *being*. What the analyst says is aimed as part of a larger whole: the psychoanalytic process. When the analyst interprets the patient, he/she does not say, *you are this ...*, but rather, *you are now doing this ...*. This view is valid for the time and circumstances, but often ephemeral due to the transformation exerted by the evolution operating throughout the analytic process, which helps the patient to transform this into another quality that, although it is stated with the conceptual umbrella of *you are now doing this ...*, is something new and different from the foregoing, governed by the "here and with me now", and so forth at each new moment.

A patient can keep recorded testimony (voice, video chat, or written) of a session in which a contentious issue was dealt with. This issue may be in reference to someone who has a connection with the patient, albeit distant. It may also be an issue involving the analyst, or it may simply contain some general confidential information. This material could eventually be used by the patient or someone of his/her acquaintance for legal purposes. Any session in which the confidentiality has been lost can be used by the patient's family to litigate against him/her if the content of the session involves him/her in a way that could merit that action.

Thus, it would be advisable for the analyst to take precautionary measures for his/her legal security. However, these are not easily applicable in the clinical practice of psychoanalysis. The success of analysis stems from the premise that the dialogue is supported by mutual trust. In in-office sessions there are also risks, although they must rarely be taken into account, given that they only arise in specific situations. This comment suggests that it is very necessary to focus one's attention on an issue linked to the development and maintenance of a sense of basic trust, which is valid both for in-office treatments and those carried out through any means of communications technology. In the former, one has the feeling, at times misleading, that he/she can "look the other in the eye" and therefore raise the degree of trust much more than in distance treatments.

Concomitant to this, it is also necessary to discourage the analyst from taking excessive precaution for each particular case due to the fact that doing so may frighten the patient or even cause him/her to distrust the analyst.

The so-called "informed consent" (Highton & Wierzba, 1991) may be a contribution to this problem although its wording should be designed so that it can be fully understood by the patient.

Other precautionary measures can be taken, such as creating ad hoc diagnostic tools that can be taken at a distance in order to be as sure as possible as to what kind of person the patient at the other end is.

From the foregoing, a couple of questions may arise:

a. When conducting distance psychoanalysis, does the degree of legal risk increase? The ability to record the sessions increases this possibility.
b. Is it possible and/or desirable to psychoanalyse someone without having interviewed him/her *face-to-face* in the analyst's office? As a conceptual answer, refer to Chapter Five, section 4: "What and who can be considered known or unknown patients?"

4   Criminal matters

Although less frequent than matters involving contracts, torts, and taxes, a distance treatment could also give rise to criminal matters. Such is the case if a patient were to commit suicide for something that the psychoanalyst did, said, or failed to do. In this case, criminal prosecution would take place in the country which has criminal jurisdiction over the incident. In criminal law, territorial jurisdiction prevails, i.e., the state in whose territory the crime took place. In common law countries, in order to determine jurisdiction for alleged crimes that are not committed entirely in the territory of one state, there are three determining legal principles. They are: the doctrines of ubiquity, objective jurisdiction, and subjective jurisdiction. The first one allows the state to assume jurisdiction over the offence if it causes effects or consequences in the territory of the state concerned. The subjective jurisdiction doctrine, which applies in countries such as Canada and New Zealand, authorizes the state to initiate criminal proceedings when any activity or element of the crime takes place in the state. The objective doctrine allows the state to assume jurisdiction when the effects of the crime take place in the state in which the crime is completed.

Several countries of the civil law system, i.e. the legal system that derives from Roman law and predominates in continental European countries and their former colonies, such as Argentina, Brazil, and Uruguay, follow the principle by which crimes committed in their territory or whose effects are produced in that territory are subject to criminal jurisdiction. This can give rise to a situation in which more than one state has criminal jurisdiction. These cases are generally resolved according to which state first initiates criminal prosecution or which has jurisdiction over the accused.

Once the state determines that it will exercise criminal jurisdiction, if the accused is not physically present in that territory, the trial may take place *in absentia*, i.e., without the accused's presence. This will take place in countries that specifically contemplate this possibility.

It may also occur that the state which intends to prosecute the accused initiates the extradition procedure to bring the accused to its territory in order to prosecute him/her.

Endnote

1. This chapter was written in association with Dr Julian Hermida, LL.M, DCL (McGill University), assistant professor of law, Algoma University, Canada.

EPILOGUE

In this work, as one might expect, I have not been able to register all my thoughts on the topic due to the fact that some of these ideas are still emerging or are in a state of spontaneous occurrences that come and go. That is to say, they have not yet been methodically processed, which gives rise to the Latin expression: *verba volant, scripta manent* (spoken words fly away, written words remain).

I have tried to convey the product of both conceptual experience and life experience that I have acquired in hours of distance analysis. This experience has also been promoted in various scientific presentations, panels, discussion groups, and presentations at international congresses, symposia, and workshops. It is also the product of dialogues with colleagues in supervising both their own clinical material and that of others who are interested in this issue.

While there are always elements to consider regarding the possible twists and turns that any rich and complex topic like this entails, I believe that those which have been developed here are sufficient so as to enable an analyst with sufficient clinical experience to initiate distance psychoanalysis. However, much remains to be done and to be written.

A systematic research of these methods within each psychoanalytic institution will bring life to all that has yet to be expressed.

The ideas presented here are constantly going through systematic research and are attentive to the criticisms and the results that will be reported regarding their multiple clinical implementations.

REFERENCES

Anderson, G. (2009). Telephone analysis. Panel at 46th IPA Congress, Chicago, July 29–August 1.

Argentieri, S. & Amati Mehler, J. (2003). Telephone "analysis": Hello, who's speaking? *Insight*, 12(1): 17–19. Available: www.ipa.org.uk/Files/media/PrevSite/Docs/NewsMagazines/IPA_ENG_12.1.pdf

Aryan, A. (2004). Setting ¿Cambios o transformaciones? Reconsideración del encuadre y de la transferencia-contratransferencia a la luz de las modificaciones tecnológicas (Setting, changes or transformations? Reconsideration of the framework and the transference-countertransference in the light of technological changes). Workshop at 43rd IPA Congress, New Orleans, March.

Aryan, A. & Carlino, R. (2009). Análisis por teléfono. Panel at 46th IPA Congress, Chicago, July 29–August 1.

Aryan, A. & Carlino, R. (2010). Desafíos *del* y *al* psicoanálisis contemporáneo. Vicisitudes de lo establecido frente a lo nuevo que va surgiendo. El psicoanálisis telefónico. Paper at VI APU Congreso Internacional y Multidisciplinario, Montevideo, Uruguay, August.

Baranger, M. & Baranger, W. (1961). La situación analítica como campo dinámico. *Revista Uruguaya de Psicoanálisis*, 4(1): 3–54.

Barrena, S. & Nubiola, J. (2007). Charles Sanders Peirce. In: F. Fernández Labastida & J. A. Mercado (Eds.), Philosophica: Enciclopedia filosófica on line (5). Available: http://www.philosophica.info/archivo/2007/voces/peirce/Peirce.html

Berenstein, S. P. de. & Grinfeld, P. (2009). Análisis por teléfono, análisis por Skype. Panel at 46th IPA Congress, Chicago, July 29–August 1.

Bion, W. R. (1957). Differentiation between psychotic and non psychotic personalities. International Journal of Psychoanalysis, 38: 266–275.

Bion, W. R. (1962). Learning from Experience. London: Heinemann. Reprinted in Seven Servants (1977). Reprinted, London: Karnac, 1984.

Bion, W. R. (1963). Elements of Psycho-Analysis. London: Heinemann. Reprinted in Seven Servants (1977). Reprinted, London: Karnac, 1984.

Bion, W. R. (1965). Transformations. London: Heinemann. Reprinted in Seven Servants (1977). Reprinted, London: Karnac, 1984.

Bion, W. R. (1967). Notes on memory and desire. Psychoanalytic Forum, 2(3): 271–280. In: E. Bott Spillius (Ed.), Melanie Klein Today, Vol. 2, Mainly Practice (pp. 17–21). London: Routledge, 1988.

Bleger, J. (1967). Psicoanálisis del encuadre psicoanalítico. Revista de Psicoanálisis, 24(2): 241–258.

Bleger, J. (1973). Criterios de curación y objetivos del psicoanálisis. Revista de Psicoanálisis, 2: 317–342.

Brainsky, S. (2003). Adapting to, or idealizing technology? Insight, 12(1): 22–24. Available: www.ipa.org.uk/Files/media/PrevSite/Docs/NewsMagazines/IPA_ENG_12.1.pdf

Cabanne, J. & Petrucci, H. (1988). La urdimbre y la trama. Psicoanálisis, 10(1): 185–196.

Cantis-Carlino, D. (2007). Soñar con el número 230 y deseo de vivir. Psicoanálisis, 39(1): 15–19.

Cantis-Carlino, D. & Carlino, R. (1987). Diálogo analítico: Un diálogo múltiple. Psicoanálisis, 9(3): 151–172.

Carlino, R. (1981). Experiencia clínica de un final de análisis. Promotion paper to be accepted as Associated Member of APdeBA, Buenos Aires, Argentina.

Carlino, R. (1986). Migraciones. El exilio y el retorno. In: XXV Symposium and XV Congreso Interno APA, 1 (pp. 121–130), Buenos Aires, Argentina.

Carlino, R. (1991). El período de comienzo (Focus on the first contacts between patients and analyst). Promotion paper to be accepted as Full Member of APdeBA, Buenos Aires, Argentina.

Carlino, R. (2000). Transformaciones socioculturales. Su incidencia en el encuentro analista-analizando. In: Actas del Segundo Coloquio Interdisciplinar. Transformaciones, Psicoanálisis y Sociedad (pp. 421–425). Barcelona: IPSI.

Carlino, R. (2002). Fronteras de llegada y fronteras de salida. In: *XXIV Simposio "El psicoanálisis y sus fronteras"* (pp. 67–80), Buenos Aires: APdeBA.

Carlino, R. (2006). ¿Psicoanálisis por teléfono? Paper at XXVI FEPAL Congress, Lima, Peru, October.

Carlino, R. (2008). Radiografía del psicoanálisis telefónico. Paper at XXVII FEPAL Congress, Santiago, Chile, September.

Carlino, R. & Torregiani, V. (1987). Contratransferencia e interminabilidad del análisis. In: *X Simposio "Las múltiples formas de la transferencia"* (pp. 88–103), Buenos Aires: APdeBA.

Cesio, F. R. (1960). El letargo: una contribución al estudio de la reacción terapéutica negativa. *Revista de Psicoanálisis, 17*(1): 10–26.

Cesio, F. R. (1962). La disociación y el letargo en la reacción terapéutica negativa. *Revista de Psicoanálisis, 19*(1–2): 20–25.

De Domini, G. (2008). Nativos digitales: tienen menos de 12 años, dominan la tecnología y los padres no los entienden. Newspaper *Clarín*, Buenos Aires, Argentina, March 9. Available: www.clarin.com/diario/2008/03/09/sociedad/s-04415.htm

Eissler, K. R. (1953). The effect of the structure of the ego on psychoanalytic technique. *Journal of the American Psychoanalytic Association*, 1: 104–143.

Estrada Palma, T. (2009). El psicoanálisis contemporáneo frente a la tecnología de telecomunicaciones. Incorporación o resistencia en la práctica psicoanalítica. Semejanzas y diferencias. Paper at 46th IPA Congress, Chicago, July 29–August 1.

Etchegoyen, R. H. (1986). *Los Fundamentos de la Técnica Psicoanalítica.* Buenos Aires: Amorrortu.

Etchegoyen, R. H. (2005). *The Fundamentals of Psychoanalytic Technique.* London: Karnac.

Ferenczi, S. (1927). The problem of the termination of the analysis. Paper at 10th IPA Congress. Innsbruck. Reprinted as: Das problem der Beendigung der Analysen in: *Internationale Zeitschrift für Psychanalyse: Offizielles organ der Internationale Psychoanalytische Vereinigung, XIV*(1): 1–10.

Ferrari, A. (2005). El ciberdiván. Newspaper *Página 12.* Buenos Aires, Argentina. Available: www.pagina12.com.ar/diario/sociedad/3-52878-2005-06-26.html

Ferrari, P. F., Rozzi, S. & Fogassi, L. (2005). Mirror neurons responding to observation of actions made with tools in monkey ventral premotor cortex. *Journal of Cognitive Neuroscience, 17*(2): 212–226. Available: www.unipr.it/arpa/mirror/pubs/pdffiles/Ferrari-Rozzi2005.pdf

Freud, S. (1900a, 1901a). *The Interpretation of Dreams. S.E.,* 4–5. London: Hogarth.

Freud, S. (1912e). *Recommendations to Physicians Practising Psycho-Analysis.* *S.E.*, *12*: 111. London: Hogarth.

Freud, S. (1913c). *On Beginning the Treatment.* *S.E.*, *12*: 123. London: Hogarth.

Freud, S. (1923a). *Two Encyclopaedia Articles. Psychoanalysis and libidotheory.* *S.E.*, *18*: 235. London: Hogarth.

Freud, S. (1926e). *The Question of Lay Analysis.* *S.E.*, *20*: 251. London: Hogarth.

Freud, S. (1937c). *Analysis Terminable and Interminable.* *S.E.*, *23*: 211–253. London: Hogarth.

Garma, A. (1974). Tres aspectos básicos de las resistencias transferenciales en las etapas finales del tratamiento psicoanalítico. *Revista de Psicoanálisis*, *3*: 9–32 (1994).

Gill, M. M. (1984). Psychoanalysis and psychotherapy: a revision. *International Review of Psycho-Analysis*, *11*: 161–179. Available: www.psychiatry-online.it/ital/10a-Gill.htm

Grinberg, L. (1986). *La Supervisión Psicoanalítica. Teoría y práctica.* Madrid: Tecnipublicaciones.

Guiard, F. (1977). Sobre el componente musical del lenguaje en etapas avanzadas y finales del tratamiento psicoanalítico. Consideraciones técnico-clínicas y metapsicológicas. *Revista de Psicoanálisis*, *34*(1): 25–44.

Guiard, F. (1979). Aportes al conocimiento del proceso post-analítico. *Psicoanálisis*, *1*(1): 171–204. *Revista Latinoamericana de Psicoanálisis*, *1*(1):193–205 (1994).

Guiard, F. (1980). Cambio de analista. Paper at XIII Congreso FEPAL, Río de Janeiro. Reprinted *Psicoanálisis*, *9*(2): 99–112 (1987).

Gutiérrez Maldonado, J. (2002). Internet y psicología. El futuro ya esta aquí. Conference at Open University of Catalonia, Barcelona, March. Available: www.psicoarea.org/internet_psic_.htm#elfuturo

Heimann, P. (1950). On countertransference. *International Journal of Psychoanalysis*, *31*: 81–84.

Helman, N. (2006). Ser o no ser. Qué hacer para ser psicoanalista. APdeBA's Ateneo, Buenos Aires, Argentina, June 20.

Highton, E. I. & Wierzba, S. M. (1991). *La Relación Médico-Paciente: el Consentimiento Informado.* Buenos Aires: Ad-Hoc.

Jones, E. (1953). *The Life and Work of Sigmund Freud: The Formative Years and the Great Discoveries, 1856–1900 Vol. 1.* New York: Basic.

Kaës, R. (1989). Alliances inconscientes et pacte dénégatif dans les institutions. *Revue de psychothérapie psychanalytique de groupe*, *13*: 27–38.

Kant, I. (1781). *The Critique of Pure Reason.* London: Everyman.

Klein, M. (1928). Early stages of the Oedipus conflict. *International Journal of Psychoanalysis*, *8*: 339–370. In: *The Writing of Melanie Klein I* (pp. 139–169). London: Hogarth, 1975.

Klein, M. (1950). On the criteria for the termination of an analysis. *International Journal of Psychoanalysis*, *31*: 204.

Kramer Richards, A. (2003). Fruitful uses of telephone analysis. *Insight*, *12*(1): 30–32. Available: www.ipa.org.uk/Files/media/PrevSite/Docs/NewsMagazines/IPA_ENG_12.1.pdf

Laplanche, J. & Pontalis, J. B. (1973). *The Language of Psycho-Analysis* (p. 367), D. Nicholson-Smith (Trans.). London: Hogarth and the IPA. [Larrea, A. (2007). El ciberdiván avanza sobre el psicoanálisis tradicional. Newspaper *Perfil*, Buenos Aires, Argentina. Available: www.perfil.com/contenidos/2007/11/18/noticia_0018.html

Leffert, M. (2003). Analysis and psychotherapy by telephone: twenty years of clinical experience. *American Journal of Psychoanalysis*, *51*(1):101–130.

Levis, D. (2005). *Amores en Red. Relaciones Afectivas en la Era Internet*. Buenos Aires: Prometeo.

Lévy, P. (1995). *Qu'est-ce que le Virtuel?* París: La Découverte. [*¿Qué es lo Virtual?* Barcelona: Paidós Ibérica, 1999.] Available: www.slideshare.net/marianamarlene/levy-pierre-que-es-lo-virtual

Liberman, D. (1962). *La Comunicación en Terapéutica Psicoanalítica*. Buenos Aires: Eudeba.

Liberman. D. (1970). *Lingüística, Interacción Comunicativa y Proceso Psicoanalítico*. Buenos Aires: Nueva Visión.

Lindon, J. A. (1988). Psychoanalysis by telephone. *Bulletin of the Menninger Clinic*, *52*: 521–528.

Lindon, J. A., Lewin, B. D., Ballint, M., Fleming, J., Gill, M., Grinberg, L., Searles, H. F., Josselling, I. M. & Wallerstein, R. S. (1972). Supervision by tape: a new method of case supervision. *Psychoanalytic Forum*, *4*: 399–452.

Ludmer, M. (2007). La técnica psicoanalítica y su entrecruzamiento con las tecnologías de la comunicación. Paper at XXIX Symposio APdeBA, Buenos Aires, Argentina, November.

Lutenberg, J. (2009). Diálogo psicoanalítico telefónico. Paper at 46th IPA Congress, Chicago, July 29–August 1.

Machado, A. (2011). *Caminante no hay Camino*. An extract from this poem: translated by James Nuss, especially for this edition.

Mantykow de Sola, B. (2007). En torno a la situación analítica y su construcción en la "situación" actual. *Psicoanálisis*, *29*(2): 313–340.

Mayans i Planells, J. (2003). El ciberespacio, un nuevo espacio público para el desarrollo de la identidad local. Inaugural Conference of III Encuentro de Telecentros y Redes de Telecentros, Peñafiel, Valladolid, Spain, October. Available: www.cibersociedad.net/archivo/articulo.php?art=158

Meltzer, D. (1967). *The Psycho-Analytical Process*. London: Heinemann Medical. [Karnac, 2008. Harris Meltzer Trust.]

Meltzer, D. (2000). A review of my writings. In: M. Cohen & A. Hahn (Eds.), *Exploring the Work of Donald Meltzer: a Festschrift* (pp. 1–11). London: Karnac.

Menninger, K. (1958). *Theory of Psychoanalytic Technique*. New York: Basic.

Merciai, S. A. (2001). Psicoterapia on-line: un vestito su misura. In: T. Cantelmi, S. Putti & M. Talli (Eds.), *@Psychotherapy, risultati preliminari di una ricerca sperimentale italiana* (pp. 113–186). Rome: Edizioni Universitarie Romane. Available: www.psychomedia.it/pm/pit/olpsy/merciai.htm

Migone, P. (1999). La psicoterapia in rete: ¿un setting terapeutico come un altro? Riflessioni da un punto di vista psicoanalitico. In: F. Bollorino (Ed.), *Psichiatria on line. Strumenti di ricerca scientifica, comunità terapeutiche, interazione tra medico e paziente* (pp. 255–265). Milan: Apogeo. Available: www.psychiatryonline.it/ital/psichiatriaonline/migone.htm

Migone, P. (2003). La psicoterapia con Internet. *Psicoterapia e Scienze Umane*, 37(4): 57–73. Available: http://www.psychomedia.it/pm/modther/probpsiter/pst-rete.htm

Moreno, J. (2002). Realidad virtual. In: *Ser Humano* (pp. 51–71). Buenos Aires: Libros del Zorzal.

Moreno, J. (2009). Cuerpo y realidad virtual. APdeBA's Ateneo, Buenos Aires, Argentina, May.

Morin, E. (1982). Más allá de la complicación: la complejidad. In: *Ciencia con Conciencia* (pp. 318–337). Barcelona: Anthropos, 1984.

Negroponte, N. (1995). *Being Digital*. New York. Vintage. *Being Digital*, e-book by Cyberdock, 2005.

Ong, W. (1992). Writing is a technology that restructures thought. In: P. Downing, S. Lima & M. Noonas (Eds.), *The Linguistics of Literacy* (pp. 293–320). Amsterdam: John Benjamins.

Ortega y Gasset, J. (1914). Meditaciones del Quijote. In: *Obras Completas I* (p. 757). Madrid: Taurus/Fundación José Ortega y Gasset.

Peirce, C. S. (1931–1958). *Collected Papers of Charles Sanders Peirce, Vols. 1–8*. C. Hartshorne, A. Weiss & W. Burks, (Eds.). Cambridge, MA: Harvard University Press.]

Polito, R. (1979). Evaluación del proceso psicoanalítico. *Psicoanálisis*, 1(1): 205–220.

Popovsky de Berenstein, S. & Sor de Fondevila, D. (1989). Función psicoanalítica y viscisitudes del vínculo transferencial. *Psicoanálisis*, 11(3): 151–172.

Prensky, M. (2001). Digital natives, Digital Inmigrants. *On the Horizon*, 9(5): 1–6. Available: http://www.marcprensky.com/writing/prensky%20-%20digital%20natives,%20digital%20immigrants%20-%20part1.pdf

Puget, J. & Berenstein, I. (1988). *Psicoanálisis de la Pareja Matrimonial.* Buenos Aires: Paidos.

Puget, J. & Wender, L. (1982). Analista y paciente en mundos superpuestos. *Psicoanálisis,* 4(3): 503–522.

Racker, H. (1948). La neurosis de contratransferencia. Paper at Argentine Psychoanalytic Association (APA), September.

Racker, H. (1952). Observaciones sobre la contratransferencia como instrumento técnico. *Revista de Psicoanálisis,* 9(3): 342–354.

Racker, H. (1953). A contribution to the problem of countertransference. *International Journal of Psychoanalysis,* 34(4): 313–324.

Racker, H. (1957). The meanings and uses of countertransference. *Psychoanalytic Quarterly,* 26(3): 303–357.

Racker, H. (1959). *Estudios sobre Técnica Analítica.* Buenos Aires: Paidós. [2nd Edition, 1969.]

Racker, H. (1968). *Transference and Countertransference.* New York: International Universities Press.

Rizzolatti, G., Fogassi, L. & Gallese, V. (2001). Neurophysiological mechanisms underlying the understanding and imitation of action. *Nature Reviews Neuroscience,* 2: 661–670. Available: www.unipr.it/arpa/mirror/pubs/pdffiles/Rizzolatti-Fogassi%202001.pdf

Rosenfeld, D. (1982). La noción de esquema corporal psicótico en pacientes neuróticos y psicóticos. *Psicoanálisis,* 4(2): 383–404.

Rosenfeld, D. (1992). *The Psychotic Aspects of the Personality.* London: Karnac.

Rosenfeld, H. (1965). *Psychotic State. A psycho-analytical approach.* New York: International Universities Press. [Spanish Edition: *Estados Psicóticos.* Buenos Aires: Hormé, 1974.]

Rosenfeld, H. (1969). On the treatment of psychotic states by psychoanalysis: an historical approach. *International Journal of Psychoanalysis,* 50: 615–631. [Spanish edition (1971): Sobre el tratamiento de los estados psicóticos por medio del psicoanálisis; un enfoque histórico. *Revista de Psicoanálisis,* 28(2): 391–431.

Rosenfeld, H. (1978). Notes on the psychopathology and psycho-analytic treatment of some borderline states. *International Journal of Psychoanalysis,* 59: 215–221.

Rudinesco, E. (2000). Hacia un nuevo psicoanálisis. Newspaper *Clarín,* Buenos Aires, Argentina, July 19.

Saul, L. J. (1951). A note on the telephone as a technical aid. *Psychoanalytic Quarterly,* 20: 287–290.

Savege Scharff, J. (2009). Report about a two-hour panel (LDG) at 46th IPA Congress, Chicago: Telephone analysis panel. Chair: Hanly, C.

(Canada); Panellists: USA: Anderson, G., Scharff, D., Savege Scharff, J.; UK/Australia: Symington, N.; Argentina: Aryan, A., Berenstein, S. P. de, Carlino, R., Ginfeld, P. & Lutenberg, J.

Searles, H. F. (1965). *Collected Papers on Schizophrenia and Related Subjects.* New York: International Universities Press. [Spanish edition: *Escritos sobre Esquizofrenia.* Barcelona: Gedisa, 1980.]

Suler, J. (2003). Presence in cyberspace in psychology of cyberspace. Available: www.users.rider.edu/~suler/psycyber/psychspace.html

Vargas Llosa, M. (2002). *La Verdad de las Mentiras.* Madrid: Alfaguara.

Wender, L., Liniado de Cvik, J., Cvik, N. & Stein, G. (1966). Comienzo y final de sesión, dinámica de ciertos aspectos transferenciales y contratransferenciales. X Symposium APA, Buenos Aires, Argentina.

Zac, J. (1971). Un enfoque metodológico del establecimiento del encuadre. *Revista de Psicoanálisis, 28*(3): 593–609.

Zac, J. (1972). Cómo se originan las interpretaciones en el analista. *Revista de Psicoanálisis, 29*(2): 217–252.

Zac de Filc, S. (2005). O Papel Continente dos Elementos Sonoros da Interpretação Psicanálise. *Psicanálise, 7*(1): 183–198.

Zalusky, S. (1998). Telephone analysis: out of sight, but not out of mind. *Journal of the American Psychoanalytic Association, 46*(4): 1221–1242.

Zalusky, S. (2003). Dialogue: Telephone Analysis. *Insight, 12*(1): 13–16. Available: www.ipa.org.uk/Files/media/PrevSite/Docs/NewsMagazines/IPA_ENG_12.1.pdf

INDEX

209